Probate Handbook

Holloway's

Probate Handbook

Seventh edition

D R LeB Holloway LLB(Hons)
formerly of the
Principal Registry of the Family Division

Oyez Longman

21/27 Lamb's Conduit Street
London WC1N 3NJ

ISBN 0 - 85120 - 840 - 1

First published 1961
Second edition 1967
Third edition 1973
Fourth edition 1976
Fifth edition 1979
Sixth edition 1982
Seventh edition 1984

Printed in Great Britain by
Butler and Tanner Ltd, Frome and London

Contents

Preface to the Seventh Edition

For new readers it is important to know that this is intended to be a handy-sized book containing the essential information required by a practitioner to enable him to deal with any non-contentious probate application, and more particularly to apply for a grant of probate or letters of administration as speedily and accurately as possible. There are detailed sections dealing with wills and the entitlement to a grant of representation, with special emphasis on the preparation of the necessary documents to lead to the grant. For this purpose precedents of the forms in common use are provided with lengthy notes to assist in their completion. There are references to relevant statutes, statutory instruments and important cases. To avoid duplication, thus keeping down the size of the book, numerous cross-references are given throughout the text. There is a questionnaire in the Appendix designed for use as an aide-memoire, firstly when considering the preparation of the papers and secondly as a check before the papers are submitted to the probate registry.

For those who are familiar with this book, may I say that the layout remains the same, with the exception that, wherever applicable, a new system of cross-referencing by reference to headings is being tried out. The text has been thoroughly revised to take account of new law and practice since the last edition. Apart from a number of relatively minor alterations in the practice, the most important changes have been those produced by the Administration of Justice Act 1982. There is a slight relaxation in the formal requirements for executing a will; the anomaly caused by the operation of s 33 of the Wills Act 1837 has been corrected so that gifts under a will which would lapse because of the pre-decease of the beneficiary and which are saved by reason of his leaving children now pass to those children; the spouse of a testator will now lose her rights as an executor and a beneficiary under the will after their marriage has been dissolved or annulled. Also the court has been given a power to order the rectification of a will in certain circumstances, and specific rules have been provided dealing with the admissibility of evidence to assist in the interpretation of wills. In these last two respects there has as yet been little opportunity for the court to give guidance on the effect of the new statutory provisions. The

Act also makes new provision for the registration of the wills of living persons and for the recognition of 'international wills', but these sections have yet to be brought into effect.

I should like to take this opportunity to thank Graham Maple in particular and other members of the Principal Registry for the help they have given me in preparing this edition.

The law and practice generally are as at 9 May 1984.

D R LeB HOLLOWAY

Table of Cases

Table of Statutes

Table of Statutory Instruments

Chapter 1

Grants of Representation

The law of England and Wales permits a person to give directions by his will for the disposal of his property after his death. If he dies without having done so, the law determines the way in which his estate is to be distributed in accordance with rules based on what are considered to be the wishes of the average testator.

The right to administer the deceased's estate is evidenced (in the case of executors) or conferred by a grant of representation issued by the court. Application for such a grant must be made to the court by the executors named in the will or, in default thereof, by the persons entitled thereto according to rules of court. Before the grant will issue, the applicant must account for any capital transfer tax payable. Generally speaking, it is necessary to produce a grant of representation in order to establish the right to recover or receive any part of the deceased's estate in the United Kingdom. Since 1 January 1972 a grant of representation issued in England and Wales in the estate of a person who dies domiciled there has been recognised not only throughout England and Wales but also in Scotland and Northern Ireland, provided that it contains a statement of the domicile. Likewise a confirmation issued in Scotland or a grant issued in Northern Ireland extends to estate in England and Wales, provided the deceased died domiciled in Scotland or Northern Ireland respectively and the domicile is stated therein (ss 1, 2 and 3 of the Administration of Estates Act 1971) (see p 219).

There are a number of statutory exemptions under which small sums registered in the deceased's name may be paid over without requiring production of the grant. These are set out in the Administration of Estates (Small Payments) Act 1965, which placed a limit of £500 on the total amount which may be paid out; see also the Trustee Savings Bank Act 1969 and the National Savings Bank Act 1971. The limit was increased to £1,500 for deaths occurring, or nominations effected, on or after 10 August 1975 or 12 August 1975, as appropriate, and to £5,000 for deaths on or after 11 May 1984. An exemption of this nature does not usually include exemption from the payment of capital transfer tax and for a transfer of assets to be made it is often a pre-requisite that a certificate is obtained from the Capital Taxes Office that capital transfer tax has been paid (Form 22 (CTT), see p 230).

In the case of moneys in the National Savings Bank, but not a trustee savings bank, or invested in National Savings Certificates or in stock held on the National Savings Stock Register or payable under the rules of certain friendly, industrial or provident societies, the depositor, investor or member is entitled to execute a nomination in respect of these moneys which on his death will take effect under the appropriate regulations. Usually the general effect of a nomination is to take the nominated property out of the deceased's estate for all purposes except liability to capital transfer tax.

Where the beneficial interest in property was held by the deceased and one or more other persons as equitable joint tenants, that interest passes by survivorship to the other tenant or tenants and does not form part of the deceased's estate for probate purposes, although it may be subject to capital transfer tax.

As from the date of death, the deceased's estate vests in the executor named in the will (unless he is a minor at the time) or, if there is no executor but an intestacy arises under the will, or if there is no will, in the President of the Family Division of the High Court of Justice until such time as a grant of representation issues, when it vests in the grantee.

1.1 Probate jurisdiction

The business of obtaining, or revoking, a grant where there is no contention as to the right thereto is known as non-contentious or common form business and includes (*a*) the passing of probates and administrations through the High Court in contentious cases where the contest has been ended, (*b*) all business of a non-contentious nature in matters of testacy and intestacy not being proceedings in any action, and (*c*) the business of lodging caveats against the grant of probate or administration. It is regulated by the Non-Contentious Probate Rules 1954, as amended. Rules specifically referred to hereinafter are denoted by the words 'Probate Rule' followed by the rule number. Non-contentious probate business is assigned to the Family Division (s 61 (1) of the Supreme Court Act 1981 and para 3 of Sched 1 thereto). In that connection the Family Division exercises jurisdiction to issue or revoke grants of representation and for that purpose decides what documents may be admitted to proof as testamentary and who is entitled to a grant subject, however, in appropriate cases to any decision of the Chancery Division made in a probate action. All other probate business has been assigned to the Chancery Division and is not dealt with in this book.

1.2 Grants of representation

Grants of representation are of three kinds:

(1) *Probate*—This issues to executors expressly appointed by a will or codicil, or to the executors according to the tenor of the will or codicil (see p 63).

(2) *Letters of administration with will annexed*—These issue in respect of wills and codicils of which no executor of any kind is appointed, or where circumstances make it impossible for the executors appointed to take out a grant of probate. Such circumstances might be—

(*a*) when, at the time it is required to prove the will, the executor is dead, or has renounced his office (see head 8.1), or has not entered an appearance to a citation calling upon him to prove the will (see head 19.2), or for good reason shown is to be passed over (see head 13.6);

(*b*) when the appointment of an executor is void by reason of uncertainty as to his identity (see p 63);

(*c*) when, subsequent to the appointment of the testator's spouse as sole executor, their marriage has been dissolved or annulled in consequence of which the appointment of the executor is to be omitted from the will (see head 2.30);

(*d*) when the executor is unable to take out probate through some disability, eg, minority (see head 9.1), incapacity to conduct his affairs (see heads 9.2(*b*) and 9.3), absence from England and Wales (see p 165);

(*e*) when the appointment of an 'executor' in the will is not in the English language and there is no person named who by the terms of the will could be regarded as an executor according to the tenor (see head 15.2(*a*)).

(3) *Letters of administration*—These issue when it is shown that the deceased died wholly intestate and also in the following special circumstances when the deceased left a will—

(*a*) when it is necessary to obtain a grant ad colligenda bona (see head 13.4);

(*b*) during the pendency of an action to determine the validity of the will (see head 13.5);

(*c*) if no response is made to a citation calling upon the persons interested thereunder to propound a purported testamentary document (see head 19.2(*c*)).

The various classes of persons entitled to apply for and obtain a grant of probate or administration in particular circumstances and the relative priorities of the claims of such persons to a grant are regulated by the Probate Rules (s 127 (2) of the Supreme Court Act 1981).

A grant of representation recites the name of the probate registry from which it issues, the name and last address of the deceased, the date of his or her death and his or her domicile at that time, and the name and address of the person or persons to whom it has been granted; it also shows whether the gross and net values of the estate do not exceed a particular figure or the actual gross and net values of the estate. In addition a grant of probate indicates the title of the grantees as executors and accounts for non-proving executors. A grant of administration (with or without will annexed) no longer gives the capacity or title in which the grantee has taken the grant, nor the manner in which persons with a prior right to the grant have been cleared off, except that it is shown how executors appointed by the will have been accounted for in appropriate cases. If the powers of administration are limited in any way, this will be recited in the grant.

Where the grantee has died and there is no chain of executorship (see head 3.1), a further grant will be necessary to deal with any part of the deceased's estate remaining unadministered. This will take the form of either a grant of double probate (see head 3.4) or a grant of letters of administration (with or without will annexed) de bonis non (see head 13.2) or cessate (see head 13.1).

A grant of probate, or of letters of administration with will annexed, may not issue until the expiration of seven days, and a grant of letters of administration may not issue until the expiration of fourteen days, from the date of death of the deceased, excluding the day of the death, except by order of two registrars. The application for an early grant should be supported by some form of evidence, whether this be an affidavit or simply a letter of explanation from the solicitor.

Where the deceased has left estate in more than one country, it may be possible to apply for a grant of representation obtained in one country to be re-sealed in another country (see head 17.2). The effect of re-sealing is to enable the grantee to administer the estate in the country in which re-sealing has been effected without having to obtain a separate grant of representation.

1.3 Enemy property

Probate Rule 36 which required that where the death took place before 6 October 1952 and a grant was to be made (i) in respect of the estate of any deceased person who was resident at the date of his death in Bulgaria, Germany, Hungary, Japan or Romania; or (ii) to any person resident in one of those countries, or to his attorney, the consent of the appropriate administrator of enemy property was first to be obtained, was revoked with effect from 1 May 1974.

1.4 How to apply for a grant

A grant of probate or letters of administration may be obtained as follows:

(1) By application through a practising solicitor (who must give the address of his place of business in England and Wales) (Probate Rule 3)—

(*a*) at the Principal Registry of the Family Division;

(*b*) at any one of the district probate registries or sub-registries.

(2) By personal application at the Principal Registry or a district probate registry or sub-registry, or a probate office (Probate Rule 4).

The jurisdiction of certain officers of Customs and Excise to deal with applications for grants of a limited nature ceased to exist on and after 1 April 1968.

(a) By application through a solicitor at the Principal Registry

Applications for any type of grant and in respect of estates of any value may be dealt with at the Principal Registry of the Family Division, Somerset House, Strand, London WC2R 1LP.

The papers to lead the grant, consisting of the oath in support (see Forms 3.2, 4.4, 5.4), the Inland Revenue account if appropriate (see head 18.2) and any other documents necessitated by the particular circumstances of the application, may be sent by the solicitor by post addressed to 'The Receiver of Papers, Principal Registry of the Family Division, Somerset House, Strand, London WC2R 1LP'. Any court fees (see Appendix 1) should be paid at the same time by enclosing with the papers a crossed cheque made payable to 'HM Paymaster General'. The court fee is based on the assessed value of the estate (for definition see p 265). No fee is payable where that value is not more than £10,000. Payment may also be made in respect of any copies of the grant which may be required. A receipt is given for the papers and for any money sent in respect of fees, and this may have to be produced on any subsequent inquiry. If the court has previously made an order to lead the grant, the order must accompany the papers, together with such affidavits in support as have not already been filed in the registry. If the amount of the estate, or the nature of the application, is such that the Inland Revenue account should be controlled, or tax paid, before the grant issues, the account must have been sent to the Capital Taxes Office for that purpose before being included with the papers to lead the grant (see head 18.3). The registry will not undertake to transmit such documents to the Capital Taxes Office.

Alternatively the papers may be left personally by the solicitor or his agent at the Receiver's Department of the registry. The same conditions apply with regard to the control of Inland Revenue accounts and to the payment of tax; the solicitor must arrange for this to be done before lodging the papers in the registry. A fee sheet is provided for the solicitor to complete and the court fees are then assessed in the Receiver's Department and are payable in the Cashier's Room (Room 22) on the ground floor. Although payment may be made by cash or by cheque, postal or money order, made out to 'HM Paymaster General', crossed cheques are preferred and will be accepted without the necessity of making any previous arrangement for their acceptance.

On receipt of the papers, whether sent by post or lodged personally, all testamentary documents are photographed and a search is made to ensure that a grant of representation has not already issued in respect of the deceased's estate and that a caveat has not been entered against the estate (see head 19.1). They are then transmitted to the Probate Department and examined by an official of that department. If in order, the grant is prepared, to which is attached a photographic copy of the will and codicils, if any. Grants are usually signed by a Probate Officer under the authority of the President of the Family Division and are then sealed with the seal of the Division. After this the grant is ready to issue, usually within two weeks from the receipt of the papers, and it will be sent by first class post to the extracting solicitor, except where the papers have been lodged by a law agent on behalf of the solicitor, when it will be available for collection. The postal address of the extracting solicitor is stated at the foot of the grant. Details of the grant are entered after issue in the calendar (see head 21.2).

A grant in respect of the estate, or part of the estate, of a deceased person will not issue out of the registry on any application if, before the grant is made, it appears to the registrar that some other application has been made in respect of that estate, or that part of the estate, and that the other application has been neither refused nor withdrawn (s 107 of the Supreme Court Act 1981). If two applications for a grant in respect of the same estate are received in the registry from persons having an equal title, the grant will usually be made to the applicant who first lodged his papers to lead to the grant. However the other applicant will first be given notice of the first application to allow him an opportunity to oppose the issue of a grant by entering a caveat (see head 19.1) or by issuing a summons for directions (see p 240 and head 20.2).

All communications to the registry should state the solicitor's reference or the name of the person dealing with the particular matter, together with a telephone number, and should give the address to which the grant is to be sent. If the papers are lodged personally these details should be inserted in the space provided on the fee sheet before lodging the papers. If it is desired as a matter of particular urgency that the issue of the grant should be expedited, the request together with the reasons for expedition should be contained in the letter accompanying the papers when these are sent to the registry by post. If the papers are lodged personally, the question of expedition should be mentioned when lodging the papers in the Receiver's Department and the solicitor will then be referred to the Principal of the Probate Department to make verbal application to him for expedition. If there is some defect in the papers, the solicitor will be informed by telephone, or by the despatch of an official communication to the address given in the solicitor's letter or the fee sheet, stating that the grant cannot issue because of a defect. Wherever possible the nature of the query will be shown briefly; otherwise the solicitor will be asked to inquire personally at the Probate Department. Complicated queries will not be dealt with through the post, even if arising in respect of an application sent through the post. Defective documents will usually be returned by post with the notification of the query, except that on occasion the solicitor will be asked to collect an original will personally. A bill for any outstanding court fees will be sent to the solicitor for payment before the grant issues.

Where application is to be made for a grant in respect of the estate of a member of the Forces whose death has occurred in warlike circumstances such that the estate is exempt from capital transfer tax, or would be so exempt if the amount of the estate were such as to render it liable to tax, a reduced court fee may be payable (Fee 3 (*a*): see p 266). Where no question of tax arises the Capital Taxes Office is not prepared to certify that the estate is exempt from tax by virtue of para 1 of Sched 7 to the Finance Act 1975. In such a case Fee 3 (*a*) will be charged on production of a certificate given by the Ministry of Defence that the circumstances of death were such as to satisfy the conditions specified in Sched 7. Inquiries should be made of the Defence Secretariat 15 (Legal Liaison), D515, Ministry of Defence, Room 8321, Main Building, Whitehall, London SW1.

Inquiries whether preliminary to the preparation of the papers to lead the grant or after their lodgment, may be made by post or personally by the solicitor or his agent to the appropriate officer of the Probate Department. However, in the case of a postal query the solicitor may be asked to attend at the registry if the matter is at all complicated. The affidavits and other documents in support of an application for a registrar's order may also be sent by post as an alternative to lodging them personally at the registry. Draft papers may be sent or lodged for settlement and advantage should be taken of this facility whenever a case presents difficulty. Affidavits to be used in support of an application for a registrar's order will not be settled. A fee of £5 is payable for settling each document. The settled drafts should be returned when the sworn papers are lodged. There is a right of appeal from the decision of the Principal of the Probate Department to one of the registrars.

An application for a second or subsequent grant, or for an order leading to the issue of such a grant, is made in the same way as an application in respect of a first grant, that is to say the papers may be sent by post to the Receiver of Papers or lodged personally at the Receiver's Department. The procedure for paying fees, notifying the solicitor of a defect in the papers and issuing the grant is also the same. Any inquiry relating to such an application may be made through the post, and draft papers relating thereto may be sent by post for settlement. The Inland Revenue account must be submitted by the solicitor to the Capital Taxes Office for control, or for assessment and payment of tax, before the papers to lead the grant are sent to, or lodged in, the registry.

If an applicant changes his solicitor in the course of the application, the new solicitor should lodge in the registry a notice of change of solicitor and should serve on the former solicitor a copy of such notice endorsed with a memorandum stating that the notice has been lodged in the appropriate registry. If there is any other party concerned, a similar copy of the notice of change should also be sent to him.

If an applicant for a grant dies at the time of making the application, the solicitor should notify the Probate Department immediately. Where notification is received before the grant has been sealed and the person who has died was the sole applicant, the application will be treated as if it had been withdrawn. However, if one of several applicants has died and a grant can properly be made to the survivor or survivors, the application will be allowed to proceed on the papers already lodged. The solicitor must produce a letter confirming the death, or a copy of the death certificate, and a note as to the death is then made on the papers. If the notification of death is received after the grant has been sealed, it must stand until revoked. It is appropriate to apply for revocation if it can be established that the grantee died before the grant was sealed. Evidence as to the death may be supplied in the form of a copy death certificate or a letter from the solicitor. Where the grantee died on the day of the date of the grant and there is some doubt as to whether he died before or after the grant was sealed, an affidavit as to the facts should be lodged with the application for revocation for consideration by the registrar. (For the procedure on an application for revocation in these circumstances, see head 16.2.) If death takes place after sealing, the grant stands and a further grant de bonis non or cessate (see heads 13.2, 13.1) must be obtained.

As to errors in the grant, see under Amendment, head 16.1.

Exceptionally a civil aid certificate may be issued under the Legal Aid Act 1974 to enable a person to obtain a grant of representation. This may occur when a grant is required to make title in an action. The certificate should be filed and the bill of costs taxed in the Division of the High Court in which the action is proceeding. If the dispute is settled before the issue of a writ, the civil aid certificate should be filed in the registry from which the grant issued (the Probate Department in the case of the Principal Registry). Bills of costs, other than those under the Solicitors Act 1974, will be taxed in the Principal Registry and the bill of costs should be lodged with the Taxing Officers' Clerk in the Principal Registry for taxation by a registrar or one of the taxing officers (Probate Rule 59). A solicitor's charges for non-contentious probate work are regulated by the Rules of the Supreme Court (Non-Contentious Probate Costs) 1956 (see also pp 138–139).

(b) By application through a solicitor at a district probate registry or sub-registry

There are eleven district probate registries in the provinces (The District Probate Registries Order 1982). In addition sub-registries have been established at a number of other places in the provinces, each sub-registry being attached to a particular probate registry. An application for a grant may be made at any one of the district probate registries or sub-registries (see list at Appendix 2). As in the case of the Principal Registry, applications for any type of grant and in respect of estates of any value may be dealt with, including an application for a second or subsequent grant, except that an application for a grant of letters of administration pending suit (see head 13.5) must be made at the Principal Registry (s 106 (2) (*a*) of the Supreme Court Act 1981). No grant can be made by a district registrar in any case in which there is contention until the contention is disposed of, or in any case in which it appears to the registrar either that a grant ought not to be made without the direction of the court or that a grant ought not to be made until any particular matter relating to the grant, or to an application for it, has been determined by the High Court otherwise than by the giving of directions. A statement of the matter in question is sent by the registrar to the Principal Registry for the necessary direction to be given (s 106 of the Supreme Court Act 1981). The procedure in a district probate registry differs in certain slight respects from that in the Principal Registry.

The papers in respect of any type of application may be lodged in person by the solicitor or his agent, or they may be sent to the district probate registry or to the sub-registry through the post. An account of the court fees payable will be sent to the solicitor in due course. They may be paid in cash or preferably by crossed cheque in favour of 'HM Paymaster General'. There must be separate cheques for each case lodged. In those cases where it is necessary to submit the Inland Revenue account to the Capital Taxes Office for control or assessment of tax (see head 18.3), it should be sent to that office before the papers to lead the grant are sent or taken to the registry. In all other cases where tax is payable, the solicitor should assess the tax himself and he may then send the Inland Revenue account, together with the warrant and a crossed cheque in respect of the tax payable to the 'Inland Revenue' either to the Capital Taxes Office, or to the registry with the papers to lead the grant and the registrar will arrange for the tax to be paid. Where tax is not payable and an account is required, it should be included with the papers to lead the grant (see also p 232).

On receipt of the papers, notice of the application is sent to the Principal Registry for a search to be made to ensure that a previous grant has not issued, that a caveat has not been entered against the estate (see head 19.1) and that no other application for the grant has been made elsewhere. On receipt of a certificate from the Principal Registry giving the necessary clearance, the papers are examined by an official of the district registry and, if in order, the grant is prepared, signed by the district probate registrar or a probate officer, sealed with the seal of the registry and sent to the extracting solicitor by first class post, whether the papers have been lodged personally at, or sent by post to, the registry, or sub-registry. If a certificate cannot be given, the district probate registrar will be advised of the reason; if there is another application for the grant, see p 6. If application is made through a sub-registry, the grant is issued, not from the sub-registry, but from the probate registry to which the sub-registry is attached. If there are defects in papers lodged through the post, the solicitor will be informed of them by letter or telephone, and the amended papers may be returned through the post. If there are defects in papers lodged personally, the practice is much the same as that followed in the Principal Registry (see p 6).

Inquiries before or after the lodgment of papers to lead a grant may be made personally or through the post at a district registry or sub-registry. Similarly, draft documents may be lodged for settlement or sent through the post.

(c) By personal application at any probate registry

Any person (other than a trust corporation) seeking to obtain a grant without employing a solicitor may apply at any probate registry or sub-registry (see Appendix 2), or at certain local probate offices served from the nearest registry. The application is made by the applicant attending personally at the registry or office. It may not be made through an agent, even if unpaid, and the applicant may not be attended by any person acting or appearing to act as his adviser. The Personal Application Department of the Principal Registry is at present situated at 5th Floor, Golden Cross House, Duncannon Street, London WC2N 4JF. The applicant may obtain from the probate registry or sub-registry a booklet of instructions (Form 48) and a set of forms including an account of the estate (CAP Form 44) which, when completed, he may return by post together with the death certificate and the will, if any, whereupon he is given an appointment to attend personally at the registry or sub-registry or at the probate office of his choice. A second attendance is sometimes necessary. A departmental fee is usually payable in addition to any court fee (see Appendix 1, Fee No 2, at p 266). An applicant may prepare the papers leading to the grant himself and lodge them at the registry unsworn, in which case up to one half of the departmental fee may be remitted (see p 265). The grant is sent to the applicant through the post when it is ready to issue.

Where an applicant requires the necessary documents to be prepared for him, he may apply through the Personal Application Department in London for the re-sealing of a Colonial grant (see head 17.2).

An application will not be accepted if the applicant has previously made an application in the same estate through a solicitor which has not been withdrawn or if it will be necessary to make an application to the court on motion or by action. Moreover, a registrar may direct that the application be made through a solicitor in any particular case; this is usual where a case presents difficult and complicated features, eg, certain applications for a discretionary grant under s 116 of the Supreme Court Act 1981 (see head 13.6) or applications for a grant to a person entrusted or entitled under foreign law (see heads 15.2(*c*), (*d*)).

1.5 Inventory and account

The duties of an administrator of an estate are detailed in s 25 of the Administration of Estates Act 1925, as substituted by s 9 of the Administration of Estates Act 1971, as being:

(i) to collect and get in the real and personal estate of the deceased and administer it according to law;

(ii) when required to do so by the court, to exhibit on oath in the court a full inventory of the estate and when so required render an account of the administration to the court;

(iii) when required to do so by the High Court, to deliver up the grant of probate or administration to that court.

Any person interested in the estate of the deceased may, after a proper period of time has elapsed from the issue of the grant of representation, make application to the court for an order that the administrator should provide an inventory of the estate and additionally that he should render an account of his administration. The application is made by summons to a registrar (see head 20.2) and should be supported by an affidavit. Should the administrator fail to obey the order application may be made to the court on motion (see head 20.3) for his committal for contempt.

Chapter 2

Wills

2.1 Validity

Before proceeding to prove a will it is first necessary to decide by what law the validity of the will in question must be tested. This is now dependent on the date of death of the testator.

(a) Death before 1 January 1964

To deal with immovable estate in England and Wales the will must have been executed in accordance with the Wills Act 1837 (see below under 'Validity under English law', head 2.3, and under 'Privileged wills', head 2.26); but where the validity of the will of a British subject can be established under the Wills Act 1861, known as Lord Kingsdown's Act, it will be valid to deal with leasehold property (*Re Grassi* [1905] 1 Ch 584). To pass other property, the will must be valid according to the law of the place where the deceased was domiciled at the date of his death (but see below).

Although the will of a British subject who has died before 1 January 1964 may not be valid according to the law of his domicile at the date of his death, it may still be possible to prove it in England and Wales, provided it can satisfy the conditions of Lord Kingsdown's Act (which was repealed with effect from 1 January 1964 by the Wills Act 1963; but see also p 15 for an instance when the Act may still be applicable in respect of the will of a person dying on or after 1 January 1964). By s 1 the will of a British subject, wheresoever domiciled at the date of his death, is valid as to personal estate in England and Wales if, having been made out of the United Kingdom (ie, as from 1 April 1923, England, Wales, Scotland and Northern Ireland), it is valid (*a*) by the law of the place where it was made, or (*b*) by the law of the place of domicile of the testator at the time it was made, or (*c*) by the law then in force in that part of Her Majesty's dominions where the testator had a domicile of origin. By s 2 a will made in the United Kingdom by a British subject is to be accepted if valid by the law for the time being in force in that part of the United Kingdom where it was made. The Act does not render valid the will of a minor who dies domiciled in a country the law of which does not permit him to make a will whilst in his minority. The grant will be limited to personalty unless the will is in English form.

The deceased must have been a British subject at the date of making the will. In determining whether he was a British subject, reference must be made to the British Nationality Act 1981 (which has for most purposes replaced the British Nationality Act 1948) and, if appropriate, to the Ireland Act 1949. It may be necessary also to have regard to the provisions of the relevant Independence Acts under which a former British colony or protectorate has attained independent status. The term 'British subject' includes naturalised citizens, but the fact and extent of their naturalisation must be set out on affidavit and supported by the production of the certificate of naturalisation; doubtful cases will be referred to the registrar.

The fact that it is possible to prove the will under Lord Kingsdown's Act by reference to English law does not of itself permit the applicant to apply under an English title if the deceased died domiciled outside England and Wales. He must still establish his title to a grant in the usual manner (see head 15.2).

Section 3 of Lord Kingsdown's Act provides that a change of domicile by the testator after execution of his will shall not operate to invalidate that will. The practice of the probate registries is to interpret this section as applying to all persons notwithstanding that they are not, and were not at the date of the will, British subjects (see *In the Goods of Groos* [1904] P 269). Reference must be made to the law of the country in which the deceased was domiciled at the time of making the will and the validity of the will established in the usual way (see head 15.1).

(For proof of the validity of a will under foreign law see head 15.1.)

(b) Death on or after 1 January 1964

The rules for recognising the validity of a will, whether made before or after 1 January 1964, of a testator who has died on or after that date, are contained in the Wills Act 1963 (but see additionally under International wills, head 2.32). The Act incorporates the provisions of the Convention on the Conflicts of Laws relating to the Form of Testamentary Dispositions concluded at the Ninth Hague Conference in 1961. The object of the Convention was to ensure that a will made in accordance with the law of any country which a testator might reasonably believe to govern its execution should receive the widest possible recognition.

As a general rule, a will dealing with movable or immovable property or both is to be treated as properly executed if it was made in accordance with the internal law of the country in which it was executed, or in accordance with the internal law of the country in which the testator was domiciled or habitually resident, or of which he was a national, either at the time of execution or at the date of his death. The internal law of a country is defined as being the law which would apply in that country in a case where no question of the law in force in any other country arose. There is, therefore, no need to consider the application of the doctrine of renvoi.

In addition to these general provisions, there are three special rules: (i) when a will has been made on board a ship (including a hovercraft) or aircraft, it will be regarded as properly executed if it conforms to the internal law of the country with which the ship or aircraft may be taken to have been the most closely connected (the fact that the ship or aircraft is registered in a particular country is relevant to establish its connection with that country but is not conclusive, eg, where a ship is flying a 'flag of convenience', or the ship or aircraft is not registered); (ii) in so far as a will disposes of immovable property, it will be treated as properly executed if it was made in accordance with the internal law of the country in which such property is situated; (iii) in so far as a will revokes an earlier will, or part thereof, the revocatory provisions will be effective if the execution of the will conforms to any law to which recourse might be had under the provisions of the Act of 1963 to establish the validity of the earlier revoked will (see p 56).

When considering for the purposes of the Act where a testator was domiciled, regard must be paid to the English concept of domicile (compare with the definition of domicile in s 41 of the Civil Jurisdiction and Judgments Act 1982). If before his death a testator had acquired a domicile of choice in a particular country, as distinct from his domicile of origin (see below), it will be necessary to show that he has taken up his residence in that country with the intention of remaining there so far as he could foresee. Should it be difficult to prove that a testator was domiciled in this sense in a country so as to enable the validity of his will to be established by the law of that country, it will often be possible to show that he was habitually resident there, thus permitting recourse to be had to that law in any event. It is to be noted also that as from 1 January 1974 a married woman's domicile is no longer dependent on that of her husband, but is to be ascertained by reference to the same factors as in the case of any other individual capable of having an independent domicile (s 1 of the Domicile and Matrimonial Proceedings Act 1973). A woman who by virtue of marriage before that date acquired her husband's domicile by dependence is treated as retaining that domicile (as a domicile of choice if it is not also her domicile of origin) unless and until she acquires another domicile on or after 1 January 1974. At birth a legitimate child takes as a domicile of origin the domicile of his father, and an illegitimate child takes that of his mother. In certain circumstances when the mother and father are living apart and the child is living with his mother, his domicile as at that time becomes that of his mother (see s 4 of the Act of 1973). A person becomes capable of having an independent domicile at the age of sixteen or on marrying under that age (s 3 of the Act of 1973).

When a testator had dual nationality, reference may be made to the law of either country of which he was a national to establish the validity of his will. Should the country of nationality consist of a number of separate territories, each having its own system of law, eg, the United Kingdom and its colonies, the particular legal system to be applied must be determined, first, in accordance with any rule in force in that country governing the choice of law in such circumstances, and, secondly, in the absence of any such rule, by reference to the legal system with which the testator was the most closely connected at the relevant time. When it is necessary to establish that the testator was closely connected with a particular territory, regard must be paid to those circumstances current at the date of his death, if the law which is to establish the validity of the will has been chosen by reference to his domicile, residence or nationality at the date of his death. Otherwise the circumstances are those current at the date of execution of the will.

The question of the choice of law will also arise when reference is to be made to the law of a country which contains two or more communities divided from each other on a tribal or religious basis and each governed by its own system of law. The same rules must be followed to decide the legal system applicable, and, if necessary, the connection of the testator with a particular community must be established.

The requirements of the legal system chosen under the provisions of the Act of 1963 are those in force at the date of execution of the will. No notice is to be taken of alterations in that law made after the date of execution unless it is provided by the law in question that the alteration thereto shall have retrospective effect so as to apply to wills which were executed at the time of execution of the will under review.

The Act of 1963 would not appear to have affected the existing practice of the court to allow proof of a will, which has already been accorded recognition by the court of the country of the deceased's domicile at the date of his death, without inquiry whether that court accepted the will's validity on some basis other than that it was executed in conformity with the internal law of that country.

Although Lord Kingsdown's Act (see head 2.1(*a*)) has been repealed with effect from 1 January 1964, it is still relevant to establish the validity of the will of a testator who had died on or after 1 January 1964 if the will was made before that date and its validity cannot be established under the provisions of the Wills Act 1963 (because the repeal of Lord Kingsdown's Act is not to invalidate a will made before 1 January 1964). In practice, since the only part of Lord Kingsdown's Act which has not been incorporated in the Wills Act 1963 is that which allows reference to be made to the law of the testator's domicile of origin, this provision will only apply in the case of a British subject who dies on or after 1 January 1964 leaving a will made before that date which is valid only by the law of the country in which the testator had his domicile of origin, such country forming part of Her Majesty's dominions.

2.2 What makes a will?

English domestic law requires that a will must be in writing (s 9 of the Wills Act 1837, as amended by s 17 of the Administration of Justice Act 1982), unless it is a privileged will (see head 2.26). Moreover, to be capable of proof any alleged testamentary document must deal with real or personal property situated in England and Wales or appoint an executor. Even if a change of circumstances, such as the death of the executor and of all the beneficiaries, has made the will inoperative, it must still be proved if a grant of representation is required, if only for the reason that it cannot be sworn that the deceased died intestate. A document which neither deals with property in England and Wales nor appoints an executor cannot be proved, even though it has been executed in the manner required by law (for an exception see *In the Estate of Wayland* [1951] 2 All ER 1041). Such a document might be one merely revoking some previous testamentary instrument (see head 2.29(*b*)). In addition, a testator must not have been under the age of eighteen years (twenty-one years if the will was made before 1 January 1970) at the time of making his will (unless it is claimed that the will is privileged: see head 2.26).

The Wills Act 1963, however, defines 'will' as including any testamentary instrument or act. Where, therefore, a person has died on or after 1 January 1964 it is necessary to consider whether any expression by him of his testamentary intentions, although made, not in writing, but by word of mouth or other means, can be set up as valid under the provisions of a foreign law to which reference may be made under the Act in the particular circumstances.

2.3 Validity under English law

When reference is to be made to the internal law of England and Wales to establish the validity of the will, for instance, because the testator died domiciled in England and Wales, the will must have been executed in accordance with s 9 of the Wills Act 1837, as amended by s 17 of the Administration of Justice Act 1982, unless it can be shown to be a privileged will (see head 2.26) or it has been executed by direction of the court on behalf of a mentally disordered person (see head 2.28). Even so, the will may be challenged on the ground that, at the date of its execution, the testator was incapable of understanding the nature of his acts or was subjected to undue influence, or it may be claimed that the will has subsequently been revoked by operation of law or by act of the testator (see head 2.29). The remaining parts of this chapter are concerned, except where otherwise stated, with the operation of the internal law of England and Wales in relation to wills. (For proof of the validity of a will under foreign law, see head 15.1, and for international wills, see head 2.32.)

Section 9 of the Wills Act 1837, as amended by s 17 of the Administration of Justice Act 1982, provides that a will is duly executed if (i) it is in writing, (ii) it is signed by the testator or by some other person in his presence and by his direction, (iii) it appears that the testator intended by his signature to give effect to the will, (iv) the signature is made or acknowledged by the testator in the presence of two or more witnesses present at the same time, and (v) each witness either (*a*) attests and signs the will, or (*b*) acknowledges his signature, in the presence of the testator but not necessarily in the presence of any other witness. 'Writing' has been defined (Interpretation Act 1978, Sched 1) as including typing, printing, lithography, photography and other modes of representing or reproducing words in a visible form, and expressions referring to writing are to be construed accordingly. In respect of the will of a testator who has died before 1 January 1983, his signature must have been made at the foot or end of the will (see head 2.5).

Defects in execution appearing on the face of a will are remedied by a properly attested codicil, but only if the codicil expressly refers to the will. In the absence of any express reference, defects in the will are not rectified by the codicil, and this is so even if the codicil is written on the same sheet of paper as the will.

Before the papers to lead a grant of probate or of letters of administration with will annexed are prepared, all the testamentary writings of the deceased should be carefully examined to ensure that they are in order and an explanation should be provided for any minor defects appearing therein.

2.4 The attestation clause

A formal statement of the facts of execution in the form of an attestation clause is not essential to the validity of a will. But if there is no such clause, or if the attestation clause is in any way defective in material particulars, proof of the execution of the document in accordance with the requirements of s 9 of the Wills Act 1837, as amended by s 17 of the Administration of Justice Act 1982, must be given.

Generally, when a will bears an attestation clause which shows that the testator signed it in the presence of the attesting witnesses, all three being present together, and that thereafter each witness signed it in the testator's presence, no evidence of due execution is called for. If the attestation clause does not establish beyond doubt that the testator signed in the presence of the witnesses and that they both signed in his presence although not necessarily in the presence of each other, an affidavit of due execution is always called for (see head 2.11 and Form 2.11). Where a will contains a printed attestation clause in which certain blanks have not been completed or certain alternative words have not been deleted (viz, 'in a presence', or 'his/her presence', or 'his or her') no evidence is required. Similarly, if the clause reads 'Signed by the said testator' followed by a space for the insertion of the testator's name, which has been left blank, evidence is usually unnecessary. However, when the clause reads 'Signed by the said' followed by a blank space, evidence may be called for unless it can be inferred from other words in the clause that the testator must have signed the will in the presence of the witnesses or there is a completed testimonium clause containing the testator's name immediately above the attestation clause. It is not sufficient for the clause to recite that the witnesses signed the will, or acknowledged their signatures thereto, at the request of the testator if it does not also show that they signed or acknowledged in his presence.

2.5 The position of the testator's signature

The position of the testator's signature in the will may sometimes raise a doubt whether the will was properly executed. Before s 9 of the Wills Act 1837 was amended by s 17 of the Administration of Justice Act 1982 it was specifically provided that the testator's signature should be 'at the foot or end' of the will. Section 1 of the Wills Act Amendment Act 1852 sought to dispel certain doubts which had arisen by indicating that if the signature appeared at or after, or following, or under, or beside, or opposite to the end of the will, it would be accepted if it appeared from the face of the will that the testator had so signed with the intention of giving effect to its contents. The result of this was that the signature might appear practically anywhere on the will, although a signature in the top margin was not accepted (*Re Stalman* [1931] WN 143). Section 1 of the Act of 1852 also provided that any testamentary disposition or direction underneath or following the signature of the testator was not a part of the will and in consequence such matter had to be excluded from probate. That is still the law in respect of the will of a testator who has died before 1 January 1983, but where the testator has died on or after that date, his signature may appear anywhere on the will so long as it is apparent that he intended to give effect to his will by that signature (s 9 of the Wills Act 1837 as amended by s 17 of the Administration of Justice Act 1982). Section 1 of the Act of 1852 has been wholly repealed, from which it follows that written matter which would previously have been automatically excluded from probate because it appeared below the testator's signature may now be included if it can be shown that such written matter formed part of the will to which the testator gave his signature.

If the signature of the testator appears at the end of the text of the will, no question will normally be raised. The fact that a blank space appears between the end of the will and the signature does not in itself call for evidence of due execution. However, in the following circumstances, evidence of due execution is usually called for:

(1) *Where the signature is not at the end of the will*—If the signature of the testator is not in the usual position following the text of the will, there should be an affidavit of due execution showing that the testator so signed 'meaning and intending' such signature to be in final execution of the will (see Form 2.11, p 28).

(2) *Where the signature appears in the testimonium or attestation clause of the will*—There should be an affidavit of due execution showing that the signature was so made 'meaning and intending' it to be in final execution of the will (see Form 2.11, p 27).

(3) *Where the signature of the testator appears below either or both of those of the witnesses*—The presumption here is that the testator signed after the witnesses had signed or acknowledged their signatures, which, if it were so, would make the will invalid. Consequently an affidavit of due execution is called for unless there is something further appearing on the

face of the will which is sufficient to rebut this presumption. For instance, in some printed will forms, a row of dots has been printed underneath the attestation clause as an invitation to the testator to place his signature there; in other will forms the word 'Signed' followed by a row of dots appears below the attestation clause. The affidavit of due execution should mention the circumstances which call for it, and state in the clearest language that the testator signed first (see Form 2.11, p 29).

(4) *Where the signature of the testator and/or those of the attesting witnesses appear on some part of the document upon which no part of the will is written*—If the signatures of the testator and of the witnesses appear on p 2 of a printed will form, which is otherwise blank inasmuch as the rest of the will is contained on p 1, and there is a proper attestation clause, no evidence is usually called for. Where the dispositive part of the will and the testator's signature occupied one side of a small sheet of paper and on the other side were the signatures of two other persons, who could not be found, but no attestation clause, it has been held that the only practical explanation of the two signatures was that they had been made for the purpose of attesting the will (*Re Denning, Harnett* v *Elliott* [1958] 2 All ER 1).

In many cases of this nature the will consists of loose sheets. The rule is that it must be established that when the will was signed all the sheets comprising it were physically connected. This connection may be by some form of fastener (*In the Goods of Horsford* (1874) LR 3 P & D 211), or the testator may have held the papers together (*Lewis* v *Lewis* [1908] P 1; *Re Little, decd* [1960] 1 All ER 387). The rule is one for the prevention of fraud, and if the evidence of the circumstances of execution clearly negatives fraud, it is not strictly applied (*In the Goods of Mann* [1942] P 146).

If the testator has made his signature not on the will but on the endorsement, it must be clearly established that the signature was so made 'meaning and intending' it to be in final execution of the will and that the witnesses signed afterwards, because prima facie the will is unsigned.

The endorsement by the testator of an envelope in which the will is placed is prima facie for the purpose of identification of the contents (*In the Estate of Bean* [1944] P 83), but if it can be established that the testator signed the envelope in the presence of the witnesses with the intention of executing the will which was before them, and which was afterwards placed in the envelope, the execution of the will is good (*Re Nicholls* [1921] 2 Ch 11; *In the Goods of Mann* [1942] P 146; compare *Re Beadle* [1974] 1 All ER 493). The witnesses must, of course, have signed their names, or acknowledged their signatures, on the will or on the envelope after the testator had made his signature.

(5) *Where the testator signed twice*—It is rare that evidence is called for merely because a testator signed his name twice, but if other matters call for the filing of an affidavit of due execution, reference should be made to the double signature in order to show which of them was made in final execution of the will (see Form 2.11, p 28). An affidavit of due execution may be accepted although it makes no reference to the double signature.

(6) *Where part of the will appears underneath the signature*—Any testamentary disposition or direction underneath or following the signature of a testator who has died on or after 1 January 1983 will be included in the probate if it can be established that the testator intended such disposition or direction to form part of his will (see Form 2.11, p 29). The fact that the text of the will is continuous apart from the space on which the signature has been inserted is a strong indication to this effect. Otherwise, and in all cases where the testator died before 1 January 1983, any such matter is not a part of the will and will be excluded from probate. The sole exception is when there is a sufficiently clear reference in the effective part of the will above the signature of the testator to the matter following the signature so as to include it in the will by incorporation (see head 2.19). Unless there is incorporation a special copy of the will omitting the matter under the signature must be prepared for the registrar's fiat (see p 23, and head 21.1).

2.6 The form of the testator's signature

The form of the testator's signature may be such as to arouse suspicion either that it was not made in final execution of the will or that at the time of making it the testator was unable to appreciate the significance of his acts. The most common instances are: (*a*) where the signature shows signs of extreme feebleness, blindness or illiteracy; (*b*) where there have been abortive efforts to sign the will or the signature is incomplete; (*c*) where the signature is by mark, initials, fingerprint or seal, or is in foreign characters; (*d*) where the will has been signed by some other person, whether he signs the testator's name or his own. In each of these cases, if the attestation clause does not set out the exact circumstances of the execution including the fact that the will was read over by or to the testator and that he understood its contents, an affidavit of due execution should be filed (Probate Rule 11). This affidavit should explain the reason for the testator having made his signature in the way in which it appears in the will and, where appropriate, it should incorporate the reading-over clause (see Form 2.11, pp 27, 28). In the case where the signature of the testator is incomplete, the affidavit should show that:

(i) he was mentally present to a degree sufficient to make him capable of executing the document and appreciating its contents;
(ii) he intended the document to be testamentary; and
(iii) what he wrote was intended to be his signature (*Re Chalcraft* [1948] P 222).

When signing his will the testator does not have to use his own name if the words he uses are intended to represent his name (see *In the Estate of Cook* [1960] 1 All ER 689: 'your loving Mother') but the name must be complete before the witnesses sign the will or acknowledge their signatures thereon (*Re Colling, decd* [1972] 3 All ER 729).

If the signature of the testator has been made by some other person, then the attestation clause should show in addition to the reading over of the will that the signing was done 'in the presence and at the direction of the testator'; otherwise an affidavit in proof of those facts will be called for (see Form 2.11, p 28). (As to signing a will on behalf of a mentally disordered person, see head 2.28.)

2.7 Signature by the witnesses

It is usually sufficient if the attestation clause shows that the will was 'attested' by the witnesses in place of the phrase 'attest and subscribe' used in the original s 9 of the Wills Act 1837 or 'attest and sign' in s 9 as amended; the subscription or signing is implicit from the witnesses' signatures. The actual signature must be of such a nature as to be descriptive of the witness, whether by a mark intended to represent the name or by initials instead of the full name (*Hindmarsh* v *Charlton* (1861) 8 HLC 160). There must be some form of physical participation by the witness in signing his name; another person may not sign on his behalf nor affix a rubber stamp bearing the witness's name, even in the latter's presence (*In the Estate of Bullock* [1968] NI 96). An acknowledgment by the witness of his previously made signature is sufficient only if the testator died on or after 1 January 1983. The signature of each witness must be made, or acknowledged, after the testator has signed, or acknowledged his signature, in the presence of both witnesses. Neither witness need sign, or acknowledge his signature, in the presence of the other witness, but such signature or acknowledgment must be made in the testator's presence. It would appear that a witness who has signed the will before the testator has made his signature, may now put matters right by acknowledging his signature after the testator has signed (in respect of deaths on or after 1 January 1983).

2.8 The date of the will

The date of a testamentary document is of the utmost importance, and where the date is missing or incomplete, or there are conflicting dates, an affidavit of due execution having particular reference thereto will be called for (Probate Rule 12 (3)) (see head 2.14 and Form 2.11, p 27). An affidavit is not necessary if the will bears two different dates, one at the commencement and the later one at the end of the will, unless the later date is in the attestation clause or is not close to the testator's signature, or conflicts with a date on the endorsement, if any, or unless the title of the applicant to the grant depends on the later date being the true one. Nor is an affidavit required if the date on the endorsement of the will is earlier than the date of the will. If the will is undated or the date is imperfect, but there is a complete date in the endorsement which there is no reason to suppose is not the true date of the will, this will be accepted and the will noted by the registry: 'Endorsement of will dated ——'. Where, however, the date on the endorsement is later than that of the will, evidence of the correct date is called for unless the discrepancy is slight and unlikely to be of material importance, when the registrar has a discretion to dispense with such evidence. Whenever it is possible, the deponent should refer to some circumstance which assists him in the determination of the date. If neither of the witnesses nor any other person who may have been present at the time of execution can give the exact date, they should arrive at an approximate date or period of time. This may be some time between two known dates, or in a certain month or season of the year. When this is the position or when no evidence at all can be given as to the probable date, an affidavit of search for any other testamentary documents which may exist must also be filed (see Form 2.14.2).

2.9 Alterations in the will

It is presumed that alterations in a will were made after execution unless there is affirmative evidence to the contrary. No alteration made after execution is valid or has any effect (save in so far as the original text cannot now be ascertained) unless it has been executed in the same manner as if it had been a will. However, a will together with the alterations therein is deemed to have been duly executed when:

(*a*) reference is made to the alterations in a memorandum appearing at the end or some other part of the will which is verified by the signatures of the testator and of the attesting witnesses at the foot or end of or opposite to the memorandum; or

(*b*) the signatures (which may be in the form of initials) of the testator and of the attesting witnesses appear in the margin of the document opposite or near to the alterations (Wills Act 1837, s 21). If the alterations are purely clerical or of small importance, the initials of the witnesses may alone be sufficient (see also below for unimportant alterations).

Alterations may also be authenticated in the following ways:

(i) by reference to them in the attestation clause as having been made before execution;

(ii) by the republication or re-execution of the document with a reference to the alterations in the clause setting out the fact of the republication or re-execution;

(iii) by the execution of a codicil which mentions the alterations, or which by its language shows that they must have appeared in the will at the time of the execution of the codicil.

If alterations are not authenticated by one of the above methods, the evidence of an attesting witness as to whether they appeared or did not appear at the time of the execution of the will must usually be obtained (Probate Rule 12 (1)). But if they were made by the person who wrote the will his evidence to that effect and that they so appeared prior to the execution of the will is generally accepted (see heads 2.11, 2.14). The registrar has a discretion to dispense with any evidence at all and to allow the will to be proved with the alterations if he is satisfied that they are of no practical importance. In the affidavit of evidence, each alteration must be specifically mentioned with reference to the line of the will in which it appears (see Form 2.11, p 29). If the evidence establishes that they appeared at the time of the execution of the will, they will form part of the will; if it shows that they did not so appear, or if no evidence either way can be obtained, they will be omitted from the will, and it must be restored to its original condition. For this purpose, an engrossment of the will, omitting all alterations which cannot be shown to have been in existence at the time of its execution and restoring all words erased or obliterated (if this is possible), must be prepared for the fiat of the registrar: 'Let probate of the will of the within named... issue in accordance with this copy', which is placed on the copy. The fiat copy (see head 21.1) is used for making the photographic probate copy, and copies of the will which may afterwards issue will follow it.

Where alterations in a will cannot be set up in this way under English law and the testator died on or after 1 January 1964, it is necessary to inquire into the possibility of establishing the validity of the alterations by reference to some other, foreign system of law with which the testator may have been connected, under the provisions of the Wills Act 1963 (see p 13 et seq). When the alteration is material or it is apparent that the testator was connected with a foreign country, the registrar may require to be satisfied that such an inquiry has been made. A certificate by the solicitor will usually suffice. (For proof of validity under foreign law, see head 15.1.)

Difficulties sometimes arise in the restoration of a will which contains erasures and obliterations. These may have been made so completely that it is impossible to read what has been erased or obliterated. This amounts to a destruction of those parts of the will, and consequently to their revocation. The will is therefore a blank so far as these words or passages are concerned, and should the registrar require a fiat copy, this and all copies will show a blank space where the erasures and obliterations appear in the original. The court will not usually allow any physical interference with the document to enable the words to be read (*Re Itter* [1948] 2 All ER 1052). However, if the doctrine of dependent relative revocation (see head 2.29(*d*)) can be invoked in the particular circumstances, it may be permissible to discover the missing words by physical means and, if successful, to have them restored to the will for probate.

2.10 Plight and condition of the will

When the general appearance of a will shows that it might have been interfered with, evidence of its condition at the time of execution and at the time of its finding may be called for (see head 2.14). An affidavit of search for other testamentary documents may also be called for. The question usually arises:

(1) *When there are signs of tearing, burning, obliteration or cancellation in any form*—In such cases there is a possibility of an attempt at revocation by destruction, and this presumption must be rebutted (Probate Rule 13). Whenever possible, the circumstances in which the will came into its present condition must be set out in the affidavit of a person having knowledge of the facts. If no evidence can be obtained, an affidavit showing whether or not the will is in the same plight and condition as when found must be provided (see Form 2.14.1). It may also be necessary to obtain evidence from an attesting witness of the state of the will at the time of execution (see head 2.14) and evidence of its custody from that time until it was found. If the signs are slight, it is advisable to ask the registrar in advance whether he will require any evidence to account for them. (See also Revocation of wills by destruction, head 2.29(*c*).)

(2) *When the will is written on a sheet of paper which has been torn or cut off a larger sheet*—There is a possibility that the sheet cut off contained other testamentary dispositions. The evidence of an attesting witness may therefore be called for to establish that the will is in the same condition as when executed (see head 2.14). If this evidence cannot be obtained, affidavits showing that it is now in the same plight and condition as when found, and of search for other testamentary documents, may be required (see Forms 2.14.1 and 2.14.2). Where the testamentary matter is complete in itself but has been written on a will form the endorsement page of which is missing, or on a sheet torn from an exercise book, the registrar may be prepared in the exercise of his discretion to dispense with evidence of plight and condition.

(3) *When the appearance of the will shows that some document has been attached to it*—This may be disclosed by the existence of pin or fastener holes or impressions, or by traces of an adhesive. If the solicitor having the conduct of the application can state of his own personal knowledge what documents were attached, his statement as to the nature of the documents and that they were not of a testamentary nature will be accepted: otherwise the affidavit evidence of the person responsible for the attachment of the papers must be obtained (Probate Rule 12 (2)) (see Form 2.14.1). When it cannot be discovered what documents had been attached, affidavits showing that the will is in the same plight and condition as when found, and of search for other testamentary documents, must be filed (see Forms 2.14.1 and 2.14.2).

(4) *When an addition appears to have been made to the will*—This usually discloses itself through a different type of writing or a differently coloured ink or having been written in pencil. These signs are not conclusive that the addition was made after the execution of the will, but the evidence of an attesting witness may have to be obtained to show whether or not the presumed addition appeared at the time of execution (see head 2.9 and Form 2.11, p 29), unless it is of no practical importance. If it did appear it will form part of the will. If no evidence either way can be obtained the consent (see Form 2.14.3) of the persons adversely affected may have to be

obtained before it is allowed to form part of the will. Otherwise it will be excluded from probate on the fiat of the registrar (see p 23).

When pencil writings of any kind appear in a will, a copy of the will or of the pages or sheets containing the pencil writing, in which that writing has been underlined in red ink (and which may be a photographic copy) must be filed for the purpose of perpetuating them (see head 21.1).

(See also Damaged wills, head 2.23.)

2.11 Evidence of execution by persons present at the time

When it is necessary that evidence should be given of the facts of the execution of a will because there is no attestation clause, or the clause is deficient, or there is some other factor present which raises a doubt that the will was properly executed, reference must first be made to the attesting witnesses (Probate Rule 10). Usually the evidence of one witness only is sufficient, provided his recollection of the circumstances is clear. If both witnesses are dead, or cannot be found, or are not conveniently available, the evidence of any other person present at the time of execution will be accepted. The affidavit should describe the entire circumstances of execution and, in addition, the deponent should be asked, if appropriate, to deal with the particular defect. When tendering the affidavit of a person other than one of the witnesses, it should be explained why the witnesses have not been contacted. Where there is a danger that the will might be lost in transmitting it with the draft affidavit to the deponent for him to swear the affidavit, application may be made to the registrar (Principal of the Probate Department in the Principal Registry) for a photographic copy of the will to be exhibited to the affidavit (Probate Rule 8).

(*Note*—In this and all following forms sections have been numbered for ease of reference to the notes appearing immediately after the form. All paragraphs of affidavits should be numbered. Affidavits used in non-contentious probate business must be in the forms required by RSC, Ord 41 (Probate Rule 65). The comments in the Practice Direction issued by the Lord Chief Justice on 21 July 1983 may also be noted in so far as they are relevant.)

Form 2.11 Affidavit of due execution

IN THE HIGH COURT OF JUSTICE,
Family Division

The Principal Registry
(or The District Probate Registry at)
In the Estate of deceased.

1 I, ,
of ,
make oath and say that

2 I am one of the attesting witnesses to the last Will and Testament

3 of ,
of , deceased,
4 the said Will, bearing date the day of , 19 , being now produced to me and marked ' ';
5 that the said deceased executed the said Will on the day of the date thereof
6 by signing his name at the foot or end thereof as the same now appears thereon, meaning and intending the same to be his final signature to the said Will
7 in the presence of me and of the other witness thereto, both of us being present at the same time:
8 that after the said deceased had so signed we attested and signed the said Will in the presence of the said deceased.
9
10 Sworn by the above-named deponent
at
this day of , 19 .
Before me
A Commissioner for Oaths (or Solicitor).

1 The full name, address and occupation or description of the deponent should be given. If the name differs materially from that which appears in the attestation clause, an explanation should be provided (see para **9**, below). Generally where a deponent is giving evidence in a professional, business or other occupational capacity, he may give instead of his private address the address at which he works, stating at the same time the position he holds and the name of his employer or firm, if any. If necessary, an application may be made to the registrar for the place of residence to be omitted from the affidavit. For occupation or description, see pp 69–70. Order 41, Rule 1 (4) of the Rules of the Supreme Court requires that where the deponent to an affidavit is, or is employed by, a party to the cause or matter in which the affidavit is sworn, this must be stated in the affidavit.

If the person giving evidence wishes to affirm, the words 'make oath and say' should be altered to 'do solemnly and sincerely affirm'; the word 'Sworn' in the jurat (para **10**) should be altered to 'Affirmed'. Evidence by an attesting witness or by any other competent person as to the signing of a will may also be given in the form of a statutory declaration provided that such evidence is directed towards proving due execution.

2 If the deponent is not one of the attesting witnesses, this paragraph should be altered to say 'I was a person present at the execution of the last Will and Testament'. Paragraphs **7** and **8** will also require slight alterations in that event. The reason why evidence is not being given by an attesting witness should be recited in para **9**, below.

When the affidavit is to speak to the execution of a codicil the words 'Codicil to the' or 'First (*or as the case may be*) Codicil to the' should be inserted before 'last Will and Testament' and corresponding alterations or additions made in the succeeding paragraphs.

3 Give the full name and last address of the deceased. If the address recited in the will differs from his last address, insert after the last address 'formerly of   ', giving the address in the will.

4 If it is necessary to deal specifically with the date of the will (see head 2.8), recite any different dates appearing in the will, or the date on the endorsement if this is material, or the fact that the will is undated, thus:

'bearing date the   day of   , 19   , in the third line thereof and the   day of   , 19   , immediately after the signature of the deceased', *or*

'bearing date the   day of   , 19   , and the further date the   day of   , 19   , on the endorsement thereof', *or*

'bearing no date', *or*

'bearing date   , but omitting the day of the month (*or as the case may be*)'.

Where the registrar has given leave for a photographic copy of the will to be exhibited to the affidavit, insert 'a photographic copy of' before 'the said Will'.

5 If it is necessary to state the exact date, this should be done viz, 'on the   day of   , 19   '. However, if the deponent is unable to swear to the exact day of the month when execution took place, he should say 'on or about the day of the date thereof' or, 'on or about the   day of   , 19   ', or 'between the   day of   , 19   , and the   day of   , 19   ', or, 'some time in the month of   , 19   , which date cannot be stated more exactly'. Reasons for the deponent being able to fix the date should be given in para **9**, below, if it is necessary to deal specifically with the date in the affidavit.

6 The exact circumstances under which the deceased's signature came to be made or acknowledged in the presence of the witnesses must be described in this paragraph, more particularly if the manner of making the signature or the place in which it was made gives rise to doubt as to due execution (see heads 2.5, 2.6). Normally it will be sufficient to use the wording which appears in the form of affidavit; the following alternatives deal with other situations which may arise:

'by making his mark, he being unable to write his name by reason of an injury to his hand' (if the reason is that the deceased was illiterate or suffering from a severe illness or blind, then it will be necessary to insert a further clause in para **9** showing whether the will was read over to the deceased and whether he appeared to understand, or had full knowledge of, the contents); *or*

'by signing his name in the attestation (*or* testimonium) clause, at the foot or end thereof as the same now appears thereon, meaning, etc'; *or*

'by acknowledging his signature as the same now appears thereon to be his final signature to the said Will'; *or* 'by signing his name immediately after the word "   " in the tenth line thereof and again on the fourteenth line thereof, as the same now appear thereon, meaning and intending the said signature on the fourteenth line to be his final signature to the said Will'; *or*

'by *CD* signing the name of the said deceased (*or* his own name) at the foot or end thereof as the same now appears thereon in the presence and at the direction of the said deceased who then acknowledged the said signature to be his final signature to the said Will.'

7 If there is any doubt as to whether the two witnesses were sufficiently 'present at the same time', for instance, because one of them was some distance away although able to see what was going on, the exact circumstances should be set out in a further clause in para **9**.

If the deponent is not an attesting witness, this paragraph should read 'in the presence of me and of *CD* and *EF*, the attesting witnesses to the Will, all of us being present at the same time'; para **8** should then read 'that after the said deceased had so signed, the said *CD* and *EF* attested and signed the said Will in my presence and in that of the deceased (*or as the case may be*).'

8 Usually both witnesses proceed to sign the will themselves in each other's presence as well as in that of the deceased, but the statute requires only that each witness should sign in the deceased's presence. If the witnesses signed at different times, this should be stated. In respect of deaths on or after 1 January 1983 it is sufficient that either or both witnesses acknowledged their signatures, already made, after the deceased signed his will and in his presence. In that case para **8** should read 'we acknowledged our signatures as the same now appear on the said Will to be our signatures in the presence of the said deceased (*or as the case may be*).' It would be advisable to explain shortly how the witnesses came to sign the will.

9 This paragraph should contain any further explanation which is required, as follows:

Change of name of witness

'And I further make oath and say that my name at the date of execution of the Will as aforesaid was *AB* but I have since married and my name is now *AC*.'

Affidavit made by person other than a witness

'And I further make oath and say that (I am informed and verily believe that) the said *CD* and *EF*, the attesting witnesses to the Will, are now both dead'; *or*

'that I have made inquiries and have caused inquiries to be made with regard to the present whereabouts of the said *CD* and *EF*, the attesting witnesses to the Will, but without success, they having moved from the addresses as stated in the Will without leaving any forwarding address.'

Date of will

'And I further make oath and say that I particularly remember the date of execution of the said Will as aforesaid because (*give reason*).'

Reading over and knowledge and approval

'And I further make oath and say that before execution as aforesaid the said Will was read over by me (*or*, by *EF* in my presence) to the said deceased (*or*, read over in my presence by the said deceased) who appeared to understand the same perfectly (*or*, who had full knowledge of the contents thereof).'

Position of signature

'And I further make oath and say that the said *EF* and I signed our names after the said deceased had signed as aforesaid and above his said signature because there was no room for us to sign our names below his signature (*or as the case may be*)'; *or*

'And I further make oath and say that the reason why the signatures of the said deceased, the said *EF* and myself appear on a sheet of paper upon which no other part of the Will is written is because there was no room for the same to be made on the last preceding page of the Will and that at the time the deceased executed the Will as aforesaid all the sheets comprising the Will including that on which the said signatures were made were fastened together as they now appear (*or*, were physically held together by the said deceased)'; *or*

'And I further make oath and say that the reason why the signatures of the said deceased, the said *EF* and myself appear in the space below paragraph 9 and above paragraph 10 of the said Will is because there was no room for the same to be made at the foot of the page on which those paragraphs are written (*or as the case may be*).'

Alterations (see head 2.9)

'And referring to the following alterations in the said Will, to wit: (*set out the nature and extent of each alteration in detail*)

I further make oath and say that the said recited alterations were made as they now appear before (*or* after) execution as aforesaid'; *or*

'that I cannot now remember whether the said recited alterations were made before execution as aforesaid'; *or*

'that I am unable to say whether the said recited alteration was made before execution as aforesaid (*and give the reason*, *eg*, because the deceased had so folded the said Will that I was unable to see any of the contents thereof save for his signature).'

10 *The jurat*—If there is one deponent it is sufficient to say 'the above-named deponent'; if there is more than one, 'both (*or* all) the above-named deponents.' If, however, the deponents swear at different times, the name of each should be inserted in a separate jurat.

The place and date of swearing must be given precisely; it is not sufficient merely to give the name of the town.

Intervention by an interpreter necessary—After the interpreter has taken the oath, there must be inserted in the jurat after the date of swearing: 'through the interpretation of , he having first sworn that he fully understood and was well acquainted with the English and languages and that he had truly and faithfully interpreted the contents of this affidavit to the said (*the deponent*) and that he would truly and faithfully interpret the oath about to be administered to the said (*the deponent*).'

Commissioner or solicitor—Affidavits may be sworn before any solicitor who holds a current practising certificate, provided that he is not acting for a party to the proceedings in which the affidavit is to be used, or is not interested in such proceedings. It is sufficient to use the description 'Solicitor'. The signature must be legible enough to allow confirmation of his office by reference to the current Solicitors' Diary. If it is difficult to decipher, it must be followed by the addition of his typed name or by use of a rubber stamp.

2.12 Other evidence in support of due execution

When the attesting witnesses are not available and no other person can be found who was present at the time of execution, the applicant for the grant must depose to that effect (see Form 2.12.1, below), and it is necessary to produce evidence sufficient to raise a presumption in favour of due execution of the will. This may take the form of an affidavit, preferably by a disinterested person, identifying the signature of the deceased on the will, together with any other part of the will written by the deceased, as being in the deceased's handwriting (see Form 2.12.2); if the applicant is the only person who would be entitled to the deceased's estate were the will not to be admitted to probate, an affidavit by the applicant to that effect and as to the deceased's handwriting may be accepted (see Form 2.12.1, below). The applicant should include in his affidavit a statement showing who are the persons who would be prejudiced by the will being proved and it may be necessary to lodge their consents duly signed and witnessed (see Form 2.12.3). The registrar may also require evidence as to the handwriting of the attesting witnesses (Form 2.12.2 can be adapted).

Even if both attesting witnesses testify to the will not having been duly executed, the court may still receive evidence to the contrary from other persons (*Re Vere-Wardale* [1949] P 395).

If, on the evidence produced to him, the registrar is satisfied that the will was not properly executed, he will mark the will 'Probate refused' (see head 2.13). If he is in doubt, he may require the applicant to apply to the court on motion for directions (see head 20.3).

Form 2.12.1 Affidavit of application in support of will
(For heading and title, see Form 2.11)

1 I, ,
of ,
make oath and say that
2 I am the sole executor named in the last Will and Testament of ,
of ,
deceased, the said Will, bearing date the day of , 19 ,
being now produced to me and marked ' ';
3 that I have made inquiries and have caused inquiries to be made with regard to the present whereabouts of *CD* and *EF*, the attesting witnesses to the said Will, but without success, they having moved from the addresses as stated in the Will without leaving any forwarding address; and that (to the best of my knowledge, information and belief) there were no other persons present at the execution of the said Will
4 And I further make oath and say that (*here state the persons who would be prejudiced by the will being proved, eg*) the said deceased died a widower without issue or parent or any other person entitled in priority to share in his estate by virtue of any enactment, that in the event of his having died intestate the only persons entitled to share in his estate would be *GH* his lawful sister of the whole blood and *KB* his lawful nephew of the whole blood, being the lawful son of *CB* his lawful brother of the whole blood who predeceased him, and that all such persons are *sui juris* (*or as the case may be*).
5
6 Sworn by the above-
named deponent
at
this day of , 19 .
Before me
A Commissioner for Oaths (or Solicitor).

1 The full name, address and occupation or description of the deponent should be given. For occupation or description, see pp 69–70. For address see note to para **1** of Form 2.11 at p 26.

If the person giving evidence wishes to affirm, 'make oath and say' should be replaced by 'do solemnly and sincerely affirm'; para **4** should be altered by substituting 'affirm' for 'make oath' and para **6** by substituting 'Affirmed' for 'Sworn'.

2 If the deponent is not an executor, the exact title under which he claims to prove the will should be inserted (see head 4.2).

If the date of the will is incomplete or there are several dates, set out the position (see the alternative wording suggested in the note to para **4** of Form 2.11 at p 27).

3 Alter this paragraph to suit the circumstances with regard to the inquiries made to find the witnesses. If they are dead, substitute 'that *CD* and *EF*, the attesting witnesses to the Will, are now both dead and that there were no other persons present etc' *or* after stating that inquiries have been made, substitute 'and I am informed and verily believe that they are both now dead and that, etc'.

If it is known that other persons were present at the time of execution, deal in the same way with the reasons why it is not possible to produce their evidence.

4 For the persons entitled on an intestacy, see head 5.3(*c*) and p 112. If these persons have consented to the will being proved, insert after the recital of their names 'who have all consented to probate of the said Will being granted to me'.

If the applicant is the only person entitled to the deceased's estate in any event, this paragraph should read 'And I further make oath and say that (eg) the said deceased died a widower without issue or parent or any other person entitled in priority to share in his estate by virtue of any enactment and I am his lawful brother of the whole blood and the only person entitled to his estate were he to have died intestate.'

5 If the deponent is also to speak to the deceased's handwriting, the contents of paras **3** and **4** of Form 2.12.2 below should be inserted here.

6 See the note to para **10** of Form 2.11 at p 29.

Form 2.12.2 Affidavit of handwriting
(For heading and title, see Form 2.11)

1 I, ,
of ,
make oath and say that

2 I have carefully perused and examined the paper writing purporting to be and contain the last Will and Testament of *AB*, of , deceased, the said Will being now produced to me and marked ' '.

3 And that I knew and was well acquainted with the said deceased for many years preceding his death and I have frequently seen him write and sign his name to paper writings and am therefore well acquainted with the manner and character of his writing.

4 And I further make oath and say that I verily believe the name *AB* written at the foot of the said Will to be of the true and proper handwriting of the said deceased.

5 Sworn by the above-
named deponent
at
this day of , 19 .
Before me
A Commissioner for Oaths (or Solicitor).

1 See the note to para **1** of Form 2.12.1 at p 31.

2 When it is the deceased's signature to a codicil which has to be identified, insert the words 'Codicil to the' or 'First (*or as the case may be*) Codicil to the' before 'last Will and Testament'; para **4** should be altered correspondingly.

3 If the deponent was the deceased's spouse, it is sufficient to say 'And that I was married to the said deceased for the years preceding his death and I have frequently, etc'.

4 If the whole of the will is in the deceased's handwriting, insert 'as well as the whole of the said paper writing with the exception of the names and addresses of the two witnesses thereto (*or as the case may be*)' after the words 'the said Will'.

5 See the note to para **10** of Form 2.11 at p 29.

Form 2.12.3 Consent

(*For heading and title, see Form* 2.11)

1 Whereas *AB*, of , deceased, died on the day of , 19 , at , having made his last Will and Testament, bearing date the day of , 19 , and in the said Will appointed *FE* the sole executor thereof.

2 And whereas the only signature of the said deceased appearing on the said Will has been made in the attestation clause thereto, both the attesting witnesses to the Will are dead and no-one else was present at the time of execution.

3 And whereas the said deceased died a widower without issue or parent or any other person entitled in priority to share in his estate by virtue of any enactment leaving *CD* and *EB* his lawful sister and brother of the whole blood respectively and the only persons entitled to share in his estate were he to have died intestate.

4 Now I the said *CD* do hereby consent to probate of the said Will being granted to the said *FE*.

5 Signed by the said *CD*
this day of , 19 ,
in the presence of

1 If there is no doubt as to due execution, the words 'and duly executed' should be inserted before 'his last Will, etc'.

This paragraph should show who is the person applying to prove the will and what is his title. If, therefore, the application is being made by a person other than an executor, it should be indicated how all the persons with a higher title have been cleared off, viz, 'appointed *FE* the sole executor, who has renounced probate thereof, and *GH* and *SH*, the residuary legatees and devisees'.

2 This paragraph should recite the circumstances which require the consent to be given, eg, that there is a defect in the will which raises a doubt as to whether it was properly executed and that it has not been possible to obtain evidence from those persons who could have directly dispelled the doubt one way or another.

3 Set out in this paragraph the names and interests of all the persons prejudiced by the will being proved including that of the person giving his consent.

4 In an appropriate case substitute 'letters of administration with the said Will annexed' for 'probate of the said Will'.

5 The consent should be signed in the presence of a disinterested witness who should then sign his name and give his address.

2.13 Wills not duly executed

In the first instance it is the duty of the solicitor having the conduct of the application to determine whether or not a will is valid and, if in doubt, to submit it to a registrar for his decision. If the registrar, having considered the evidence, is satisfied that a will, containing the signature of the testator and of two witnesses, nevertheless has not been duly executed he will mark the will 'Probate refused' (Probate Rule 10). If in doubt he may refer the matter to the court on motion. The application to the registrar is made ex parte (through the Probate Department if made at the Principal Registry), supported by the affidavits of both, or one, of the attesting witnesses. It is advisable to obtain the evidence of both witnesses if they are conveniently available. Each witness must depose so far as he is able to the exact circumstances under which the deceased and the witnesses signed the will (see Form 2.13, below). If the testator did not sign his will in the presence of the witnesses, then they must be asked whether he acknowledged his signature in their joint presence. Acknowledgement may be express or implied; thus it is sufficient if the witnesses could have seen the testator's signature on the will if they had looked (*Daintree* v *Butcher and Fasulo* (1888) 13 PD 102).

If the will is marked 'Probate refused', it is retained in the registry, together with the supporting affidavits, to be filed with the papers to lead any other grant that may subsequently issue in the estate of the same deceased. There is no fee for the registrar's fiat nor for filing any affidavit.

Application for refusal of probate may be made at the same time as the papers to lead to a grant are lodged; in the Principal Registry all the papers are left with the Receiver of Papers.

If it is found after a grant has issued that the will was not duly executed, application should be made (through the Record Keeper if made in the Principal Registry) for an order revoking the grant (see head 16.2) and, if satisfied, the registrar will also mark the will 'Probate refused'.

Form 2.13 Affidavit to lead to refusal of probate

(For heading and title, see Form 2.11)

1 I, ,
of ,
make oath and say that

2 I am one of the attesting witnesses to the purported last Will and Testament

3 of ,
of , deceased,

4 the said Will bearing date the day of , 19 , being now produced to me and marked ' ';

5 And I further make oath and say that on or about the day of , 19 , the said deceased visited me at my shop at , produced the said Will to me and asked me to witness his signature thereto; that the said deceased thereupon signed his name at the foot or end thereof as the same now appears thereon meaning and intending the same as his final signature to the said Will, in my presence and I thereupon attested and signed the said Will in the presence of the said deceased; that at the time of execution as aforesaid, the said deceased and I were the only persons present in my said shop; that after I had so signed, the deceased took his Will away saying that he would get a second witness to sign it later on; that I have never met *EF* the other witness thereto [*or* that I know *EF* the other witness thereto but he was not present at that time, *or as the case may be*].

6 Sworn by the above-
named deponent at
this day of , 19 .
Before me,
A Commissioner for Oaths (or Solicitor).

1, 2, 3 and **4**—see the notes to the corresponding paragraphs of Form 2.11, pp 26–27.

5 This paragraph should set out the exact circumstances under which the deponent came to act as a witness to the will or to be present at the time of purported execution. It is never sufficient to say merely that 'the deceased did not sign his name nor acknowledge his signature on the said Will in my presence'.

6 See the note to para **10** of Form 2.11, at p 29.

2.14 Who may give evidence concerning the state of a will or as to its date, etc

If evidence is required as to the condition or appearance of a will at the time of its execution, or as to its date, or as to the knowledge and approval of the testator, it is advisable in the first place to refer to the attesting witnesses and, if they are not available, then to any other person who was present at that time (see Form 2.11). One exception is when the evidence is required to establish whether or not alterations appeared in the will at the time of its execution. If these were made before the execution of the document by the person who wrote or engrossed it (either in correction of a mistake made by him or on the instructions of the testator), the evidence of that person will be accepted, and no reference need be made to the attesting witnesses. Moreover, if a date later than that appearing on the will has been inserted in error on the endorsement of the will, the evidence of the person who made the mistake will usually be sufficient. The registrar has a discretion to accept an affidavit from any person he may think fit in these circumstances (Probate Rule 14). (As to the date of a will, see also head 2.8, alterations, head 2.9, and plight and condition, head 2.10)

It is important to note that, when an attesting witness or any other person present at the time of execution gives any evidence concerning the terms, condition or date of execution of a will, or as to the knowledge and approval of the testator, he must also depose to its due execution, even though the validity of the execution is not in question (Probate Rule 14) (see Form 2.11).

When no evidence of this nature is available, it may be necessary to file an affidavit as to the plight and condition of the will when found, or an affidavit of search for other testamentary documents, or both (see Forms 2.14.1 and 2.14.2, below), together with the consents of the persons prejudiced (see Form 2.14.3, below).

Form 2.14.1 Affidavit of plight and condition
(For heading and title, see Form 2.11)

1 I, ,
of ,
make oath and say that
2 I am the sole executor named in the last Will and Testament of , of , deceased, the said Will, bearing date the day of , 19 , being now produced to me and marked ' '.
3 And referring to the fact that the said Will has a torn left-hand edge and pinholes in the top left-hand corner I further make oath and say that
4 when I was going through the said deceased's private papers at his home at shortly after his death on the day of , 19 , I found the said Will folded in an envelope addressed to me by name as Executor; attached to the Will by a pin through the top left-hand corner was a slip of paper in the deceased's handwriting containing instructions with regard to cremation which said paper I removed; with that exception the said Will is now in all respects in the same condition as when found by me, namely with a torn left-hand edge.
5
6 Sworn by the above-
named deponent
at
this day of , 19 .
Before me
A Commissioner for Oaths (or Solicitor).

1 See the note to para **1** of Form 2.12.1 at p 31.

2 If the deponent is not an executor, insert the exact title under which he claims to prove the will (see head 4.2), or if he is not applying for a grant, give a short explanation as to why he should be the person making the affidavit, eg, by reason of his relationship to the deceased, and the fact that he resided in the same house, or as the case may be.

3 Here set out the condition of the document which requires to be explained (see head 2.10).

4 Here recite the finding of the will and, if possible, account for its present condition or else give the history of its custody up to the time when it was found.

5 If the deponent was present at the time of execution, whether as an attesting witness or otherwise, he must also depose to due execution of the will (see Form 2.11).

6 See the note to para **10** of Form 2.11 at p 29.

Form 2.14.2 Affidavit of search
(For heading and title, see Form 2.11)

1 I, ,
of ,
make oath and say that
2 I am the sole executor named in the last Will and Testament of , of , deceased, the said Will being now produced to me and marked ' '.

3 And referring to the fact that the said Will bears no date I further make oath and say that both the attesting witnesses thereto are now dead (to the best of my knowledge, information and belief), there were no other persons present at the execution of the said Will, and I have been unable to obtain any information concerning the date of execution of the said Will.

4 And that I have made inquiry of *LM*, the solicitor of the said deceased, and I have also made diligent and careful search in all places where the deceased usually kept his papers of importance, in order to ascertain whether he had or had not left any other Will, codicil, or testamentary paper, but that I have been unable to discover any such Will, codicil or other testamentary paper and I know of no other person who might have kept papers for the deceased. And I lastly make oath and say that I verily believe that the said deceased died without having left any Will, codicil or testamentary paper whatever other than the said Will hereinbefore referred to by me.

5

6 Sworn by the above-
named deponent
at
this day of , 19 .
Before me
A Commissioner for Oaths (or Solicitor).

1 See the note to para **1** of Form 2.12.1 at p 31.

2 If the deponent is not an executor, insert the exact title under which he claims to prove the will (see head 4.2).

3 Here set out the circumstances which call for an affidavit of search (see pp 23, 42, 43, 45) and the reason why direct evidence is not obtainable.

4 Detail all the persons from whom inquiries could be made and the results of such inquiries or the reason why an inquiry has not been made of them. Set out also any other testamentary papers found if necessary exhibiting them to the affidavit and explaining why it is not sought to prove them.

5 If the deponent was present at the time of execution of the will, whether as an attesting witness or otherwise, he must also depose to due execution of the will (see Form 2.11).

6 See the note to para **10** of Form 2.11 at p 29.

Form 2.14.3 Consent

(For heading and title, see Form 2.11)

1 Whereas *AB*, of , deceased, died on the day of , 19 , at having made and duly executed his last Will and Testament, bearing date the day of , 19 , and in the said Will appointed *FE* the sole executor thereof.

2 And whereas the following alterations appear in the said Will, to wit:— and no evidence can be obtained as to whether the said alterations were made previous or subsequent to execution of the said Will.

3 And whereas *CB* widow the relict of the said Deceased is the sole residuary legatee and devisee named in the said Will and would be prejudiced by effect being given to the said alterations.

4 Now I the said *CB* do hereby consent to probate of the said Will as containing the said alterations, being granted to the said *FE*.

5 Signed by the said *CB*
this day of , 19 ,
in the presence of

1 If the person applying to prove the will is not the executor, insert the exact title under which he is claiming the grant (see head 4.2).

2 Set out the nature and extent of each alteration in detail or otherwise set out the circumstances which require the consent to be given, ie, the particular condition of the will which requires an explanation and the inability to give a satisfactory explanation (see also head 2.22, as to proof of a copy will).

3 Set out in this paragraph the names and interests of all persons prejudiced by the will being proved as it stands including that of the person giving his consent.

4 In an appropriate case substitute 'letters of administration with the said Will annexed' for 'probate of the said Will'.

5 The consent should be signed in the presence of a disinterested witness who should then sign his name and give his address.

2.15 Omission of offensive or libellous words or passages in a will

When a will contains offensive or libellous words or passages, application may be made to the court for their exclusion from the probate. It is not possible to expunge them from the will (*Re Maxwell* (1929) 45 TLR 215).

The words to be omitted must not be dispositive, and must be clearly of an offensive or libellous character. It is sufficient if they are offensive in the sense that they are most objectionable, even though they do not refer to a particular individual (*In the Goods of Bowker* [1932] P 93). It is sufficient reason if they are offensive to, libellous, scandalous or blasphemous of, the testator's family or of a group of individuals.

A contested application must be made to a registrar by summons (see head 20.2). An uncontested application should be made to the registrar of the probate registry at which application for the grant is to be made, ex parte by lodging the affidavits in support, exhibiting the will or codicil in question, together with any consents in writing of persons not under disability who might be prejudiced by the order (Form 2.14.3 can be suitably adapted). The registrar may make the order asked or he may require the application to be made by summons to a judge (p 253) or to the court on motion (head 20.3).

After an order has been obtained in this way, a typed copy of the will excluding the offensive words must be lodged with the papers to lead to the grant, together with a copy of the order. A fiat signed by the Principal of the Probate Department or by the district registrar (see p 23) is placed on the copy will.

2.16 Rectification of a will

The court has in the past exercised jurisdiction in particular but limited circumstances to order that words other than those of an offensive nature be omitted from the probate of a will, for instance where they have been inserted by mistake in a will and were not brought to the notice of the testator, or in certain circumstances even when the words were read by or to the testator (*Re Morris, Lloyds Bank Ltd* v *Peake* [1970] 1 All ER 1057), or where there has been a wrong reference in a codicil to a numbered clause in the will (*In the Goods of Swords* [1952] P 368), or to a previous will which has been revoked by a later will, and the testator was unaware of the error (see also under Revocation of wills, at p 55). The court has never assumed the power to supply words omitted from a will by mistake. An application for the court to exercise its discretion was made in the same way as an application to omit words of an offensive nature (see above).

Now, under s 20 of the Administration of Justice Act 1982, if the court is satisfied that a will is so expressed that it fails to carry out the testator's intentions in consequence of a clerical error or of a failure to understand his instructions, it may order that the will is to be rectified so as to carry out his intentions.

An application under s 20 may be made only in respect of the will of a testator who has died on or after 1 January 1983. Save by leave of the court no such application may be made later than six months after the date of issue of a grant of representation in respect of the deceased's estate. Protection is given to the deceased's personal representatives if they have distributed any part of the estate which is subsequently affected by an order for rectification, after six months have elapsed from the date of issue of the grant to them.

So far there has been very little guidance on the extent to which the court will use its power under s 20 to order rectification of a will. Clearly the court may now direct that words and figures are to be added to the text as well as omitted from it. For instance, if it can be shown that the amount of a legacy has in error been written in for a much smaller amount than the testator intended, this mistake can be corrected. But if a testator whilst fully approving words written in his will did not realise their real significance, this may not qualify for rectification.

An application for rectification of a will, which it is known will be opposed, is made to the Chancery Division by the issue of a writ beginning a probate action (see RSC, Ord 76). The commencement of the action operates to prevent the sealing of a grant (see p 235). A copy of an order for rectification made in such proceedings is sent to the Principal Registry for filing, and a memorandum of the order is endorsed on, or annexed to, the grant of representation if one has issued. Otherwise, a copy of the order must accompany the papers to lead the grant following upon determination of the action.

If it is thought that an application for rectification will not be opposed, it may be made in the Family Division to a registrar of the Principal Registry (through the Probate Department) or, if the application for the grant is to be made in a district probate registry, to any district probate registrar, unless a probate action has commenced (Probate Rule 55(1)). Unless otherwise directed, notice of the application must be given to every person interested under the will whose interest might be adversely affected by the proposed rectification. The applicant must lodge an affidavit in support setting out the grounds of the application and exhibiting any comments in writing which have been received from persons to whom notice of the application has been given. The evidence to be adduced to the registrar must show clearly in what respects it is said that the testator's intentions were not understood, or the nature of any alleged clerical error. In this connection, extrinsic evidence may be allowed to assist in the interpretation of the will (see head 2.17). If the registrar is satisfied that notice has been given to all persons affected and that the application is unopposed, he may order the will to be rectified. If the registrar is not so satisfied, he may direct that the application be made on summons to a registrar of the Principal Registry or to a judge (see head 20.2), or if it is clear that the application is opposed, the applicant will be referred to the Chancery Division (see above).

2.17 Interpretation of wills

Questions relating to the interpretation of wills usually fall within the jurisdiction of the Chancery Division, but will often be determined by the Family Division when it is a matter of ascertaining the person or persons entitled to prove the will, for instance whether a gift is one of the residuary estate or the identity of the person to whom a gift is made (see p 86).

The general rule has been that if the words used by the testator in their ordinary sense have a clear meaning when applied to the facts, the court will not allow extrinsic evidence to be adduced to show that those words were not used in their ordinary sense. There are, however, certain instances when such evidence has been allowed, but usually excluding declarations by the testator as to his intentions. Thus, if there is any doubt as to the identity of beneficiaries, the extent of the gift, or the meaning of any term used, eg 'money', evidence of the surrounding circumstances may be given so that the court may be placed in the same position as the testator at the time he made his will. Also, if by reference to the context of the will it appears that certain words were not used by the testator in their ordinary meaning, extrinsic evidence may be given to show that the words were used in some other sense. Such evidence will also be permitted if there is a partial misdescription in the will of persons or property. Again, if the description of a beneficiary given in the will fits two or more persons, extrinsic evidence including on this occasion declarations of intention by the testator, will be admitted to identify the person whom the testator intended to benefit.

In respect of the will of a testator who has died on or since 1 January 1983, s 21 of the Administration of Justice Act 1982 lays down general rules as to the evidence which may be given to assist in the interpretation of the will. Now, in so far as (*a*) any part of a will is meaningless, (*b*) the language used in any part of a will is ambiguous on the face of it, (*c*) evidence, other than evidence of the testator's intention, shows that the language used in any part of a will is ambiguous in the light of surrounding circumstances, extrinsic evidence, including evidence of the testator's intention, may be admitted to assist in its interpretation.

As with the new jurisdiction to order rectification of a will, the extent to which s 21 of the Act of 1982 may be used has yet to be clarified by the court. Certainly it would appear that evidence of the testator's intention, including declarations by him, will now be admitted whenever it can be shown that there is some uncertainty as to the meaning of the language used by him in his will.

2.18 Codicils

The same rules apply to codicils as to wills, and the remarks on the latter are equally applicable to codicils.

Codicils are generally proved with the will to which they refer. If this cannot be done (as when the existence of a codicil is unknown at the time of proof of the will), the codicil may be proved separately at a later date, provided that:

(i) it does not alter or revoke the appointment of executors made by the will; and

(ii) the grant made in respect of the will was one of probate.

If these conditions are not fulfilled, the grant made in respect of the will must be revoked and the will and codicil again proved together. This will usually be done in the registry in which the will was originally proved (but see p 215). If there is a dispute only as to the validity of a codicil, which does not affect the appointment of executors, and it is urgently necessary for part of the estate to be administered, probate of the will only will be granted to the executors on the understanding that a full distribution of the estate will not take place until the question of the validity of the codicil has been resolved.

Provided that a codicil expressly refers to or confirms the will, it has the effect of republishing the will from the date of execution of the codicil (Wills Act 1837, s 34), save in so far as republication may defeat the testator's intentions or is specifically excluded by statute. So also a will which has been revoked may be revived, if it has not been destroyed, by a codicil which shows an intention to bring about that result. This situation often arises where an earlier will, revoked expressly by a later will, is then apparently confirmed by a still later codicil. The effect may be that the second will is itself revoked, particularly if the earlier will contains a revocation clause (*Re Pearson* [1963] 3 All ER 763). Sometimes all the testamentary documents are required to be proved, leaving it to a court of construction to interpret the testator's wishes as to the disposition of his estate. In this connection it may now be possible to adduce extrinsic evidence, including evidence of the testator's intention, to assist in interpreting any ambiguity (see head 2.17).

When a codicil is revoked by a later codicil it should not be destroyed, for its production may be called for when application for probate is made. It will then be for the registrar to decide whether the revoked codicil shall be included in the testamentary papers admitted to probate. Normally, it will not be included in the probate unless it alters the terms of the will or of a preceding codicil. This is an important matter, for the bare revocation of a codicil which has altered the terms of preceding testamentary documents does not revive the parts of the previous documents which were revoked (Wills Act 1837, s 22; *In the Goods of Hodgkinson* [1893] P 339). In all cases of doubt, the opinion of the registrar should be obtained in advance.

If a revoked codicil cannot be produced when called for, evidence of the reason why it cannot be produced, and of its contents, must be given. If it has been destroyed, the evidence of the person who destroyed it or witnessed its destruction must be obtained. When this evidence cannot be obtained, search must be made for the revoked codicil, and this must be evidenced by affidavit (see Form 2.14.2).

If a will has been partially revoked by a codicil which itself has been revoked by destruction, a registrar's order should be obtained admitting the codicil to proof as contained in a draft or reconstruction thereof; the grant is not in this instance limited until a more authentic copy is proved (see head 2.22 at p 46).

It sometimes happens that a codicil misquotes the date of the will to which it refers, or misquotes the number of codicils preceding it (as when it is described as a second codicil when in fact it is the third). Unless the person who made the error in preparing the codicil is available to make an affidavit in explanation, either of these errors calls for an exhaustive search for other testamentary documents in general, and for the document dated as mentioned in the codicil, or for the codicil which appears to be missing from the sequence of testamentary documents, in particular. The making of this search and its results must be set out in an affidavit, usually by the applicant for the grant (see Form 2.14.2).

2.19 Incorporation of documents

When a will contains a reference to another document which is not itself capable of proof as a testamentary document although its provisions are dispositive, it must be considered whether that document should be incorporated in the will (Probate Rule 12 (2)). Thus, a testator may refer in his will to a list setting out his wishes for the disposal of his personal belongings to various relations and friends or he may direct in his will that his residuary estate be administered in accordance with trusts set up by a previous settlement. A will or codicil, the attestation of which has been defective, may be set up by incorporation if it is specifically referred to in a later codicil which has been properly executed. Moreover, there is no need to produce evidence of foreign law to establish the validity of a foreign will if there is a codicil thereto which confirms the will and has been executed in conformity with English law provided that law can be applied. To determine whether a document qualifies for incorporation, two rules should be applied:

(i) it must be established that the document was in existence at the date of the instrument which refers to it; and

(ii) the document must be capable of being identified by the reference to it as a specific written document in the executed testamentary instrument.

As a result of the first rule, it is evident that a reference to a document which is to be drawn up at a future date can be ignored, and this is so even though there is a codicil of a later date which confirms the instrument containing the reference. If the document is declared to be in existence, though in fact it is not, but it comes into existence before the execution of a later document which confirms the will or codicil containing the reference to the document, it will be incorporated.

If the testator directs expressly that the document is not to form part of his will or that its contents are not binding, there can be no incorporation. When there is doubt as to whether a document should be incorporated, the registrar should be asked for his directions. If he is not satisfied that the two rules mentioned have been fully complied with, he may direct that the document is to be filed but not incorporated. In such a case, no reference need be made to it in the oath or elsewhere.

A deed may be of such length that it cannot conveniently be incorporated in the will. The incorporation of a part of, or an extract from, a deed is undesirable. The registrar may direct that a deed be incorporated if it is sufficiently short but usually he will require an examined copy of the deed, or part of it, verified by affidavit, to be filed with the papers in place of incorporation.

The document to be incorporated should be identified by affidavit; this can often be effected by an additional paragraph in the oath. If there is a reference in the will to another document which cannot be found and the question of incorporation arises, an affidavit of search must be filed (Form 2.14.2 may be adapted for this purpose). When there is a reference in the will to the will of another testator in such a way as to require incorporation, and that will has already been proved the probate thereof should be lodged with the papers and the registry will then place a note identifying the will to be incorporated on the will which is being proved and on the probate copy thereof.

A statement for the purposes of the Inheritance (Provision for Family and Dependants) Act 1975 is not incorporated unless it is testamentary. It need not be produced and should be retained by the executors, but if mention is made of it in the will it is advisable to lodge with the papers to lead the grant a letter or certificate by the solicitor to the effect that the statement is not dispositive.

2.20 Two or more wills

Since a will is 'the aggregate of a man's testamentary intentions' (*Lemage* v *Goodban* (1865) LR 1 P & D 57), it may be contained in more than one document. This may occur:

(*a*) when a document is referred to in a will or codicil in such a manner as to call for its incorporation (see above); and

(*b*) when two or more executed documents constitute one will.

The commonest example of the second class is when a testator makes one or more codicils to his will (see head 2.18). However, testators often make separate wills for different classes of property, eg, one will may dispose of only one item or class of property, and another of the remaining property, as when the first document deals with personal estate, and the other with real estate. In this case the documents are of equal testamentary value and together constitute one will, neither being complete without the other.

Alternatively, a will may be made disposing of property in England and Wales and another disposing of property abroad. If it is clear that the intention of the testator was that the two wills should be quite independent one of the other, and that intention has in fact been carried out, it is usual for the English will alone to be proved; a copy of the foreign will duly authenticated should be lodged in the registry to be placed with the original English will (*In the Goods of Murray* [1896] P 65). It is always advisable in these circumstances to obtain the decision of the registrar beforehand. The court has on occasion allowed both wills to be proved together (*In the Estate of Wayland* [1951] 2 All ER 1041) but both wills must be valid according to the appropriate law (see head 15.1).

(See also under Revocation of wills, By another writing, head 2.29(*b*).)

2.21 Duplicate and draft wills

If a will has been executed in duplicate, only one part is proved but the duplicate must be lodged with the papers to lead the grant; this is handed back to the applicant's solicitor after examination with the original. If only one part can be found, the absence of the other part must be satisfactorily accounted for by affidavit because, otherwise, the presumption arises, if the missing part was in the testator's possession, that he destroyed it intending to revoke it (see under Revocation by destruction, head 2.29(*c*)). Since the will is effectively revoked by the destruction of one part only (*Boughey* v *Moreton* (1758) 3 Hag Ecc 191), the remaining part cannot be proved unless the presumption can be rebutted.

Sometimes a testator has executed the draft of a will as his original will. In proving an executed draft of a will, inquiries must be made to ascertain whether an engrossment was prepared, and if one was prepared, whether it was executed. This evidence must be given by the affidavit of a person having knowledge of the facts, who is generally the solicitor to whom the testator gave instructions for the preparation of the will. Where it is established that no engrossment was ever prepared, the draft will is the original will and is described as such, but it must be shown that the testator executed it intending it to be testamentary (*Re Meynell* [1949] WN 273). When an engrossment has been made, the question of its execution arises. If it was not executed, that fact must be sworn to and, if possible, the reasons why it was not executed given; if it was executed, its whereabouts must be ascertained. If it cannot be found and it is established that the draft of the will was executed by the testator at the same time as the engrossment, the same presumption arises as in the case of duplicate wills where one part is missing (see above). Sometimes there is uncertainty as to whether the engrossed copy was executed. This situation calls for the most searching inquiries, and the results must be embodied in an affidavit showing that all possible inquiries (which must be detailed) and a search in all places where the testator kept his important papers have been made (Form 2.14.2 may be adapted for this purpose).

2.22 Will lost or not available

Where the will is not available or has been lost, a copy, completed draft, reconstruction or declaration of its contents may be proved on production of an order of the court (Probate Rule 53) (see also nuncupative wills, head 2.26(*d*)). However, if the reason for the will not being produced is that it is retained in the custody of a foreign court or official, no order is necessary provided that a duly authenticated copy of the will is submitted for proof (see p 206).

The application for an order is made in the first instance to a registrar of the Principal Registry or it may be made to any district probate registrar if the application for a grant is to be made at a district probate registry. The registrar may make the order or direct that the application should be made by way of summons to a registrar or a judge, or to the court on motion. The registrar will not usually make an order himself if the original will cannot be proved to have been in existence after the testator's death or if the consents of all the persons prejudiced cannot be obtained because they object or are not sui juris or are under some other disability. The manner of application is for the papers to lead the order to be left at the Probate Department of the Principal Registry, or at the district registry. No attendance by the solicitor is necessary. (For the procedure by way of summons, see head 20.2, and on motion, see head 20.3.)

Most of the facts in support of the application will have to be deposed to by the person who seeks to establish the copy or declaration. When certain of the facts are within the knowledge of other persons, they must of course depose to them. In a normal application the following are the documents required:

(*a*) An affidavit of the facts of the disappearance of the will (this must establish, if appropriate, that it was whole and unrevoked and in existence after the death of the testator; if this cannot be proved, the evidence must rebut the presumption that the testator revoked the will by destruction (see *Re Davies decd* (1978) 128 NLJ 735)): any peculiar facts connected with the disappearance of the will, eg, its destruction or misplacement; the efforts made to find the original will (when an advertisement has been published, copies of the newspapers containing the advertisement should be exhibited to the affidavit); the circumstances under which the copy it is sought to prove was made, or, if it is sought to establish a declaration of the contents of the will, the circumstances which enable the declarant to remember the contents of the will so accurately (in the latter case it is generally found convenient for him to reconstruct the will; the copy or reconstruction must be exhibited to the affidavit); the names and exact relationships of the persons adversely affected by proof of the will and whether or not they are sui juris or under any other disability (if any of these persons are dead at the time of the application, it must be stated whether their personal representatives have been constituted; such persons are, in the majority of cases, those who would be entitled if the testator had died intestate); the value of the estate involved in the application.

(*b*) An affidavit of due execution (see Form 2.11). (As to the persons who may make this affidavit, see p 25.)

(*c*) The signed and witnessed consents (if obtainable) to the proof of the copy or declaration of such of the persons adversely affected by proof of the will as are not under any disability (see Form 2.14.3).

(*d*) Affidavits in corroboration of any of the facts set out in the previous affidavits.

When an order is made admitting a copy or declaration of the contents of a will to probate, the subsequent grant will be limited either until 'the original or a more authentic copy of the will be proved' or according to the particular circumstances. Should the original will be found subsequent to the issue of the limited grant, it would seem that there is no power in the court to require a further grant to be obtained, although such a course may be advisable, especially if the will as proved in the form of a copy or declaration differs in some respects from the original will.

2.23 Damaged wills

When a will or codicil is found to have been so damaged, for instance by fire or water, that it is doubtful whether it can or should be submitted for probate, the solicitor should leave it with the registrar of the registry where application for a grant is to be made (the Principal of the Probate Department in the case of the Principal Registry) for his decision. Whenever possible an examined copy should be lodged with the original document, a similar copy being retained by the solicitor. The question whether it would be possible to obtain a photographic copy by special process should be left to be decided by the registrar.

If the document is so damaged that it is evident that it cannot be accepted for probate, application must be made to the registrar for an order that a copy or draft thereof should be admitted to probate. The procedure is the same as that to be followed when a will or codicil has been lost (see above), but at the discretion of the registrar the production of evidence of due execution and of the consents of persons prejudiced may be waived. The remains of any damaged document should always be lodged in the registry when application is made for the order to admit a copy or draft of the will, and these will be retained in the registry upon the issue of a grant. The grant will be limited 'until a more authentic copy be proved'.

For this procedure to be applicable it is of course necessary to show that the damage was not caused by the testator in an attempt at revocation, otherwise different considerations will arise (see heads 2.10 and 2.29(*c*)).

2.24 Joint and mutual wills

A testamentary document which contains the dispositions of two persons who have both executed it is termed a joint will. It should be proved on the death of each testator except that a joint will which deals solely with joint property or is expressed to take effect only on the death of the survivor should not be proved until the survivor has died. A codicil made by only one testator is proved on the death of that testator. The will is not given out of the registry after the first application and the second application should be made at the same registry. Should proof of due execution be called for, it must be shown that the will was duly executed by both testators. On an application to prove the will for the first time, the solicitor should give the date of birth of the other testator, or his date of death as appropriate.

Mutual wills are wills made by two persons who give each other mutual rights in each other's property. Each is proved on the death of its testator unless it is in the form of a joint will.

A joint or mutual will may be revoked by either testator, but if revoked without notice to the other testator or after his or her death a trust may arise in respect of benefits derived by the survivor under the will of the other testator or in respect of the survivor's own property (*Re Hagger* [1930] 2 Ch 190; *Re Green* [1951] Ch 148; *Re Cleaver* [1981] 1 WLR 939).

2.25 Conditional wills

When a will is expressed to be conditional on the occurrence of an event or in certain stated circumstances, it must be established that the event has occurred, or that the circumstances exist, before the will may be admitted to probate. A distinction must be drawn between a will which is expressed to be operative on the fulfilment of a condition and a will which sets out the reason why it was made. Thus, if a testator says: 'Should I die tomorrow my will is...' the document is inoperative unless his death occurred on the morrow. But if he says: 'All men are mortal and no one knows how soon his life may be required of him. Lest I die before the next sun, I direct...' the will gives the reason why it was made and it will be operative whether he dies before the next sun or not (*Burton* v *Collingwood* (1832) 4 Hag Ecc 176; *In the Estate of Vines* [1910] P 147).

Where a will is expressed to be operative in the event of the simultaneous deaths of the testator and some other person, the term 'simultaneous death' is held to be death in such circumstances that the ordinary man would infer that the deaths were simultaneous. The presumption laid down by s 184 of the Law of Property Act 1925 and the rule in *Hickman* v *Peacey* [1945] AC 304 do not of necessity apply (*Re Pringle* [1946] Ch 124; but see *Re Rowland* [1962] 2 All ER 837).

When the expressed condition has been fulfilled, or when the stated circumstances exist, the fact must be sworn to in a concise paragraph in the oath. If the requirement has not been fulfilled, or if there is a doubt as to whether the will is conditional or whether the condition has been fulfilled, a separate affidavit deposing to the relevant facts should be submitted to the registrar. Where the condition is clearly inoperative or the registrar has decided that it has not been fulfilled, the document and the affidavit, if any, are retained in the registry to be kept with the oath to lead any subsequent grant that may issue in respect of the estate of the deceased.

If the conditional document refers to an earlier testamentary document, whether by date or not, the effect may be to republish the earlier document (see p 41), or, if it has not been duly executed, to incorporate it (see p 42). On that ground alone the conditional document is entitled to be proved even if the expressed condition has not been fulfilled.

2.26 Privileged wills

The formalities usually required for the execution of wills (see head 2.3) do not apply to a soldier or member of the Royal Air Force in actual military service, or to a member of Her Majesty's naval or marine forces not only at sea but also when he is so circumstanced that if he were a soldier he would be in actual military service, or to a mariner or seaman at sea (s 11 of the Wills Act 1837; Wills (Soldiers and Sailors) Act 1918). If the deceased died on or before 6 February 1918 this privilege can be claimed only in so far as the will disposes of personal estate, but if the deceased died after that date, an informal will made by him is effective to dispose of both personal and real estate and to appoint a testamentary guardian in respect of his minor children. If the privilege is exercised and it is sought to prove an informal will, the facts which justify the exercise of the privilege should be set out in detail in the oath or in a supplementary affidavit (see Form 2.26). The privilege only attaches to persons domiciled in England and Wales at the time of making the will, and consequently the domicile at that time must be sworn to in the oath. But when the circumstances are such that it is possible to refer to a foreign law system to establish the validity of the will (see p 13), it would seem that any similar privilege conferred by that law may be claimed (for proof of validity under foreign law, see head 15.1).

(a) Actual military service

The term 'actual military service' has the same meaning as 'active service', and both terms are confined to such military service as is 'directly concerned with operations in a war which is, or has been, in progress, or is imminent' (*Re Wingham* [1948] 2 All ER 908, at p 911). Any male or female who is serving or has been called up for service in a war falls within the term, and the privilege of making an informal will attaches to them. It is not necessary that they should be actively engaged with the enemy, nor under orders to proceed to an active theatre of war. It is sufficient if they are in captivity or internment, or merely in course of being trained to fight. After hostilities have ended, the privilege may still attach, eg, when soldiers garrison occupied countries (*In the Estate of Colman* [1958] 2 All ER 35). The privilege has been held to extend to a soldier serving in Northern Ireland at a time of terrorist activities on the basis that whether he was in actual military service depended, not on the character of the opposing operations, but on the nature of his activities and the unit or force to which he was attached (*Re Jones, decd* [1981] 1 All ER 1). Wherever there is a doubt as to the privilege, the benefit should be given to the soldier. The decision in *Re Wingham* has greatly extended the scope of the privilege, and very many of the former decisions as to what constitutes 'actual military service' are no longer of authority.

Where the privilege is claimed because a sailor of the Royal Navy or a marine was 'so circumstanced that if he had been a soldier he would have been in actual military service', the circumstances in which he was situated at the date of the will must, therefore, be as outlined in the preceding paragraph.

(b) At sea

For a mariner or seaman to make a valid privileged will, he must be 'at sea' at the time of making it. He is deemed to be at sea if he is at sea in the course of a voyage, in a port at which his ship has called in the course of a voyage (*In the Goods of Lay* (1840) 2 Curt 375), on a ship engaged in river trade (*In the Goods of Patterson* (1898) 79 LT 123), on a ship on harbour duties (*In the Goods of M'Murdo* (1868) LR 1 P & D 540), on a ship proceeding up a river in the course of a voyage commenced by a sea voyage (*In the Goods of Austen* (1853) 2 Rob 611), on leave ashore (*In the Goods of Newland* [1952] P 71), or under orders to join his ship (*In the Goods of Wilson* [1952] P 92). It has recently been held that a seaman who made his will at home whilst on leave, having been discharged from one ship and not having been posted to another, was not 'at sea' within the meaning of s 11 of the Act of 1837 (*Re Rapley's Estate* [1983] 3 All ER 248).

The term 'mariner' comprises all ratings forming the crew of a modern ship, and so includes a ship's doctor (*In the Goods of Saunders* (1865) LR 1 P & D 16), a purser (*In the Goods of Hayes* (1839) 2 Curt 338), or even a female typist (*In the Goods of Hale* [1915] 2 Ir R 362). The nature of the service must be 'sea service'.

(See also p 52 as to seamen's wills.)

(c) Age of testator

Members of the classes of persons who may make a privileged will may do so even if they are under the age of eighteen years. No objection will be raised to the privileged will of a minor unless he is under the age of fourteen years, which is generally recognised as the lowest age at which a member of the privileged classes mentioned may make a will, but his age must be stated in the oath. When the will of a member of a privileged class appears to have been executed in accordance with s 9 of the Wills Act 1837, and the evidence in support of the privilege is insufficient to establish that the testator was 'in actual military service' or 'at sea', the will is, of course, invalid if he was under the age of eighteen (or twenty-one if the will was made before 1 January 1970) at the time he made it.

(d) Form of a privileged will

There is no set form of will, and any informal document or statement may be accepted. It need not be signed nor witnessed, and may even be a memorandum written by some other person of a statement made by the testator (*In the Goods of Scott* [1903] P 243), written instructions given by the testator to his solicitor (*In the Estate of Rowson* [1944] 2 All ER 36; *Re Beavis* (1941) unreported), the draft of a will amended by the testator (*Re Wood* (1941) unreported), a statement made by the testator (*Re Stable* [1919] P 7; *In the Estate of Spark* [1941] P 115), or a personal letter. When the will is contained in a letter of a personal nature, the registrar may direct that only that part of it which is testamentary is to be proved. The complete letter must be filed, and the testamentary portions will be embodied in a fiat copy signed by the registrar (see p 23). This will be open to inspection, but the original letter may not be examined except on good reason being shown.

Application must first be made for an order admitting an oral or nuncupative will to proof (Probate Rule 53). The procedure is the same as that for lost wills (see head 2.22).

The essential requirement of a privileged will is that the document or statement must have been intended to be testamentary. A direction as to how a business should be conducted (*In the Estate of MacGillivray* [1946] 2 All ER 301), or a statement as to what a testator thinks he has done with his property (*In the Estate of Beech* [1923] P 46), cannot, therefore, be admitted as a testamentary document.

When there is some doubt as to whether a will is privileged or not, the matter should be referred to a registrar. If it is decided that the document is not privileged it will be retained in the registry for inclusion with the papers to lead any subsequent grant.

(e) Alterations

Alterations appearing in a privileged will are deemed, in the absence of evidence to the contrary, to have been made whilst the testator was still 'in actual military service' or 'at sea'. They will, therefore, be of full effect (*In the Goods of Tweedale* (1874) LR 3 P & D 204); but if the will is unattested it must be shown by affidavit evidence that the alterations are in the testator's handwriting or, if not in his handwriting, that he knew of and approved them (see below). If witnesses have signed the will, it is within the registrar's discretion to allow the alterations to be set up in the usual way, if necessary by requiring affidavit evidence in support (see p 22). The possibility must also be borne in mind of establishing the validity of an alteration by reference to another system of law under the Wills Act 1963 (see p 13).

(f) Revocation

If at the time of revocation of a will the circumstances are such that the testator would be entitled to make a privileged will, then the revocation is effective although made with the same lack of formality, that is by any informal document or statement which indicates a clear intention on the part of the testator to revoke his previous will (*In the Estate of Gossage* [1921] P 194). However, a testator who has made a valid privileged will whilst under the age of eighteen years may now revoke the will whilst still under that age without the circumstances having to be such that he would be entitled to make a privileged will (s 3 (3) of the Family Law Reform Act 1969). Revocation would have to be by one of the usual methods of revocation available to a non-privileged testator (see head 2.29).

(g) Evidence required

The circumstances by reason of which it is claimed that the will is privileged should be set out in detail in the oath, or in a supplementary affidavit (see Form 2.26, below). In addition, evidence of the handwriting and signature of the testator may be required (see Form 2.12.2). If there are two or more witnesses to the will, no evidence is usually required; if there are no witnesses or only one witness, the evidence of one or more disinterested persons to prove the testator's handwriting and signature will be called for. The registrar has a discretion in the matter (Probate Rule 15) and, if the applicant is the only person who would be entitled to the deceased's estate were the will not to be admitted to probate, an affidavit by the applicant to that effect and as to the deceased's handwriting may be accepted. If the testator signed by mark, evidence that he knew and approved the contents will be required (see Form 2.11, p 29).

Form 2.26 Affidavit in support of privileged will
(For heading and title, see Form 2.11)

1 I, ,
of ;
make oath and say that

2 I am the sole executor named in the last Will and Testament of , of , deceased, who died on the day of , 19 , the said Will, bearing date the day of , 19 , being now produced to me and marked ' ';

3 And that the said deceased made the said Will whilst he was a soldier in actual military service, being at the date thereof domiciled in England.

4 And I further make oath and say that at the date of the said Will the said deceased was a Corporal in the 2nd Battalion of the Regiment under orders to proceed to the zone of active military operations in Italy.

5 Sworn by the above-named deponent
at
this day of , 19 .
Before me
A Commissioner for Oaths (or Solicitor).

1 See the note to para **1** of Form 2.12.1 at p 31.

2 See the note to para **2** of Form 2.12.1 at p 31. If the will was made orally, insert before 'the said Will' the words 'a reconstruction of' or as appropriate.

3 Here give the qualification of the deceased which it is claimed entitled him to make a privileged will, viz, soldier (*or* airman) in actual military service, seaman at sea, or as the case may be.

4 Give the detailed circumstances which are relied upon to establish the claim that the will was made on a privileged occasion, viz, in the case of a soldier or airman that he was a member of the (auxiliary) forces, and serving or called up for service in a war, giving his rank, unit and place of service at the date of the will; in the case of a sailor, marine or seaman, that he was at sea, or in a port during the course of a voyage, stating the name of the ship (and the port, if appropriate) and other relevant circumstances (see subhead (*b*) above).

5 See the note to para **10** of Form 2.11 at p 29.

2.27 Seamen's wills

The wills of seamen (including petty officers) and mariners (including non-commissioned officers) were at one time not valid to pass naval assets forming part of the estate unless they had been made in conformity with the provisions of the Navy and Marines (Wills) Acts 1865 to 1939. These special provisions have now been repealed (Navy and Marines (Wills) Act 1953), except that they still apply (*a*) to restrict the operation of the will of a seaman or marine who died on or before 14 August 1953 and (*b*) to render valid any will made in conformity therewith on or before that date, which would otherwise be invalid.

A seaman or marine who makes a will during his service must deposit it with the Ministry of Defence (Navy Department). When application is to be made for a grant in respect of the estate of a person who has at any time served as a seaman or marine, inquiry must first be made to the Inspector of

Seamen's Wills, Ministry of Defence, Pay and Pensions Division, HMS Centurion, Grange Road, Gosport, Hants PO13 9XA, as to the existence of a will in his custody, and the Inspector's certificate must be lodged with the papers to lead the grant (Probate Rule 17). The certificate is not required if (*a*) the deceased had made a will revoking all previous wills after leaving the service, or (*b*) the deceased was at the date of his death a pensioner from the service.

2.28 Wills of mentally disordered persons

There is another instance when the usual formalities for the execution and attestation of a will under English domestic law are not applicable. By s 103 (1) (*dd*) of the Mental Health Act 1959 (added by s 17 (1) of the Administration of Justice Act 1969) the court has power to give directions for the execution for a patient—that is a person who by reason of mental disorder is incapable of dealing with his property—of a will, or codicil, making any provision, whether by disposing of property or exercising a power or otherwise, which could be made by the patient if he were not mentally disordered. For the considerations to be borne in mind in making such a will, see *In re L (WJG)* [1966] 1 Ch 135. The power of the court is not to be exercised if the patient is a minor, or unless the judge believes that the patient is incapable of making a valid will for himself. The will must be expressed to be signed by the patient acting by the person authorised by the court to sign on his behalf. The latter must sign the will both with the name of the patient and with his own name in the presence of two or more witnesses present at the same time; those witnesses must then attest and sign in the presence of the authorised person; finally the will must be sealed with the seal of the Court of Protection (see [1970] 1 All ER 15). Apart from s 9 dealing with the manner of execution and attestation, the other provisions of the Wills Act 1837 apply to such a will as if the patient had signed the will for himself. The will has the same effect as if the patient had been capable of making a valid will and had executed the will according to the provisions of the Wills Act 1837, save that (i) it is not effective to dispose of immovable property other than in England and Wales, and (ii) where the patient is domiciled in Scotland or Northern Ireland or a country or territory outside the United Kingdom at the time of execution, it is effective to dispose of any property or matter only if, in respect of that property or matter, any question of the patient's testamentary capacity would fall under the law of his domicile to be determined in accordance with the law of England and Wales.

It is to be noted that where this special procedure has not been followed, the fact that the deceased died in a mental hospital does not call for any special evidence as to the mental condition of the testator, unless it can be presumed from the face of the will that there might be lack of testamentary capacity. Such a presumption would arise if the contents of the will were most unreasonable, or showed lack of coherent thought, or if there was uncertainty as to the status or capacity of the attesting witnesses. In the absence of such special circumstances, the onus of establishing that the testator was not of testamentary capacity is on the person disputing the will.

2.29 Revocation of wills

(a) By marriage

With two exceptions, a will is revoked by the marriage of the testator (Wills Act 1837, s 18, as amended by Law of Property Act 1925, s 177, and as from 1 January 1983 by Administration of Justice Act 1982, s 18(1)). At the date of the marriage the testator must be domiciled in a country by the law of which marriage revokes a previous will (*In the Goods of Reid* (1866) LR 1 P & D 74; *Re Martin* [1900] P 211).

The exceptions are:

(*a*) Where a disposition in a will has been made in the exercise of a power of appointment. Such a disposition will take effect in spite of the testator's subsequent marriage unless the property so appointed would in default of appointment pass to the testator's personal representatives. A grant will issue in respect of that part of the will which exercises the power of appointment.

(*b*) Where a will has been made in contemplation of a marriage which has in fact taken place.

(i) In respect of wills made between 1 January 1926 and 31 December 1982 the position is governed by s 18 of the Wills Act 1837, as amended by s 177 of the Law of Property Act 1925. A will expressed to have been made in contemplation of a marriage will not be revoked by the solemnisation of the marriage contemplated. A reference in the will to marriage generally is insufficient (*Sallis* v *Jones* [1936] P 43). The reference must be to marriage to a particular person, although it need not be expressed in those specific words; thus a residuary gift to 'my fiancee' was held to be sufficient (*In the Estate of Langston* [1953] P 100); the test was, was the will as a whole expressed to be made in contemplation of the marriage which has in fact taken place? (*Re Coleman* [1975] 1 All ER 675).

(ii) In respect of a will made on or after 1 January 1983 reference must now be made to s 18 of the Wills Act 1837 as substituted by s 18(1) of the Administration of Justice Act 1982 (s 177 of the Act of 1925 has been expressly repealed). Where it appears from the will that at the time it was made the testator was expecting to be married to a particular person and that he intended that the will should not be revoked by that marriage, then the will is not revoked by his subsequent marriage to that person. If, however, in such circumstances it appears only that the testator intended that a disposition in the will should not be revoked by his marriage to that person, the disposition will take effect notwithstanding the marriage, and any other disposition in the will will also take effect, save in so far as it appears from the will that the testator intended that other disposition to be revoked by the marriage. Any ambiguity in the language of the will may be resolved under s 21 of the Administration of Justice Act 1982 (see head 2.17).

It follows that the decision in *Re Coleman* has now been reversed. If a testator has shown by the language used in his will that he intended the whole or any part thereof to survive a particular marriage, then it will be presumed that the whole will was intended to survive save in so far as a contrary intention is indicated in respect of any specified part.

The facts necessary to establish that the will comes within one of these exceptions should be recited in the oath.

A voidable marriage is sufficient to revoke a will, even if the marriage is subsequently annulled, because the annulment does not have effect back to the date of the marriage (*Re Roberts decd* [1978] 3 All ER 225).

(b) By another writing or testamentary act

A will may be revoked expressly or in general terms by another will or codicil, duly executed, or by any writing by which the testator has declared his intention to revoke his will and which has been executed in the manner prescribed for the execution of a will (Wills Act 1837, s 20). In the latter case the writing is not proved but must be lodged in the registry with the papers to lead the grant, and the grant will bear a notation referring to the writing (*Toomer* v *Sobinska* [1907] P 106; *Re Spracklan's Estate* [1938] 2 All ER 345). (For revocation of, and by, a codicil, see head 2.18.)

The fact that a document is described as 'the last Will and Testament' or similarly is of little importance, for that statement does not bring about the revocation of earlier testamentary documents (*Simpson* v *Foxon* [1907] P 54; *Kitcat* v *King* [1930] P 266). To revoke an earlier testamentary document, the later document should revoke it by express words, but it may impliedly revoke it by disposing of all the estate of the testator. Of two testamentary documents *wholly* inconsistent with each other, the later revokes the earlier. When two testamentary documents are only *partially* inconsistent, both must be proved, either as a will and codicil or as two documents constituting one will, as the circumstances warrant, the later document revoking the earlier to the extent of the inconsistency (*Townsend* v *Moore* [1905] P 66).

The fact that the testator has written the word 'Cancelled' across his will does not amount to a sufficient revocation unless the circumstances in which the word has been written are in accordance with the procedure prescribed for the execution of a will (*Stephens* v *Taprell* (1840) 2 Curt 458).

If a general revocatory clause has been included in a will by mistake, the court may allow the clause to be omitted from the probate (see *Re Phelan, decd* [1971] 3 All ER 1256; *Re Luck decd* [1977] WAR 148 (Western Australia) commented upon in *New Law Journal*, 2 November 1978, at p 1077 et seq) (see also under Rectification of a will, head 2.16). Moreover, if it can be shown that such a clause was inserted conditionally upon the testator disposing of the whole of his estate in the new will, and the will is defective in this respect, the court may allow an earlier will to be proved with the later will omitting the revocatory clause and any inconsistent passage in the earlier will (*In the Estate of Cocke* [1960] 2 All ER 289; *Re Crannis decd* (1978) 122 SJ 489; also see below under Dependent relative revocation).

When a testator has died on or after 1 January 1964 it must be considered whether his will has been revoked by any means by which he has expressed an intention so to do, not only in writing but also orally or in some other way, provided such means are in conformity with a system of law to which reference may be made under the Wills Act 1963 (see p 13). Moreover, although a will containing a clause revoking an earlier will may not have been validly executed according to any law to which reference might be made under the general provisions of the Wills Act 1963, yet provided that the will has been executed in accordance with any law by which the validity of the earlier will could have been established under the same statutory provisions, the revocatory clause (but not the rest of the will) will be treated as effectively revoking the earlier will, or the relevant part thereof. When the earlier will is wholly revoked in this way, the revocatory document is not proved but must be lodged in the registry with the papers to lead the grant. If the earlier will is only partly revoked, both documents are proved as together constituting the testator's will. In both instances the evidence establishing the validity of the revocatory clause must be lodged with the papers (see pp 205–207).

(c) By destruction

A will may also be revoked by the burning, tearing or otherwise destroying the same by the testator, or by some person in his presence and by his direction, with the intention of destroying the same (Wills Act 1837, s 20). Destruction of a will is not an effective revocation if carried out by some other person on the instructions of the testator, but not in the latter's presence (*In the Estate of De Kremer* (1966) 110 SJ 18). The destruction need not be complete but if there has been only partial destruction it is usually necessary to prove the intention on the part of the testator to revoke the will. The tearing of a will is more a question of degree and of the conditions in which the will was kept after execution. Partial tearing which leaves all the words of the will distinct and legible does not of itself raise a presumption of an intention to revoke, though the circumstances in which it occurred must be explained (*Re Cowling* [1924] P 113). Where a portion of a will has been torn off, its importance in relation to the rest of the will must be considered. The question is whether the portion torn out is independent of the rest of the will and whether the rest of the will was intended to stand. Thus where a testator cut out certain legacies or the clause appointing executors, it was held that the rest of the will could stand

(*In the Estate of Nunn* (1936) 80 SJ 267; see also *Re Everest* [1975] 1 All ER 672). But if pages of a will are torn out, the whole is held to have been revoked (*Treloar* v *Lean* (1889) 14 PD 49), and this is so even if other executed papers are substituted (*Leonard* v *Leonard* [1902] P 243). Any sign of tearing or burning or other form of attempted destruction in a will which it is sought to prove must be satisfactorily explained (see head 2.10).

If a will or codicil cannot be found after the death of the testator and it was last in his custody, there is a presumption that he has revoked it by destruction provided that he retained his mental capacity during the relevant period of time (see also Duplicate and draft wills, head 2.21).

Where an erasure or obliteration which cannot be set up under the Wills Act 1837 is nevertheless of such a nature that the original words of the will are not apparent, there is a revocation as to that part of the will (see also p 23 and below).

(d) Dependent relative revocation

Where a testator would appear to have revoked his will, it is sometimes possible, by invoking the doctrine of dependent relative revocation, to establish that the revocation was intended by the testator to be conditional upon the happening of some other event and that, because that event did not in fact take place, the revocation was ineffective. To invoke the doctrine successfully, evidence of the testator's intention at the material time must be produced. Thus, a testator was presumed to have destroyed his will in the belief that he had nothing to leave when he had forgotten that he was entitled to inherit an interest in his sister's estate if she pre-deceased him, which she did (*Re Carey decd* (1977) 121 SJ 173). Again, the destruction of one will in the belief that a later will was validly executed may be shown not to amount to revocation when it transpires that the later will is invalid (*In the Estate of Davies* [1951] 1 All ER 920; *In the Estate of Botting* [1951] 2 All ER 997). But, if the testator did not intend that the dispositions made in the earlier will should take effect in any circumstances, proof of an intention to make a new will, or the actual making of a will which turns out to be invalid, is not sufficient to render the revocation ineffective (*Re Jones* [1976] 1 All ER 593). It is advisable in such cases to obtain the direction of the registrar as to whether, and in what form, an application to the court should be made.

The doctrine may also be used to restore parts of a will which have been obliterated; in that case, it is permissible to use all available means, including physical interference with the document, to discover the original wording (*Re Itter* [1950] P 130 (CA): infra-red photography).

(See also as to the omission of a general revocatory clause, at p 55.)

2.30 Effect on will of dissolution or annulment of marriage

Where a testator has died on or after 1 January 1983 having made a will, whether before or after that date, and subsequent to the making of that will his marriage has been dissolved or annulled or declared void by a decree of a court, the will takes effect as if any appointment of the former spouse as an executor, or executor and trustee, has been omitted, and any devise or bequest to the former spouse has lapsed, subject always to there being no contrary intention expressed in the will (s 18A(1) of the Wills Act 1837, added by s 18(2) of the Administration of Justice Act 1982). Any question of interpretation will be dealt with under s 21 of the Administration of Justice Act 1982 (see head 2.17). If a life interest has been given in the will to the former spouse, then any interest in remainder, whether vested or contingent, will have immediate and absolute effect (s 18A(3) of the Wills Act 1837).

The effect of the lapse of a gift of the residuary estate to a former spouse in consequence of the marriage having been dissolved has recently been considered by a judge of the Family Division (*In the Estate of Piotr Cherrington decd* (1984) 128 SJ 302). The question arose because, having appointed his wife his sole executrix and left her the residuary estate, the testator went on to nominate other executors and residuary beneficiaries in the event of his wife predeceasing him. It was held that in the particular circumstances and in order not to frustrate what seemed clearly to be the testator's intentions, the word 'lapse' was to be equated with 'predecease' rather than with 'being of no effect'. The executors substituted if the wife predeceased the testator were in consequence entitled to apply for probate of the will.

The former spouse's right, if any, to apply for financial provision under the Inheritance (Provision for Family and Dependants) Act 1975 remains unaffected (s 18A(2) of the Act of 1837).

Section 18A(1) will presumably have effect when the testator's marriage has been dissolved or annulled by the decree of a court of another country. The recognition of foreign decrees of divorce is governed by the Recognition of Divorces and Legal Separations Act 1971, as extended by the Domicile and Matrimonial Proceedings Act 1973 (for details see pp 117–118, and as to decrees of nullity see p 118). In as much as s 18A(1) refers to 'a decree of a court', the question arises whether it will apply when a marriage has been ended by extra-judicial proceedings.

For the wording of the oath in these circumstances see p 76 (probate) and pp 91–92 and 101 (letters of administration with will annexed). An office copy of the decree absolute or an official copy of any foreign decree, with a notarial translation if appropriate, should be lodged with the papers to lead the grant.

2.31 Exercise of power of appointment by will

The exercise of a power of appointment by a will is not effective until the will has been proved in this country. Usually the will can be shown to have been validly executed (in the case of a testator who has died on or after 1 January 1964) by reference to one of the legal systems available under the general provisions of the Wills Act 1963 (see p 13). Difficulties may arise, however, if the will has not been validly executed. Where the testator died on or after 1 January 1964 a will, otherwise invalid, is to be treated as valid in so far as it exercises the power of appointment, if it has been executed in conformity with the law governing the essential validity of the instrument containing the power. If the testator died before 1 January 1964, the exercise of the power by a will invalid in other respects will be regarded as effective only if the instrument is governed by English law and the will is in English form. In such cases, a grant of letters of administration with that part of the will which exercises the power of appointment annexed will issue to the persons entitled on an intestacy, or if the testator has made another will a grant in respect of both wills may issue to the persons entitled thereto; if necessary such a grant limited to dealing with the property affected by the exercise of the power will issue to the appointees of the power. A similar situation may arise when the will exercising the power has been revoked, save as to the exercise of the power, either by a later will disposing of the testator's estate or by his subsequent marriage (see head 2.29).

If the instrument creating a power of appointment requires certain formalities to be observed in the exercise of that power, the fact that the will which has exercised the power was not executed in accordance with those formalities does not by itself provide a sufficient reason for regarding the will as invalid in so far as it has exercised the power. Where the testator has died on or after 1 January 1964 this principle applies to all wills including those the validity of which is to be established by reference to a foreign law. Where the testator died before that date, however, it is applicable only to wills validly executed in accordance with English law.

2.32 International wills

The Annex to the Convention on International Wills concluded at Washington in 1973 contains rules providing for a uniform law on the form of an international will. Although the Annex has now been given the force of law in the United Kingdom by s 27 of the Administration of Justice Act 1982, that section has not been brought into effect to date. As soon as s 27 becomes effective, it will be possible for a will which cannot be established as valid under any of the provisions of the Wills Act 1963 to be proved in this country so long as it can be shown to comply with the rules relating to international wills.

An international will is valid as to form no matter where it was made, or where the assets are situated, or what was the nationality, domicile or residence of the testator. The essential requirements are:

(*a*) the will must be in writing, by hand or any other means, and may be expressed in any language, but it does not have to be written by the testator himself;

(*b*) at the time of execution the testator must declare in the presence of two witnesses and an 'authorised person' (see below) that the document is his will and that he knows the contents, but he does not have to disclose the contents to any of those persons;

(*c*) the testator must sign his will, or acknowledge his signature previously made, in the presence of the two witnesses and of the authorised person;

(*d*) the two witnesses and the authorised person must thereupon attest the will by signing it in the presence of the testator;

(*e*) if the testator is unable to sign, he must explain the reason for his not being able to do so to the authorised person who must make a note of this on the will; if the law under which the authorised person is designated permits the testator to direct another person to sign on his behalf, the testator may so direct.

All signatures have to be made at the end of the will. If the will is made up of several sheets, each sheet must be numbered and must be signed by the testator, or by any person signing on his behalf, or failing that by the authorised person. The date of the will is the date when the authorised person signs the will and he must enter this date at the end of the will.

After the will has been executed in this fashion, the authorised person is required to complete and attach to the will a certificate to the effect that the obligations of the law relating to international wills have been complied with. The certificate must be in the form set out in the Annex to the Convention or substantially similar (see Form 2.32, below). It is the duty of the authorised person to keep a copy of the certificate and to give the testator another copy. Unless there is evidence to the contrary, this certificate is conclusive evidence as to the formal validity of the will as an international will. However, if the certificate cannot be produced at the time the will is being proved, or if it contains an irregularity, the formal validity of the will is not affected. Presumably it will then have to be established in some other way that the will satisfies the conditions relating to international wills. The various affidavits and other forms required in respect of wills executed in accordance with s 9 of the Wills Act 1837 (see Forms 2.11, 2.12.1–2.12.3 and 2.14.1–2.14.3) may be modified for this purpose.

Form 2.32 Certificate to be attached to an international will

CERTIFICATE

(Convention of October 26th, 1973)

1 I, [*name, address and capacity*], a person authorised to act in connection with international wills

2 Certify that on [*date*] at [*place*]

3 [*testator*] [*name, address, date and place of birth*] in my presence and that of the witnesses

4 (*a*) [*name, address, date and place of birth*]
(*b*) [*name, address, date and place of birth*]
has declared that the attached document is his will and that he knows the contents thereof.
5 I furthermore certify that:
6 (*a*) in my presence and in that of the witnesses
(1) the testator has signed the will or has acknowledged his signature previously affixed;
[*or if appropriate:*
(2) following a declaration of the testator stating that he was unable to sign his will for the following reason

I have mentioned this declaration on the will, the signature has been affixed by [*name, address*]];
7 (*b*) the witnesses and I have signed the will;
8 (*c*) [*if appropriate*] each page of the will has been signed by and numbered;
9 (*d*) I have satisfied myself as to the identity of the testator and of the witnesses as designated above;
10 (*e*) the witnesses met the conditions requisite to act as such according to the law under which I am acting;
11 (*f*) [*if appropriate*] the testator has requested me to include the following statement concerning the safekeeping of his will:

12 PLACE
13 DATE
14 SIGNATURE and, if necessary, SEAL

In the absence of rules relating to the specific safekeeping of wills, the authorised person must ask the testator whether he wishes to make a statement concerning the safekeeping of his will. If the testator expressly so requests, the place where he intends that his will should be kept has to be set out in the certificate to be given by the authorised person. By virtue of s 28 of the Act of 1982 international wills may be deposited for safekeeping in this country in the manner provided by s 23 of the same Act (see Chapter 22).

Miscellaneous provisions relating to international wills are as follows:

(*a*) if the wills of two or more persons are contained in the one instrument, that document cannot be accepted as an international will;
(*b*) there are no special rules relating to the revocation of an international will which may be revoked in the ordinary manner (see head 2.29);
(*c*) the fact that a will cannot be set up as an international will does not prevent its formal validity from being established under any other appropriate law.

Persons authorised to act in connection with international wills (authorised persons) in the United Kingdom are (*a*) solicitors and (*b*) notaries public (s 28(1) of the Administration of Justice Act 1982). Any person authorised under s 6(1) of the Commissioners for Oaths Act 1889 to do notarial acts in any foreign country or place may act in such country or place as an authorised person (s 28(2) of the Act of 1982).

Chapter 3

Executors

Probate of a will issues only to an executor and he has a prior right to prove the will. His powers arise from the will and not from the grant of probate; nevertheless it is necessary that he should prove the will because it is only by production of the probate that he can prove his title, or bring an action in respect of the testator's estate. He may be expressly appointed by the will, or codicil, or he may have been given such duties under the terms of the will that it can be presumed that he was intended by the testator to be responsible for the administration and distribution of the estate in accordance with the directions expressed in the will. This latter person is called an executor according to the tenor of the will, or codicil. The duties he is called upon to perform must be of an executorial character (*In the Goods of Fry* (1827) 1 Hag Ecc 80; *In the Goods of Brown* (1910) 54 SJ 478). Thus a direction to pay the testator's debts has been held to be sufficient but not a direction to pay them out of a particular fund; the appointment of a trustee 'to get in all my property' is enough but not a bare appointment of trustees.

An executor need not be expressly named in the will. If the testator has appointed in his will a named person with power himself to nominate an executor, any such exercise of the power is effective and the nomination should be lodged with the papers to lead the grant.

An appointment which is ambiguous may be void for uncertainty, eg 'any two of my sons' or '*A* or *B*' (but possibly not '*A* and/or *B*': see *Re Lewis* [1942] Ch 424). If there are two separate appointments of executors it has been assumed that the testator intended all the persons named to act together unless there was some indication in the will to the contrary, eg if the later appointment was of a 'sole executor' it would be deemed to revoke the earlier appointment but possibly not in the case of a 'sole execut*rix*'. It is now possible, in respect of the will of a testator who has died on or after 1 January 1983, to adduce extrinsic evidence, including evidence of the testator's intentions, to assist with the interpretation of any language in the will which is ambiguous on the face of it, or which is shown by evidence, other than evidence of the testator's intention, to be ambiguous in the light of surrounding circumstances (see head 2.17). In appropriate circumstances it may be necessary to apply for rectification of the will (see head 2.16). Enquiry should be made of the registrar to ascertain his requirements in any particular case.

The restriction that a grant of representation should not be made to more than four persons has been slightly relaxed on and after 1 January 1982. Probate is not to be granted to more than four executors in respect of the same part of the estate of a deceased person (s 114 (1) of the Supreme Court Act 1981). This means that if four general executors have been appointed, a fifth executor whose powers are limited to dealing with a particular part of the estate may not be joined in the grant unless one of the general executors steps down (*In the Estate of Holland* [1936] 3 All ER 13, still applies). But if, for instance, a literary executor is appointed as well as four other executors whose powers are limited to dealing with all the estate excluding the literary estate, all five persons may now apply to be joined in a single grant. Unless the exception applies, power must be reserved to the excess executors to prove the will (see Power reserved, head 3.3). When one of several executors is proving the will, the others must be accounted for, either by having power reserved to them (see head 3.3) or by renunciation (see head 8.1). An executor who has been substituted in the event of the original executor failing to prove the will may apply on the original executor renouncing probate.

Probate will not be granted to an executor who is a minor (see head 9.1(*a*)) nor to an executor who by reason of mental or physical incapacity is incapable of managing his affairs (see heads 9.2(*b*) and 9.3). A trust corporation which has been appointed executor may take a grant in its corporate capacity, although the oath is sworn by its duly appointed nominee (see p 196). If the testator has appointed as sole executor a corporation which is not a trust corporation, the corporation may take a grant only through its nominee or attorney and this will be a grant, not of probate, but of letters of administration with will annexed (see head 14.2). If an individual has been appointed as executor with a corporation which is not a trust corporation, he may take a grant of probate alone (see p 76).

Where one corporate body takes over the business of, or merges with, another such body, it is usually arranged (eg, in a private Act of Parliament) that an appointment as executor of the body taken over shall henceforth be treated as an appointment of the composite body. Details of the provision whereby such change of executorship was effected must be recited in the oath (see p 201). A trust corporation which by virtue of the Companies Act 1980 has re-registered as a public company and now carries the suffix 'public limited company' or its abbreviation 'plc' in its name will not be required to explain any consequential difference between its present title and that given in the appointment in the will. Nor will such a corporation normally be required to produce evidence of registration under the Act.

Sometimes executors are appointed by description, as when the holder of an office or the members of a firm are appointed. Different considerations have applied in these two cases in the absence of any clear intention set out in the will. Where the holder of an office has been appointed, the person entitled to act as executor is the holder *at the date of the death of the testator* (*In the Estate of Jones* (1927) 43 TLR 324); where a firm has been appointed it is only the members of the firm *at the date of the will* who may act (*In the Goods of Fernie* (1849) 6 Notes of Cases 657; and for a detailed discussion of the problem see *Re Horgan, decd* [1969] 3 All ER 1570). Where a will containing the appointment of a firm has been republished by a codicil, it is the members at the date of the codicil who are qualified. Now, however, in respect of the will of a testator who has died on or after 1 January 1983, extrinsic evidence, including evidence of the testator's intention, may be adduced to assist in the interpretation of a will which is in part meaningless or the language of which is ambiguous (see head 2.17).

The powers of an executor may be limited by the terms of the will or his appointment may be made subject to certain conditions (see also p 75). Thus, he may be appointed 'for life or until re-marriage', or he may be empowered to deal only with 'the estate in England', or he may be appointed for a particular purpose, eg, as literary executor to deal with the literary assets. In all such cases the grant will be similarly limited. If the appointment is conditional it must be shown in what way it has become effective. A special case arises where there was land vested in the testator which was settled previously to his death and which remained settled land notwithstanding his death. In that event, the trustees of the settlement at the date of death, if not specifically appointed as such by the deceased's will, are deemed to be the special executors as to the settled land and they may apply for and obtain probate in respect of the settled land (see head 12.1). If the general executors are not also the trustees, they will take a grant of probate save and except the settled land.

In a case where foreign law is applicable, provided the will is valid by that law and the appointment of an executor therein is written in the English language, he will be accepted as having full rights of executorship and no inquiry need be made as to whether his powers are limited in extent or duration under the foreign law. If an appointment purporting to be that of an executor is in a foreign language a grant of probate will not issue to such person unless he can show that the will sets out his duties in terms sufficient to make him an executor according to the tenor (see head 15.2(*a*)). A foreign corporation which has been appointed executor in a will has the same rights as an English corporation which is not a trust corporation (see above and p 210; for an exception see pp 195–196).

3.1 Chain of representation

When an executor who has proved the will of his testator dies leaving part of the estate unadministered, it is not always necessary to obtain a further grant in respect of the testator's estate. It is provided that an executor of a sole or last surviving executor of a testator is the executor of that testator (Administration of Estates Act 1925, s 7) and he has the same rights and duties in respect of the testator's estate as had the original executor when he was living. This chain of representation is only maintained if the executor of the sole or last surviving executor proves the latter's will, but subject thereto, may continue indefinitely. The chain is broken if an executor dies intestate, or fails to appoint an executor in his will, or his executor fails to prove his will; it is not broken, but remains suspended, if a temporary grant of letters of administration with will annexed is issued, provided that probate is subsequently granted. Difficulty sometimes arises when an executor to whom power has been reserved (see head 3.3) is still alive when the surviving proving executor dies. The chain of representation will still pass to the executor of the latter but may be broken at any time by the executor to whom power has been reserved taking a grant of double probate. If the executor to whom power has been reserved renounces his right to a grant of probate, or dies without proving, or fails to take a grant after citation (see head 19.2), the possibility of the chain being broken in this way is removed. But if there is no executor of the surviving proving executor, the chain is suspended until the executor to whom power has been reserved takes a grant of double probate and no person may take a grant of letters of administration with the will annexed unless such executor dies without proving or renounces or is cited or is passed over by an order under s 116 of the Supreme Court Act 1981 (see head 13.6).

Because a grant of probate issued in Northern Ireland in respect of a testator who is recited in the grant as having died domiciled there is to be treated as if it had originally issued in England and Wales (see p 220), there can be a chain of representation through that grant whether it issued before or after 1 January 1972. A similar situation does not apply to Scottish confirmations (see s 1 (3) of the Administration of Estates Act 1971), in respect of which there can be no chain of representation. Provided both grants of probate have been re-sealed in England and Wales under the Colonial Probates Act 1892, the proving executor of a deceased proving executor will represent the original testator through a chain.

3.2 Oath for executors

Every application for a grant must be supported by an oath contained in an affidavit sworn (or an affirmation) by the applicants (Probate Rule 6 (1)). It is by means of this document that the executors establish their right to a grant of probate. It must be completed with the greatest care, because errors may call for it to be amended and re-sworn, unless they are of a minor nature, when a certificate by the solicitor will be accepted.

Form 3.2 Oath for executors
(*For heading and title, see Form* 2.11)

1 ,
of ;

2 make oath and say that believe the paper writing now produced to and marked by to be the true and original last will and testament
3 of
late of
formerly of deceased, who
4 died on the day of , 19 , aged years, domiciled in
5 and that to the best of knowledge, information and belief there was no land vested in the said deceased immediately before his death which was settled previously thereto (and not by his will) and which remained settled land notwithstanding his death.
6 And further make oath and say that
7 the execut named in the said will
8 and will (i) collect and get in the real and personal estate ( ) of the said deceased and administer it according to law; (ii) when required to do so by the court, exhibit on oath in the court a full inventory of the said estate ( ) and when so required render an account of the administration of the said estate to the court; and (iii) when required to do so by the High Court, deliver up the grant of probate to that court;
9 and that to the best of knowledge, information and belief
[the gross estate passing under the grant does not exceed £ , and the net estate does not exceed £ , and that this is not a case in which an Inland Revenue Account is required to be delivered]
[the gross estate passing under the grant amounts to £ , and the net estate amounts to £].
10
11 Sworn by the above-
named deponent
at
this day of , 19 .
Before me
A Commissioner for Oaths (or Solicitor).

The name and address of the extracting solicitor should appear in the top right-hand corner of the oath. If the solicitor's office reference is inserted immediately following his name, the reference will be included, following the solicitor's name, at the foot of the grant without any special request.

1 This paragraph should commence 'I' or 'We' followed by the full names, addresses and occupations or descriptions of the deponents. They must appear in the order set out in the appointment of executors in the will. If it is desired that this order should be varied (as when a trust corporation desires its name to appear first in the grant) a letter of request to that effect, signed by all the executors, may be filed with the papers. If the oath recites the names of the executors in an order other than that given in the will, and no letter of consent is filed, it will be assumed that by subscribing to the oath the executors have given an implied consent to the change in the order.

(1) *Names*—The true and correct names of each of the executors must be given. If any of these differ from those given in the appointment of executors in the will, an explanation must be given. Where there is a slight discrepancy it will be sufficient to say 'in the will called (*or if it is a mistake*

in the spelling of a name "written") '. When there has been a change of name, the facts should be recited, thus:

(*a*) by deed poll, 'formerly who changed my name by deed poll dated the day of ' (the deed poll should be lodged for inspection);

(*b*) on marriage, 'formerly and in the will called spinster' (or as the case may be);

(*c*) on becoming a peer, 'formerly and in the will called '.

If the name has been changed by habit and repute, the change should be explained as follows: 'That I was formerly known as (old name) but assumed the name of (new name) on or about the since when I have never used the name of (old name) but have always been known as (new name).'

Serious discrepancies between the true name and that given in the appointment of executors call for proof of identity. This is normally given by the executor whose identity is in question, and takes the form of either an explanatory paragraph in the oath or a separate affidavit dealing with the matter. (As to trust corporations, see pp 64 and 201.)

No explanation is required if all the forenames of the executor are correctly represented by initials, and the omission of a middle name may be explained by reciting 'in the will called ', but the inversion of forenames or the omission of the first forename, whether the names are given in full or by initials, always calls for proof of identity. The manner of proof is dependent upon the extent of the discrepancy. If the address of the executor is given in the will, the simplest proof is the sworn statement that the deponent was the only person bearing the forenames or initials given in the will, living at that address at the date of the will. Identity may also be established by the sworn statement that the deponent was a close friend of the testator and a person likely to be appointed an executor. If the testator had informed the deponent of his appointment, it should be so sworn; if he told some other person that he had appointed the claimant an executor, such person should make an affidavit to that effect. If the discrepancy is in the name of a child of the testator, it must be sworn that the deponent is the only child bearing or known by the name given in the will. It is never sufficient to state merely that the applicant is the same person as the person named in the will.

Errors in the recital of relationship are fairly common, and testators often give a relationship which in fact only exists between the person named and the spouse of the testator, eg, a testator may call an executor 'his nephew' when in fact he is a nephew of the testator's wife. This should be stated in the oath or affidavit of identity, and it must be further sworn that the testator never had a lawful nephew of that name. If an entirely non-existent relationship is given, proof of identity must take the form of establishing:

(i) that the testator had no relative of that name of that degree of relationship; or

(ii) if he had, that such person was to the knowledge of the testator dead at the date of the will; and

(iii) such facts as will establish that the deponent was the person intended to be appointed an executor.

Where the executrix is described simply as 'my wife', it must be stated that the applicant was the lawful wife of the deceased at the date of the will. If this statement has been omitted, a certificate by the applicant's solicitor to the effect that he has seen the marriage certificate confirming the applicant's claim will be accepted. Similarly, where the testator has appointed 'my son' as executor, it must be shown that the applicant was the only lawful son of the deceased at the date of the will.

If the executor has been appointed under the description of 'Mr (or Captain) Smith', he must give proof of identity as indicated above. Similarly, where 'Mr and Mrs J Smith' have been appointed executors and application is being made by Mrs Smith, she must state that she was the lawful wife of 'John Smith' at the date of the will.

An executor described in the appointment as 'the younger' or 'junior' should be so described unless he is the son of the testator.

(See also note to para **6** at p 74).

(2) *Addresses*—The full private and permanent postal address of each executor must be given. An accommodation address, such as c/o , or a club, hotel, or bank will not be accepted unless it is sworn, or certified by the solicitor, that no further or better address can be given, giving the reason, or it is shown that an apparent accommodation address is in fact the permanent residential address of the deponent. A solicitor, chartered accountant or similar person administering the estate in a professional capacity may give his professional address only. Moreover when it would be an advantage in administering the estate for the grant to show the business address of any other grantee, there is a discretion to allow this to be inserted, but the residential address must also be recited in the oath. In any case of doubt an inquiry should be made at the registry. Former addresses need not be given unless required to establish the identity of an executor. The private address of a member of the forces should be given but, if none, his rank, number, unit and station will be accepted. See also note to para **1** of Form 2.11 at p 26.

(3) *Occupations or descriptions*—The occupation of a deponent, male or female, must be given, or if he or she has none, his or her description (RSC, Ord 41, r 1 (4), and Probate Rule 65).

(i) *Males*—The occupation must be given in precise language. University degrees or letters denoting membership of learned societies will not be accepted unless it is clear that the deponent follows the profession to which they relate. A professional qualification will be sufficient, as also will service ranks. The term 'gentleman' will not be accepted unless amplified by the further statement 'of no occupation'. The description 'of independent means' will not be accepted by itself. If the applicant is retired, he should state his previous occupation qualified by the word 'retired' or else say 'of no occupation', although 'retired' alone may be accepted. A 'clerk in Holy Orders' should be described as such and the name of the deponent should be prefixed with the title 'Reverend'. In all other cases where the term 'clerk' is used, the exact type of clerk (mercantile, solicitor's or the like) should be specified, although 'clerk' may be accepted without inquiry. A knight or peer should describe himself as such and need not give his occupation; a knight should state whether he is a baronet or knight bachelor or indicate the Order to which he belongs. An applicant who describes himself as a student should state that he is of full age.

(ii) *Females*—A woman is now properly described by reference to her occupation in precise language (see above). If she has no occupation her status may be given; a spinster or widow is described as such; a divorced woman as 'single woman, formerly the wife of ____'; a married woman should be described as such, and not by giving the name of her husband (although the latter description will be accepted). A female whose marriage has been annulled may be described by the status she had immediately before the ceremony of marriage took place. 'Feme sole' is now accepted as sufficient provided that the title of the applicant to the grant does not depend on her status.

The wife of a knight is properly described as 'Lady' unless she is entitled in her own right to a higher mode of address. To avoid the inconvenience which sometimes arises because the occupation or status of a grantee is no longer inserted in the grant, it has been arranged that if the mode of address of a female applicant is given in the oath as 'Mrs', 'Miss', etc, that prefix will be included in the grant. The appropriate prefix will also be included in the grant whenever the status of a female grantee appears in the oath.

The occupation or description may be supplied or amplified by the certificate of the solicitor having the conduct of the application.

2 Although this paragraph makes the oath binding, it deals mainly with the identification of the documents put forward for proof. If the deponents wish to affirm, the words 'make oath and say' must be altered to read 'do solemnly and sincerely affirm', and a corresponding alteration made in para **6** and the jurat at the foot of the oath. The identification of the documents is completed by 'marking' which consists of the signature of the executors and the person before whom the oath is sworn being written on each of them (Probate Rule 8). If they are all contained on the same sheet of paper, one 'marking' is sufficient; if they are on separate paper writings, each must be 'marked'. When a document in Welsh or in a foreign language is being proved, it is the original which must be marked and not the translation which accompanies it. Whenever possible, the marking should be placed away from the text of the document, because if the document is thereby made unsuitable for photographic reproduction, the registry may call for an engrossment (see head 21.1). When an engrossment copy has to be lodged, for instance because alterations cannot be shown to have been made before execution of the will (see p 23), or because an order has been made for rectification of the will (see head 2.16), it is the original will which is marked. The registrar has a discretion to allow a photographic copy of the original will to be marked by the applicant when there is a danger that the original might be lost in sending it to the applicant (Probate Rule 8); application for leave should be made to the Principal of the Probate Department of the Principal Registry or to the district registrar. In that case the words 'a true photographic copy of which is' should be inserted immediately after 'paper writing'; both the copy and the original document must be lodged with the papers to lead the grant.

When an original will is being proved, it is described as in the printed words with the addition (when necessary) of the words 'with codicils thereto'. If two or more wills are being proved or another document is to be incorporated in the will, the words 'as contained in paper writings A, B, etc' are added after the word 'testament'.

As to codicils, it is important to remember that a codicil which has been revoked by a later one may have to be proved. In any case its production will be called for. The rule is that if the revoked codicil alters the terms of the will or of a previous codicil it must be proved, notwithstanding that it was later revoked (see p 42).

It sometimes happens that the original testamentary document is not being proved. In such a case this paragraph of the oath should speak of the document as being 'the true last will and testament', the word 'original' being deleted, and the nature of the document given in the words 'as contained in '. This position may arise in the following circumstances:

(1) *Official copy of a will proved*—This situation arises when the original will is in the custody of a foreign court or notary, and it is not possible for it to be given out (see pp 45, 206). In the oath the document to be proved is described as 'the true last will and testament as contained in a true and official copy thereof'. The copy must bear the seal, if any, of the court or notary. (As to proof of the validity of a foreign will, see head 15.1.)

(2) *Copy of a lost or damaged will proved*—When an order has been made admitting a copy of a lost or damaged will or a declaration of its contents to probate, the document is described as 'the true last will and testament as contained in a copy thereof', *or* 'in a photographic copy thereof', *or* 'in a completed draft thereof', *or* 'in paragraph of the affidavit of sworn herein on the day of , 19 ', *or* 'in the exhibit marked " " to the affidavit of sworn herein on the day of , 19 '.

The last two descriptions are also used in respect of the nuncupative (oral) will of a soldier, airman or seaman which is being admitted to proof as a privileged will (see p 50). As a rule the wording of the order of the court should be followed. (For the circumstances under which the contents of a lost will may be admitted to probate, see head 2.22; for damaged wills, see head 2.23.)

3 The full name and address of the testator must be given in this paragraph. The true and proper name of the testator must *always* be given. Where there has been a change of name by habit and repute only, and it has not been recorded by the filing of a deed poll, the true name is often taken to be that in which the birth was registered, or in the case of a married or divorced woman, the surname of her husband or former husband (the adopted name will usually require to be inserted in the grant as an alias). But where there has been a complete abandonment of the former name over a period of time, the true name is the name by which he was known at the date of death. If there is any doubt reference should be made to the registrar. If the will has been made or executed in some other name, or if the testator held property in some other name, and it is convenient to include that other name in the grant, then that name must follow as an alias. The paragraph would then read, eg, 'John Charles Smith otherwise John Smith otherwise John Smythe'. The facts which justify the inclusion of an alias must be deposed to either in a separate affidavit or in the oath in para **10** (see p 79). An explanation will not be required merely because the signature of the deceased omits some of his names; however, any major variation must be explained (see head 2.6). It is usually sufficient to state that the signature appearing in the will was the usual form of signature of the deceased.

The address of the testator must have been his usual residential address. An accommodation address will not be accepted unless it is further sworn that no better address can be given. If the form of the deceased's address has changed since the date of the will, this should be explained, viz, 'formerly known as and in the will described as   '. If the testator made his will while serving in the armed forces and inserted his rank, regimental number and unit instead of an address, these should be stated in order to complete the identification.

Where the latest in date of the testamentary documents to be proved gives an address different from the last address of the testator, that is the only former address that need be given. All others may be ignored. If the oath omits to account for the discrepancy, an explanation will not be required by the registry unless there is some doubt as to the identification of the testator.

It is sometimes desired that a number of addresses of the testator shall appear in the grant of representation. These must all be sworn to and a request for their inclusion in the grant made in a letter from the solicitors. In no case will more than four addresses be included.

Ecclesiastical designations, the description 'clerk in Holy Orders', and titles of honour should be given. The status of females is no longer included in the grant (save where it is necessary for the purpose of clearing in cases of administration) and accordingly need not be included in the oath.

4 The date of death must be set out as it appears in the certificate of death. Generally, the production of the certificate of death is not called for, though the circumstances of a particular case may make this necessary (see head 7.1).

In cases where there is uncertainty as to the exact date of death, as when the body of the testator was found some days after his disappearance, the fact of death is sworn to thus: 'who was known to be alive on the day of , 19 , and whose dead body was found on the day of , 19 '.

Presumed death—Where it is necessary to presume death, the evidence necessary to support the presumption is dependent upon the circumstances of the disappearance of the testator. The various types of cases are dealt with at p 142. The wording of the order of the court should be followed; leave is usually given to swear that the death occurred 'on or since the day of , 19 ', which would be the last day upon which the testator was known to have been alive.

Place of death—The place of death is no longer included in a grant of representation and in consequence does not have to be inserted in the oath.

Age at death—The age of the deceased must now be stated in the oath. If the exact age is not known, the best estimate possible should be given.

Domicile—Unless otherwise directed by the registrar, the domicile of the deceased must be stated in the oath (Probate Rule 6 (4)), and it will be included in the grant. A statement in the oath that the deceased died domiciled 'in England', or 'in Wales', or 'in England and Wales', will result in the domicile being recited in the grant as 'in England and Wales'. In those countries which have a federal constitution, eg, the USA, the law may vary in different parts and care should be taken to swear that the testator died domiciled in a particular State in the federal country. If there is any possibility of doubt as to the domicile, an affidavit setting out the facts upon which the claim is made should be filed in support of the statement in the oath. (As to domicile generally, see p 14.)

Domicile must also be sworn to in the following special circumstances:

(*a*) When the will is an informal document made when the testator was in actual military, naval or air service, or made whilst he was a mariner at sea, his domicile at the date of making the will must be stated (see p 48).

(*b*) When the validity of the will falls to be established by the law of the testator's domicile at some time other than at his death, the domicile in question must be given, eg, when there has been a change of domicile since the making of the will and it is necessary to establish its validity by reference to the law of the country in which the testator was domiciled at the time of making the will (see pp 13–15). The relevant facts should be given either in a separate affidavit or in para **10** of the oath.

5 This paragraph is required only when the testator died on or after 1 January 1926. If he died before that date it should not be inserted. Care must be taken in its completion, for errors may call for the re-swearing of the oath.

If there was no settled land, the paragraph should be left as printed. If there was settled land, then the word 'no' must be deleted and, whether it is intended that the grant shall include or exclude such land, the rest of the paragraph left as printed; this is so even if the land has subsequently ceased to be settled land. If it is intended that the grant shall exclude the settled land, it is sufficient merely to state that there was such land vested in the testator and the settlements need be neither disclosed nor identified. However, para **9** of the oath must be qualified by inserting in the appropriate spaces 'save and except settled land'. If the grant is to include or be limited to the settled land, details of the settlement must be given, eg, 'under the will of , proved in the Registry on the day of , 19 ', *or* 'under an indenture of settlement dated the day of , 19 ', *or* 'under a compound settlement arising out of an indenture of settlement dated the day of , 19 , and the will of proved in the Registry on the day of , 19 ' (or such documents as give rise to the compound settlement). (For examples of settlements of this nature, see *Re Taylor's Estate* [1929] P 260; *Re Sharpe's Deed of Release* [1939] Ch 51.)

When settled land was vested in the deceased as tenant for life jointly with another person, who survives the deceased, it should be stated that 'there was no settled land vested solely in the said deceased immediately before his death, etc'.

If there was other settled land, in respect of which the applicants are not entitled to a grant, this fact must be stated.

(For the practice relating to settled land grants, see Chapter 12.)

6 The relationship, if any, of a grantee to the deceased is no longer stated in the grant unless it is necessary for the purpose of establishing title or identification. In consequence the relationship need not be set out in the oath save for those reasons. For instance, when the appointment of executors in the will gives a relationship which does not exist or is erroneous, the oath should recite it—'I am in the said will erroneously called a of the said testator'. The question of identity will, of course, arise, and if it can be established by a concise paragraph, such a paragraph should appear in para **10** (see pp 68–69, as to the manner of establishing identity).

If the facts required to prove identity do not lend themselves to a short concise statement, a supplementary affidavit should be filed.

7 The applicants must swear that they are the executors named in the will. This should be done in accordance with the terms of the appointment. When they are unusual it is advisable to follow the wording of the will. The most usual manner of swearing is:

One executor named—The sole executor (or executrix).

All the executors named are male—The executors.

All the executors are female—The executrices.

Some male, some female—The executors.

The applicants are the surviving executors—The surviving executors.

Some executors have renounced probate—One (*or* two *or* three) of the executors named in the said will, the other executors named therein having renounced probate thereof. (The fact of renunciation need not be recited but the instrument of renunciation must be filed with the papers.)

Power is to be reserved to some executors—One (*or* two *or* three) of the executors named in the said will. (The fact that power is being reserved need not be mentioned in the body of the oath, the marginal note 'Power reserved to the other executors' being sufficient; see head 3.3.)

Contingent appointment of executor—Having attained the age of eighteen (twenty-one) years (*or such other fact as results in the fulfilment of the contingency*), the sole executor named in the said will (*or* the executors named in the said will, the said having attained the age of eighteen (twenty-one) years).

(It is to be noted that the appointment of an executor contingent upon attaining the age of twenty-one years is not affected by the reduction of the age of majority by the Family Law Reform Act 1969. If, however, the appointment is expressed to be dependent upon the executor attaining full age or ceasing to be an infant or a minor, the construction of such phrases is governed by whether the will was made before 1 January 1970 or on or after that date. It is the date of the will or codicil which contains the appointment which is relevant, and the fact that a codicil made after 1 January 1970 confirms a will made before that date does not alter the position.)

Some executors appointed by the will, others by the codicil—The executors named in the said will and codicil.

Limited appointment of executors:

(*a*) *As to status and/or time*—The executrix for life or widowhood (*or* the executors named in the said will but as to the said for life or widowhood only).

Being resident in Great Britain (*or as the case may be*) at the date of death of the said deceased, the sole executor named in the said will (*or* the executors named in the said will, the said being resident in Great Britain at the date of death of the said deceased (*or as the case may be*)).

(*b*) *As to place*—The executor for England and Wales named in the said will (*or as the case may be*) (*or* but as to the said only so far as concerns the estate of the said deceased situate in England and Wales (*or as the case may be*)).

(*c*) *As to purpose*—But as to the said only so far as concerns the winding up of the business of of the said deceased (*or as the case may be*).

The applicants are original executors, there being a substitution of executors in certain circumstances—The executors named in the said will as therein mentioned.

Application by an executor appointed without apparent limitation but other executors have been substituted on his death—An executor for life.

Substituted executors, after death—The executors substituted in the said will, mentioned in the said will having died in the lifetime of the said testator (*or as the case may be*).

Substituted executors, after divorce or annulment—The executors substituted in the said will, the marriage of the said deceased with mentioned in the said will having on the day of 19 been dissolved (*or* annulled) by final decree of the High Court of Justice (*or* of the County Court) in England and Wales (*or as the case may be*) and that thereby the said will takes effect as if the appointment of the said as sole executor named therein were omitted and the gift to the said as the residuary legatee and devisee named in the said will has lapsed (see head 2.30).

The will appoints the spouse of the testator and one other person as executors and the testator's marriage has subsequently been dissolved or annulled (see head 2.30)—One of the executors named in the said will, the marriage of the said deceased with having on the day of 19 been dissolved (*or* annulled) by final decree of the High Court of Justice (*or* of the County Court) in England and Wales (*or as the case may be*) and that thereby the said will takes effect as if the appointment of the said as the other executor named therein were omitted.

The will appoints one person sole executor and in the event of his predeceasing the deceased another person as sole executor; application by the second-named executor—The sole executor named in the said will, mentioned in the said will having died in the lifetime of the said deceased.

Executors according to the tenor—The executors according to the tenor of the said will.

Special executors as to settled land (see head 12.1)—The executors named in the will and the trustees of the said settled land at the date of death of the said deceased and as such the special executors as to the said settled land.

When a testator has appointed as executors an individual and a corporation which is not a trust corporation, on an application by the individual for a grant of probate, the oath should contain a concise statement (in para **10**, or immediately before para **6** as convenient) as follows: 'That the said deceased in his said will named and Company Limited as executors and that the said Company Limited is not a trust corporation as defined by Rule 2(2) of the Non-Contentious Probate Rules 1954.' Alternatively power may now be reserved to the corporation, leaving the question whether the corporation is or is not entitled to a grant of probate to be determined should any subsequent application be made on its behalf for a grant of representation.

8 Unless there is some special limitation on the extent of the estate to be administered little need be done to this paragraph, which sets out the duties of the personal representatives of the deceased (see head 1.5). If there was settled land vested in the testator, the words 'save and except settled land', 'limited to settled land', or 'including settled land' should be inserted in the brackets provided, as the circumstances of the case warrant, and also in the brackets in para **9**. In other cases the limitation is described, as appropriate.

9 The value of the estate to be inserted is that of the estate passing by means of the grant. In those cases in which the deceased died on or after 1 April 1981 and an Inland Revenue account is not required to be delivered because the estate is an 'excepted estate' (see p 228) it is sufficient merely to say that the gross estate passing under the grant does not exceed £40,000 (or £25,000 if the deceased died before 1 April 1983) and that the net estate does not exceed either £10,000 (in which event no probate fee is payable), or £25,000 (when a flat probate fee of £40 is payable), or £40,000 (when a flat probate fee of £80 is payable) as the case may be. In those circumstances the first paragraph in square brackets should be completed and the second paragraph ignored. Failure to recite in an appropriate case that it is not one in which an account has to be delivered will require the oath to be amended to insert this clause and resworn. Where the deceased died on or after 1 April 1981 and the circumstances are not as recited above, or where the deceased died before 1 April 1981, the values of the gross estate and of the net estate passing under the grant must be stated; in that event the first paragraph in square brackets should be ignored and the second paragraph completed. (See also under 'Nil estate' at p 81.)

Estate passing under the grant—This must be the 'free' estate and therefore excludes property in which the deceased had only a limited interest at the time of his death, joint property devolving by survivorship, donationes mortis causa, life interests and the like. The test is not whether capital transfer tax is payable on the property, but whether the production of the grant is necessary to establish a claim to it. Ex gratia payments (eg, a Civil Service death gratuity, unless nominated) to the personal representative of the testator must therefore be included but gifts inter vivos and nominated property are excluded. When the testator died possessed of freehold or leasehold property, the gross value must be included without the deduction of mortgages. If the grant includes settled land, the value includes that of the settled land.

Scope of the property—Where the testator died domiciled in England and Wales, the scope of the property passing by means of the grant varies according to the date of death, as follows:

(*a*) *Death before 1 January 1898*—The personal estate in the United Kingdom of Great Britain and Ireland.

(*b*) *Death after 31 December 1897, but before 22 November 1921*—The personal estate in the United Kingdom of Great Britain and Ireland and the real estate (other than copyholds and customary freeholds) in England and Wales.

(*c*) *Death on or after 22 November 1921, but before 1 April 1923*—The personal estate in Great Britain and Ireland (exclusive of Northern Ireland) and the real estate (other than copyholds and customary freeholds) in England and Wales.

(*d*) *Death on or after 1 April 1923, but before 1 January 1926*—The personal estate in Great Britain (ie, England, Wales and Scotland) and the real estate (other than copyholds and customary freeholds) in England and Wales.

(*e*) *Death on or after 1 January 1926, but before 1 January 1972*—The personal estate in Great Britain (ie, England, Wales and Scotland) and the real estate in England and Wales.

(*f*) *Death on or after 1 January 1972*—The personal and real estate in England and Wales, Scotland and Northern Ireland.

When the testator was domiciled out of England and Wales, the value of the estate to be inserted is that of the real and personal property situated in England and Wales only.

'*Nil estate*'—Provided that sufficient reason can be shown, a grant will issue in respect of a 'nil estate'. The facts calling for the grant should be stated in the oath in para **10** (see p 81).

'*Estate so far as at present can be ascertained*'—It sometimes happens that a full statement of the estate of a testator cannot be made at the time of the application for probate. If the applicant discloses in the Inland Revenue account that he has not been able to ascertain the precise amount or value of the estate or he wishes to show the amount of the estate as being 'so far as at present can be ascertained', the Inland Revenue account should include a statement as to why a full disclosure cannot be made, and must be submitted to the Capital Taxes Office for the concurrence of the Commissioners of Inland Revenue in the issue of the grant to be obtained. They will call for an estimate of the value of the estate in question and may require tax to be paid on the basis of that value, on the understanding that the matter will be rectified by a corrective account at a later date. The value to be inserted in the oath should be based on an estimate of the final value of the estate, not merely a total of the assets the value of which has been ascertained. When the final value of the estate has been ascertained, a corrective account must be submitted to the Capital Taxes Office. No increase or decrease in the value of the estate will be noted on the grant and further court fees by reason of any increase in the estate do not have to be paid. If, however, the circumstances are such that the highest estimate of the value will not take the total estate out of the category of an 'excepted estate' so that an Inland Revenue account is not required (see p 228), it will be sufficient merely to describe the gross estate passing under the grant as not exceeding £40,000 (or £25,000 in respect of a death before 1 April 1983) and the net estate as not exceeding £10,000, or £25,000, or £40,000, as appropriate, incorporating for this purpose the best estimate of the unascertained value.

Community of property—When community of property exists under the law applicable to the testator (generally in countries where Dutch or Roman-Dutch law prevails), this paragraph of the oath should be altered to read: 'That the whole of the estate in England and Wales (*or as the case may be*) in respect of which a grant is now required amounts in value to the sum of £ to the best of my knowledge, information and belief and that £ (*generally one-half*) of that sum has accrued to the surviving spouse by reason of the existence of community of property under the law of the place of domicile of the said deceased at the date of the marriage (*or as the case may be*).' The grant will then be made in respect of the whole of the estate, though court fees will only be chargeable in respect of one-half (or as the case may be) of the property subject to community of property. In the case of an 'excepted estate' (see pp 77 and 228), the wording should be suitably altered if appropriate.

10 The purpose of this paragraph is to disclose matters relevant to the application which do not conveniently fall to be dealt with in previous paragraphs of the oath. If this cannot be done, separate affidavits should be filed. The following are examples of the use of this space:

Clearing off—An executor may be appointed to act subject to a condition or on the occurrence of an event. The fulfilment of the condition or the occurrence of the event may be deposed to in this space:

(*a*) Where an executor is appointed subject to his being in the United Kingdom at the date of death of the testator: 'That the said was resident in the United Kingdom at the date of death of the said testator', *or* 'That mentioned in the said will was absent from the United Kingdom at the date of death of the said testator'.

(*b*) Where an executor is appointed subject to his having attained a certain age at the date of death of the testator: 'That the said attained the age of years in the lifetime of the said testator', *or* 'That mentioned in the said will had not attained the age of years at the date of the death of the said testator'.

(*c*) Where an executor is appointed to act when he attains a certain age: 'That the said has attained the age of years'. (If the person named has not attained the necessary age or is still in his minority, see head 3.3, under Power reserved. See also under Contingent appointment of executor, p 75.)

Alias—A testator's alias may not appear in a grant unless he made his will in that name or the applicant can give some valid reason for the inclusion of the alias, usually because the testator held property in that name. When these conditions exist the following paragraph may be inserted here: 'That the true and proper name of the said testator was John Charles Smith but that he made and duly executed his said will in the name of John Smith, and certain property, to wit, is vested in him in the name of John Smythe.' At least one property held in the alias name must be specified. If the alias cannot be established by such a short summary, or has been omitted from the oath, a supplementary affidavit should be filed.

Conditional wills—The facts by reason of which a conditional will is operative may be stated here (see head 2.25).

Privileged wills—The facts on which the applicant relies as constituting the document a privileged will may be set out here (see head 2.26 and Form 2.26).

Validity of wills established by decree—When a will has been declared valid by the decree of a competent court, it must be so recited in the oath:

(*a*) *Chancery Division*—'That on the day of , 19 , in an action entitled Mr Justice , one of the Justices of the Chancery Division of the High Court of Justice sitting at the Royal Courts of Justice, Strand, London (*or as the case may be*) pronounced for the force and validity of the said will (*or* ordered that the said will be rectified by virtue of s 20(1) of the Administration of Justice Act 1982, etc).'

(*b*) *County Court*—The recital in the oath should read: 'That on the day of , 19 , His Honour Judge sitting at the County Court for holden at , in an action entitled against , did order (*follow the terms of the order*).'

When an action has been tried in the High Court an office copy of the judgment or order of the court is sent to the Principal Registry by the Chief Master, together with any testamentary documents in respect of which probate or administration with will is to be granted, appropriately endorsed. The original documents will be handed out to the applicants in exchange for a photographic copy, and, after marking by them, should be lodged with the other papers to lead to the grant, together if appropriate with an engrossment of the will in its rectified form. If application for the grant is being made in a district probate registry, an official copy of the decree should accompany the papers. When the will has been the subject of proceedings in a county court, the registrar of the court will endorse the testamentary documents pronounced for or against and send them together with any order or decree made and his certificate to the registrar of the nearest probate registry.

When a will has been declared valid by a decree, that fact is recited in the body of the grant of probate; when a grant issues in accordance with the order of a county court judge, the grant bears a notation 'By order of the county court at dated the day of , 19 .'

Grant issues by order—When a grant issues by any order of the court, the fact of the making of the order and its substance must be recited in the oath.

(*a*) *Order on motion*—'That by order on motion made by the Family Division of the High Court of Justice on the day of , 19 , it was ordered that .'

(*b*) *Other order*—'That by order of Mr Justice (Mr Registrar) (*or* the District Probate Registrar) made on the day of , 19 , it was ordered that .'

A copy of the order issued from the registry must accompany the papers. No reference will be made to it in the body of the grant. If the order is for rectification of the will, an engrossment of the will in the form in which it is to be proved must also be lodged (see head 2.16).

Validity of will under foreign law—See pp 73 (Domicile), 205–209.

Nil estate—If a grant is required to issue in respect of a nil estate, the reason should be stated here, eg, 'That the purpose for which the grant now sought is required is to make title to property (viz,   ) of which the said deceased was tenant for life' (*or* 'is to constitute a personal representative of the said deceased in order to pursue (*or* defend) an action (to be) brought under the Law Reform (Miscellaneous Provisions) Act 1934'). It would seem appropriate to express the gross and net value of the estate as 'nil' (see para **9** at p 77). There is jurisdiction in the court to make a grant of representation although the deceased left no estate but it has been said that it is contrary to principle for a grant to issue in respect of the estate of a person who has died domiciled in some other country and leaving no assets within England and Wales (*Aldrich* v *A-G* (*Rogers intervening*) [1968] 1 All ER 345).

Previous grants—If there have been previous grants in the estate of the deceased which have been revoked or have ceased to be operative, the relevant facts should be recited, eg, 'That the grant of   issued out of   Registry on the   day of   , 19   , was revoked by order dated the   day of   , 19   '; 'That the grant of letters of administration with the said will annexed of the estate of the said deceased issued out of the   Registry on the   day of   , 19   , to   for the use of   during his minority has ceased and expired by reason of the attainment of the age of eighteen years by the said   ' (see also head 13.1); where a grant is being applied for by substituted executors, the original proving executors having been appointed for life only, 'That the grant of probate of the said will issued out of the   Registry on the   day of   , 19   , to   the executors for life named therein has ceased and expired by reason of the death of the said   ' (or whatever contingency brings the grant to an end). The original or an office copy must accompany the papers when application is made in the Principal Registry, or whenever application is made in a registry other than that from which the previous grant issued.

11 See the note to para **10** of Form 2.11 at p 29.

3.3 Power reserved

If one out of several executors does not wish to take out probate, power may be reserved to him to take out probate at some future time. If more than four executors are appointed by a will, probate will only be granted to four of them, power being reserved to the others to take out probate (but see p 64 for an exception). When one out of several executors is under some legal incapacity (such as minority or mental illness), power will be reserved to him to prove the will when the incapacity ceases.

If it is desired or necessary that power should be reserved to an executor, the oath to lead the grant must be marginally endorsed, 'Power reserved to the other executor(s)'; 'Power reserved to the other executor when he shall attain the age of eighteen years'; 'Power reserved to the other executor when he shall regain his mental capacity' (or as the case may be). In the last-mentioned case the incapacity must be proved in the usual manner (see head 9.2(*a*)). If the identity of the executor to whom power is to be reserved cannot be ascertained at the time the will is proved, power will be reserved 'to the other executor' without naming him (see note to para **7** at p 76). However full details of the position of the executors must be given in the oath.

Power can be reserved only to executors who are of equal degree to the proving executors, so that when probate is granted to an executor for life, power may not be reserved to the executors appointed to act on his death.

When power has been reserved it is sometimes necessary, in order to deal with the assets, to obtain a certificate that no grant of double probate has issued in the meantime. Application may be made by letter to the Record Keeper, Principal Registry of the Family Division, Somerset House, Strand, London, WC2R 1LP.

3.4 Double probate

When an executor to whom power has been reserved wishes to prove the will, he may apply for a grant of double probate at the Principal Registry or at any one of the district probate registries. A grant of double probate is general in its terms and confers the fullest powers on the executor. It differs from the first grant of probate only in that the value of the estate shown on it is that of the unadministered estate. The executor to whom power was reserved may demand of the proving executor particulars of the estate (*Re Griffin* (1910) 54 SJ 378).

Where only one out of several executors to whom power has been reserved applies for double probate, it will bear the endorsement that power is again reserved to the other non-proving executors.

The appropriate form of Inland Revenue account is at present CAP Form A-5C and this must be sent in all cases to the Capital Taxes Office (see p 231). When the Inland Revenue account has been returned suitably endorsed, the papers should be lodged in the usual way (see pp 5, 9). An office copy of the previous grant, obtained from the registry, should accompany the papers when application is made in the Principal Registry, or whenever application is made in a registry other than that from which the previous grant issued, unless the original grant can be lodged.

Form 3.4 Oath for double probate
(For heading and title, see Form 2.11)

1
of
2 make oath and say that believe the paper writing now produced to and marked by to be the true and original last will and testament
3 of
late of
formerly of , deceased, who
4 died on the day of , 19 , aged years, domiciled in
5 and that to the best of knowledge, information and belief there was no land vested in the said deceased immediately before his death which was settled previously thereto (and not by his will) and which remained settled land notwithstanding his death;
6 And that on the day of , 19 , probate of the said will issued out of the Registry to and two of the executors named in the said will, power to take a like grant being reserved to the other executor named in the said will
7 And further make oath and say that of the said deceased and
8 the other execut named in the said will
9 and will (i) collect and get in the real and personal estate ( ) of the said deceased and administer it according to law; (ii) when required to do so by the court, exhibit on oath in the court a full inventory of the said estate ( ) and when so required render an account of the administration of the said estate to the court; and (iii) when required to do so by the High Court, deliver up the grant of probate to that court;
10 and that to the best of knowledge, information and belief the gross estate left unadministered and passing under the grant amounts to £ and the net estate amounts to £ .
11
12 Sworn by the above-
named deponent
at
this day of , 19 .
Before me
A Commissioner for Oaths (or Solicitor).

The name and address of the extracting solicitor should appear in the top right-hand corner of the oath, together with his office reference if this is required to be included in the grant.

1 See the note to para **1** of Form 3.2, at p 67.

2 See the note to para **2** of Form 3.2, at p 70. The original will may be marked, but as that involves the attendance of the executor at the registry, it is usually more convenient to mark an office copy of the will (or if not available a sealed and certified copy of the will). If available the probate copy of the will in the original grant may be marked, but this will result in it being retained in the registry. If a copy of the will is being marked, the oath should refer to 'the true last will and testament as contained in an official copy thereof'. (See also the note to para **8** of Form 13.1, at p 185.)

3, 4 and **5** See the corresponding notes to Form 3.2, at pp 72–74.

6 The making of the previous grant must be recited. The proving executor then identifies himself (in para **8**) as 'the other executor named in the said will' or as the case may be. If the reservation of power was the result of the incapacity of the executor, proof of his present capacity must be given. If the reason was minority, it must be stated that he has now attained the age of eighteen years; if it was mental incapacity, it must be stated, and shown by medical evidence on affidavit, that he has regained his mental capacity. When power was reserved on the occurrence of a vacancy among the proving executors, the fact of the vacancy must be established: 'That the said   is now dead whereby a vacancy occurs among the proving executors'.

7, 8 and **9** See the notes to paras **6, 7** and **8** of Form 3.2, at pp 74–77.

10 See the note to para **9** of Form 3.2, at p 77. The executor swears to administer the whole of the estate, but the value shown in the oath will be that of the unadministered estate valued as at the date of the Inland Revenue account. The procedure in respect of 'excepted estates' is not applicable.

11 and **12** See the notes to paras **10** and **11** of Form 3.2, at pp 79–81.

Chapter 4

Letters of Administration with Will Annexed

Letters of administration with will annexed will issue when a will is to be proved and the grant is to be made to a person who is not an executor. This may occur when a will appoints no executor; when the executors appointed are dead, have renounced, have been cited without effect (see head 19.2) or have been passed over by order of the court (see head 13.6); when the appointment of an 'executor' is in a foreign language (see head 15.2(*a*)); when they are in such a position that they can prove the will only through their attorney (see Chapter 10) or nominee (see head 14.2) when they are minors (see head 9.1(*a*)) or otherwise incapable of taking a grant (see head 9.2(*b*)); or where the appointment of a sole executor has to be omitted by reason of the subsequent dissolution or annulment of the testator's marriage (see head 2.30).

A grant may not issue to more than four persons in respect of the same part of the estate (see p 64). If life or minority interests arise under the will, it will usually be required to be made to at least two individuals or to a trust corporation with or without an individual (see head 6.2). The applicant or applicants may be required in special circumstances to provide a guarantee by sureties for the proper administration of the estate (see head 11.1).

4.1 To whom granted

The title to a grant of letters of administration with will annexed is determined by the extent of the interest of the applicant under the terms of the will. The greatest interest is deemed to be in the residue of the estate (*Atkinson* v *Barnard* (*Lady*) (1815) 2 Phillim 316; *In the Goods of Gill* (1828) 1 Hag Ecc 341), and regard must be had to the person interested in it in preference to all other interested persons. This fact should be fully recognised, for even if there is no residue of any value, the persons entitled to it whether under the express terms of the will or under the rules of intestacy are, with one exception (see p 95), preferred to legatees and devisees of the major portion of the estate.

The term 'residue' covers all the estate of the testator which is not the subject of specific, general or demonstrative legacies or devises. Such gifts, even though they constitute all the estate of any value which the testator owned, cannot be considered to be gifts of residue. The question of whether or not a particular gift amounts to a gift of residue often presents a difficult problem which could be solved hitherto only by reference to the intention of the testator as expressed by the terms of his will. Now, in respect of the will of a testator who has died on or after 1 January 1983, where any part of a will is meaningless, or the language used in any part is ambiguous on the face of it, or is shown to be ambiguous in the light of surrounding circumstances by evidence, other than evidence of the testator's intention, extrinsic evidence, including evidence of the testator's intention, may be admitted to assist in the will's interpretation (see head 2.17). It is advisable, whenever there is ambiguity of phraseology which might affect the title of the applicant for a grant, to obtain the opinion of the registrar before the papers to lead the grant are prepared.

Certain words and phrases have been judicially interpreted (eg, 'money', 'effects', 'belongings'), but as these interpretations are usually qualified by the context of the particular will in question they cannot be followed blindly (see, for instance, *Perrin* v *Morgan* [1943] AC 399; *Re Barnes's Will Trusts* [1972] 2 All ER 639).

There is often difficulty when a testator gives one person what would appear to be an absolute interest in the residuary estate and then proceeds to cut down that interest by a gift over of what remains. At one time it was considered that where the original gift was expressed to be absolute the gift over was void unless there were words clearly indicating an intention to restrict enjoyment of the gift by the legatee either in time or by recourse to the capital (*Re Jones* [1898] 1 Ch 438; *Re Gouk* [1957] 1 All ER 469). The court then said that in each case the will must be looked at as a whole to discover the construction which would most effectively express the intentions of the testator (*Re Last* [1958] P 137). Now extrinsic evidence may be used to help in the interpretation (see head 2.17). But in the case of a testator who has died on or after 1 January 1983, it has to be presumed in the absence of any contrary intention that if the testator has given property to his spouse in terms which in themselves would give an absolute interest to that spouse, but by the same instrument has purported to give his issue an interest in the same property, the gift to the spouse is absolute in spite of the purported gift to the issue (s 22 of the Administration of Justice Act 1982).

The general principle to be applied when a will contains two separate gifts of the same thing is that the later gift cancels out the earlier. In the case of a double gift of the residuary estate, however, it has been said that the first gift should be regarded as effective, the second gift being inserted in case the first should lapse (*Re Gare* [1952] Ch 80). This is now subject to the production of extrinsic evidence as to the testator's intention (see head 2.17) and, in appropriate circumstances, to the operation of s 22 of the Administration of Justice Act 1982 (see above).

4.2 Order of preference—death on or after 1 January 1926

The order of preference for the purpose of the issue of a grant of representation in respect of a death on or after 1 January 1926 where the deceased left a will is determined by Probate Rule 19 as follows:

(i) the executor;

(ii) any residuary legatee or devisee holding in trust for any other person;

(iii) any residuary legatee or devisee for life;

(iv) the ultimate residuary legatee or devisee, including one entitled on the happening of any contingency, or, where the residue is not wholly disposed of by the will, any person entitled to share in the residue not so disposed of (including the Treasury Solicitor when claiming bona vacantia on behalf of the Crown) or, subject to para (3) of Rule 25, the personal representative of any such person: provided that—

(*a*) unless a registrar otherwise directs a residuary legatee or devisee whose legacy or devise is vested in interest shall be preferred to one entitled on the happening of a contingency; and

(*b*) where the residue is not in terms wholly disposed of, the registrar may, if he is satisfied that the testator has nevertheless disposed of the whole or substantially the whole of the estate as ascertained at the time of the application for the grant, allow a grant to be made (subject however to Rule 37, see p 95) to any legatee or devisee entitled to, or to a share in, the estate so disposed of, without regard to the persons entitled to share in any residue not disposed of by the will;

(v) any specific legatee or devisee or any creditor or, subject to para (3) of Rule 25 (see p 94), the personal representative of any such person or, where the estate is not wholly disposed of by the will, any person who, notwithstanding that the amount of the estate is such that he has no immediate beneficial interest therein, may have a beneficial interest in the event of an accretion thereto;

(vi) any specific legatee or devisee entitled on the happening of any contingency, or any person having no interest under the will of the deceased who would have been entitled to a grant if the deceased had died wholly intestate.

Each of the interests mentioned must be considered and, if necessary, disposed of in the oath to lead the grant, before a lower interest can establish a claim. The classes of interests must be dealt with in detail and in order of their priority.

(a) Executors

Executors must be cleared off by the recital of the fact that none has been appointed or of the particular circumstances which prevent any executors appointed applying for probate (eg, their death in the lifetime of the testator or subsequently, their renunciation or non-appearance to a citation, their incapacity, and the like).

(b) Residuary interests

Residuary interests are of the following kinds:

(*a*) residuary legatees and/or devisees in trust (Probate Rule 19, class (ii));

(*b*) residuary legatees and/or devisees for life (Probate Rule 19, class (iii));

(*c*) ultimate residuary legatees and/or devisees, including any such residuary legatee or devisee who is entitled on the happening of any contingency, and where the residue of the estate is not wholly disposed of, the persons entitled to share in the residue not so disposed of, as on an intestacy (Probate Rule 19, class (iv));

(*d*) the personal representatives of the persons indicated in (*c*) above (Probate Rule 19, class (iv)).

If a life or minority interest arises under the terms of the will, and there is only one member of the class first entitled to the grant, a member of the next lower class must be joined unless the circumstances are such that the registrar can be persuaded that it is expedient to appoint an individual as sole administrator (see head 6.2). Any number of applicants of a class may apply for a grant without reference to the other members of the same class, unless the gift is a joint gift to them all. In that event, the consent of those other members to the applicants taking the grant must be obtained. Moreover, unless the registrar directs otherwise, a residuary legatee or devisee whose legacy or devise is vested in interest is preferred to one entitled on the happening of a contingency (Probate Rule 19 (iv)). Thus where application for a grant is made by a contingent residuary legatee or devisee and there are other residuary legatees or devisees with a vested interest who are not joining in the application, they must be 'cleared off' by renunciation or by direction of the registrar (on application being made to him ex parte before the papers to lead the grant are prepared). Strictly a life interest does not arise when a joint tenancy is created by a gift of residue; nevertheless, it may be desirable for the application for the grant to be made by two or more persons, or by a trust corporation. For a grant to a trust corporation, see head 14.1(*b*).

Failure of gift—By virtue of s 15 of the Wills Act 1837, a person taking a beneficial interest under a will loses that benefit if he, or his spouse, attests the execution of the will; in consequence, he also loses his right to a grant as a beneficiary but may take a grant in some other capacity (Probate Rule 20). The identity of the beneficiary must be ascertainable at the date of execution of the will for the rule to operate against him (*Re Royce's Will Trusts* [1959] Ch 626). The benefit is saved if subsequently the testator makes a codicil which is attested by different witnesses and which has the effect of republishing the will (*Anderson* v *Anderson* (1872) LR 13 Eq 381). If a person has signed his name at the end of a will, there is a presumption that he did so as a witness thereto. The presumption is particularly strong if the signature is placed in such a position as would seem to indicate that the person making it signed as the first or second witness. Evidence may be given to rebut this presumption and, if satisfied that a beneficiary signed the will not as a witness but, for instance, at the request of the testator in approval of its contents, the court will allow the signature to be omitted from the probate copy of the will, provided that the will was properly attested by two other persons (*Kitcat* v *King* [1930] P 266; *In the Estate of Bravda* [1968] 2 All ER 217). Even if the beneficiary or his spouse signed the will as a witness, in the case of a testator dying after 30 May 1968 the benefit will be saved provided that there are at least two other persons who have duly attested the will and that neither of the latter mentioned persons is a beneficiary or the spouse of a beneficiary (Wills Act 1968). If an application for a grant of letters of administration with will annexed is to be made by a beneficiary, or the spouse of such a person, claiming the benefit of the Wills Act 1968 it should be indicated in the papers to lead the grant that no other witness is a beneficiary under the will or the spouse of a beneficiary. If this is done no evidence as to execution is called for and the will is admitted to proof without further inquiry. If however another witness is also a beneficiary there may be a dispute with that other beneficiary witness. The onus is upon the applicant in those circumstances to establish, if he can do so, that he, or the person through whom he claims, was not a witness to the will so that his signature should be omitted from the probate copy of the will. Where there is a dispute, a discretionary grant under s 116 of the Supreme Court Act 1981 (see head 13.6) may issue, leaving the dispute to be dealt with by the court after the issue of the grant.

Effect of murder or manslaughter—There is a rule of public policy (the forfeiture rule) which precludes a person who has unlawfully killed another from acquiring a benefit in consequence of the killing. Thus a person found guilty of murder or manslaughter may not benefit from the estate of his victim, under either the will or an intestacy (*In the Estate of Crippen* [1911] P 108; *Re Callaway* [1956] Ch 559). It is to be noted that a person who puts forward a successful defence of insanity is found 'not guilty by reason of insanity' (Criminal Procedure (Insanity) Act 1964). Under s 2 of the Homicide Act 1957, a person charged with murder is allowed to put forward a plea of diminished responsibility and if this is accepted by the court he will be convicted of manslaughter. A person so convicted on a plea of diminished responsibility is similarly disqualified from taking a benefit under the will, or on the intestacy of the person he has killed (*Re Giles, decd* [1972] 1 Ch 544).

As from 13 October 1982 the court has had power to modify the forfeiture rule in individual cases. Where it has been found that the rule has precluded a person who has unlawfully killed another from acquiring an interest in property passing on the death of that other, the court may make an order modifying the effect of the rule if it is satisfied, taking all relevant circumstances into account, that there is justification for such modification (s 2 of the Forfeiture Act 1982). The modification may affect only part of the total beneficial interest in property (s 2(5) of the Act). Any application for modification must be made within three months from the date of conviction and may be made even if the unlawful killing occurred before 13 October 1982 with the proviso that no order is to affect any interest in property acquired by some other person before that date by reason of the operation of the forfeiture rule. No application is allowed in the case of a person who has been convicted of murder.

Where no application has been made for a modification order, then, unless a renunciation of the right to a grant has been obtained, application for a grant to issue to some other person with an inferior right or who has acquired a beneficial interest by reason of the forfeiture is made under s 116 of the Supreme Court Act 1981 (see head 13.6) with notice to the person disqualified from taking a benefit. Proof of the commission of the offence is effected by exhibiting a properly authenticated copy of the certificate of conviction (s 11 of the Civil Evidence Act 1968). An application for a grant by the disqualified person in these circumstances would have to be accompanied by the consents of the persons with an inferior right to the grant or who have acquired a beneficial interest. If, however, the disqualified person has obtained a modification order, a grant will be made to him, if entitled thereto, in the usual manner.

Trust interests (Probate Rule 19, class (ii))—Where a will gives the residuary estate to named persons on certain trusts, they are preferred to the other persons entitled to the residue of the estate. There must be a gift to them, and their bare appointment as 'trustee' is insufficient.

Life interests (Probate Rule 19, class (iii))—The persons entitled to life interests in the residue are next entitled. If there is a succession of life interests, they are preferred in the order in which they appear in the will. Where the spouse of the testator has been given a life interest in the residuary estate and their marriage has subsequently been dissolved or annulled so that, subject to any contrary intention, the interest has lapsed (see head 2.30), the spouse should be cleared off (for wording see pp 91–92). In those circumstances the interest in remainder is treated as if it had not been subject to the life interest, and if contingent as if it had been absolute (s 18A(3) of the Wills Act 1837, as inserted by s 18(2) of the Administration of Justice Act 1982).

Ultimate interests (Probate Rule 19, class (iv))—These interests may be immediate absolute interests or interests substituted on the termination of life interests. In the former case the beneficiaries are described as 'residuary legatees and/or devisees named in the will'; in the latter as 'residuary legatees and/or devisees substituted by the will'. Additionally since 1 May 1974 this class includes contingent residuary legatees and devisees, although they may not take a grant unless residuary legatees or devisees with a vested interest are 'cleared off' (see p 88). Generally, a reversionary interest, following a life interest, vests in the reversioner on the death of the testator, notwithstanding that the reversioner may die during the lifetime of the life-tenant. Sometimes, however, the bequest is qualified by a proviso as to survival or by a gift over in the event of the reversioner's death before that of the life-tenant. In that case the reversionary interest is contingent during the lifetime of the life-tenant and does not vest until it falls into possession. On an application for a grant by the reversioner before his interest has vested he should be described as 'the contingent residuary legatee and/or devisee substituted'. If the reversioner in these circumstances applies for a grant after his interest has vested, he should be described as 'the residuary legatee and/or devisee named in the said will as therein mentioned'. If there is any doubt as to the position, the direction of the registrar should be obtained.

When a will contains no bequests or devises other than a residuary bequest to one person, and it is desired that a spes grant may be made to the next of kin of that person (see head 8.4), he is described as the 'universal legatee and devisee named in the will'.

When the residuary gift is made to the members of a class, the membership must be clearly established in the oath. Thus, where the gift is to the children of the testator, they must be described as the 'lawful children of the testator and *as such* the residuary legatees and/or devisees named in the will (*or* substituted by the will *or as the case may be*).' (As to the extent to which the description 'children' includes adopted, legitimated and other children, see p 93.) Where the residuary gift is made subject to a condition, compliance with the condition must be shown in the oath, eg, 'that I am the residuary legatee and/or devisee named in the will having attained the age of eighteen years (*or as the case may be*).'

Interests in undisposed residue (Probate Rule 19, class (iv))—The rules speak of residue which is not wholly disposed of. This may give rise to a number of possibilities:

(i) There is no disposition of the residue at all.
(ii) The disposition of the residue has failed.
(iii) The disposition of the residue is partial or has partially failed.
(iv) The exact disposition cannot be ascertained.

If there is *no disposition of the residue* of the estate it must be sworn in the oath 'that there is no residuary legatee or devisee named in the said will'. There is an intestacy as to it, and the persons who would have been entitled, had the testator died intestate, are first entitled to the grant (see p 114). Where a testatrix made a will revoking all previous wills and thereafter only expressed the wish that her husband should not succeed to her estate, it was held that the will effectively disposed of her estate in favour of the persons entitled as on an intestacy, excluding her husband (*Re Wynn decd* [1983] 3 All ER 310).

Where *the disposition of the residue has failed*, the reason for the failure must be given, eg, 'that   the residuary legatee and/or devisee named in the will died in the lifetime of the testator' or 'that the gift to   as the residuary legatee and/or devisee (for life) named in the will has lapsed by reason of the fact that the marriage of the said deceased with the said was on the day of 19 dissolved (*or* annulled) by final decree of the High Court of Justice (*or* of the County Court) in England and Wales (*or as the case may be*)'. If the gift was made subject to a condition, the failure to comply with the condition must be recited. The persons entitled as on an intestacy are first entitled to the grant (see p 114) unless the testator has substituted other beneficiaries in the event of failure (for the special case where a gift to a former spouse has lapsed by reason of the dissolution or annulment of the marriage and there is a substitution in the event of the spouse predeceasing the testator, see head 2.30 and p 76, Substituted executors). A bequest does not lapse if there is a clearly expressed contrary intention in the will.

When there is an intestacy as to the residuary estate, or part thereof, and the deceased died on or after 1 January 1953 leaving a surviving spouse, the value of any benefit conferred on that spouse by the will, apart from personal chattels, must be deducted from the amount of the statutory legacy (see pp 112–113) to determine whether the spouse is entitled to the whole of the undisposed of estate or whether the next of kin are entitled to share therein (Administration of Estates Act 1925, s 49 (1), as amended by the Intestates' Estates Act 1952). When the deceased left issue this may affect the question whether a life interest arises. It would seem probable that the benefit includes property abroad (*Re Osoba, decd* [1978] 2 All ER 1099; (CA) [1979] 1 WLR 247).

Where a surviving spouse is given a life interest in the residuary estate, but the will makes no disposition of the estate on the death of the tenant for life, there is a partial intestacy and the combined effect of the will and the spouse's statutory legacy (see pp 112–113) is to entitle the spouse to be paid the statutory legacy immediately and to receive the income on the remainder, if any, for her life (*Re Bowen-Buscarlet's Will Trusts* [1971] 3 All ER 636).

If the gift lapses by reason of the death of the beneficiary in the lifetime of the testator, regard must be had to two possibilities: that the beneficiary was a child or other issue of the testator or exceptionally that the gift was made in discharge of a moral obligation. Where the gift is to a child or other issue of the testator by name or by such a description that he can be identified (as 'to my two children'), and such child or other issue dies in the lifetime of the testator leaving issue who are alive at the time of the testator's death, s 33 of the Wills Act 1837 in its original form or as substituted by s 19 of the Administration of Justice Act 1982 must be borne in mind. Section 33 originally provided that in those circumstances, unless an intention to the contrary appeared in the will, the beneficiary named was to be deemed to have died immediately after the testator, the consequence being that the gift did not lapse but fell into the estate of the beneficiary and his personal representative was entitled to the grant (subject to Probate Rule 25 (3): see p 94). Where, however, the testator has died on or after 1 January 1983, then, subject to a contrary intention appearing in the will, the gift takes effect as a gift to the issue of the beneficiary living at the testator's death. Furthermore, where the will of a testator who has died on or after 1 January 1983 contains a gift to a class of persons consisting of children or remoter issue of the testator, and a member of that class dies before the testator leaving issue, then, subject to a contrary intention appearing in the will, the gift takes effect as if the class includes the issue of deceased members living at the testator's death. Issue of a deceased beneficiary take in equal shares the share which their parent would have taken. Where the testator has died on or after 1 January 1970 the expression 'child or other issue' includes any illegitimate child of the testator and anyone who would rank as such issue if he, or some other person through whom he is descended from the testator, had been born legitimate; moreover the reference to the issue of the intended beneficiary includes a reference to anyone who would rank as such issue if he, or some other person through whom he is descended from the intended beneficiary, had been born legitimate (s 16 (1) of the Family Law Reform Act 1969). In that context 'illegitimate child' included a person legitimated within the meaning of the Legitimacy Act 1926 or a person recognised under that Act or at common law as having been legitimated. The situation has not been altered by the Legitimacy Act 1976 which repealed the Legitimacy Act 1926 and under which a legitimated person, and any other person, is entitled to take any interest as if the legitimated person had been born legitimate. In respect of deaths on or after 1 January 1976 'child' includes also an adopted child (Children Act 1975, to be repealed in due course and continued by the Adoption Act 1976). Where the testator has died on or after 1 January 1983, for the purposes of applying s 33 as amended, the illegitimacy of any person is to be disregarded, and a child conceived before the testator's death but born living thereafter is to be taken as living at the testator's death.

When it can be shown that the gift is more in the nature of the discharge of a moral obligation than a mere bounty (eg, to a creditor in payment of a statute-barred debt: *Stevens* v *King* [1904] 2 Ch 30; or in satisfaction of a debt already compounded in bankruptcy proceedings: *Turner* v *Martin* (1857) 7 De GM & G 429), there is no lapse. The gift falls into the estate of the deceased beneficiary, whose personal representative is entitled to the grant (subject to Probate Rule 25 (3): see p 94). It is to be noted that where a gift is made to two or more persons without words of severance, and the interest of one lapses, it passes to the other beneficiaries.

Where a will only *partially disposes of the residue* of the estate, or where there is a partial failure of the disposition (see above as to lapse of a gift), the rules on intestacy apply to the devolution of the estate which is, or has become, undisposed of. In such cases, two classes of persons are entitled to the grant of representation: the legatees or devisees of the part of the residue effectively given, and the persons entitled as on an intestacy to the undisposed or ineffectively disposed portion of the residue. Members of either class may take the grant and there is no preference in favour of either, even if the interest of the residuary legatees or devisees is contingent.

Whenever the rules on intestacy apply, the applicants prove their claim in a manner similar to that in a case of total intestacy (see pp 91 and 114). The 'clearing off' of prior interests must therefore be properly done; eg, when the applicants claim the grant as brothers or sisters of the whole blood of the testator, it must be sworn that he died a widower (*or* widow *or* bachelor *or* spinster) without issue or parent, and without any other person entitled in priority to share in his estate by virtue of any enactment. Moreover, where the deceased died before 1 January 1926 leaving real estate, the heir at law must be considered (see head 5.1(*b*)).

Sometimes the *disposition of the residue of the estate cannot be ascertained* because the will is couched in such ambiguous language that it is not possible to determine to whom, or how, or when the gift is given. Whenever these circumstances occur the oath should state 'that the gift of the residuary estate of the said deceased is void by reason of uncertainty', and a grant may be made to the persons who would have been entitled had the testator died intestate. It is advisable to obtain the opinion of the registrar in advance before preparing the papers to lead the grant on the basis of an ambiguity (head 2.17 and p 86). When the disposition of the residue cannot be ascertained at the time when application for a grant has to be made because the gift is dependent upon a condition, as when it is to take effect as the beneficiaries attain the age of eighteen years and none has attained that age, there is now no difficulty because a grant may be made to the contingent residuary legatees and devisees, or to their guardians if necessary without having to clear intermediate classes (see p 88).

When the devolution of the residue turns on the rules of intestacy and the testator had no relatives of the classes entitled to share under those rules it falls to the Crown as bona vacantia. In these circumstances the representative of the Crown has the same right to take a grant as any other person entitled to share in the residue not disposed of, and if any other person intends to apply for a grant, notice of the intended application must be given by the applicant to the Treasury Solicitor, or the Solicitor for the Duchy of Lancaster or the Duchy of Cornwall in appropriate cases.

Personal representatives of persons entitled to the residue (Probate Rule 19, class (iv))—If a beneficiary entitled to an absolute interest in the residue survives the testator, the interest becomes vested and on the death of the beneficiary passes to his personal representatives. Such personal representatives have a right to a grant, subject to the rule that, unless the registrar directs otherwise, the grant will be given to a living person in preference to the personal representative of a deceased person who would, if living, have been entitled in the same degree (Probate Rule 25 (3)). This results in the situation that if all the persons entitled to the residue are dead, a grant may be made to the personal representatives of any of them; but if only some are dead, preference is given to the living beneficiaries, who must be 'cleared off' by direction of the registrar (on application being made to him ex parte) before a grant will be made to the representative of a dead interest. It would appear that now the personal representative of a deceased contingent residuary legatee and devisee has a right to a grant (Probate Rule 19 (iv)).

Passing over persons entitled to undisposed residue—Where the residue is not in terms wholly disposed of but the testator has disposed of the whole or substantially the whole of his estate as known at the time of the application for the grant, the registrar has a discretion to allow a grant to issue to a legatee or devisee who is given either the whole of, or a share in, the known estate, without regard to the persons entitled to share in the undisposed residue (Probate Rule 19 (iv)). The oath should recite the clearance of executors, describe the applicant as 'a legatee named in the said will' and contain the further statement in para **10** (see Form 4.4) immediately after the gross amount of the estate 'all of which is disposed of by the said will', *or* 'of which £ is disposed of by the said will', as appropriate. In a case where no Inland Revenue account is required to be lodged (see p 228) sufficient details as to the values of the estate, the applicant's share, etc, should be given to support the application for the exercise of the registrar's discretion. A specific application is not usually required where the whole of the estate has been disposed of by the will and the applicant receives a substantial benefit. In other cases the application is made to the registrar, or in the Principal Registry to the Principal of the Probate Department. He will want to be satisfied that the interest of the person entitled to the undisposed of estate is small enough to justify his being passed over and that the legatee or devisee has a substantial interest in the estate, and he may call for further evidence or require notice to be given to the person entitled to the undisposed of estate. It must be remembered that, if there are no kin or no known kin, notice of the intended application should be given to the Treasury Solicitor on behalf of the Crown (Probate Rule 37).

(c) Legatees, devisees and creditors, etc

This class comprises:

(*a*) Legatees, devisees and creditors.

(*b*) The personal representatives of the persons indicated in (*a*) above.

(*c*) Where the estate is not fully disposed of, any person who, notwithstanding that the amount of the estate is such that he has no immediate beneficial interest therein, may have a beneficial interest in the event of an accretion thereto (see p 116) (Probate Rule 19, class (v)).

When all persons having any immediate or future beneficial interest in the residuary estate have been cleared off, together with their personal representatives, and subject to the proviso in favour of legatees and devisees where the residue has not been wholly disposed of (see above), a grant may issue to a member of these three classes. There is no preference between members, and application may be made by a member of one of them without reference to members of the other classes. Before proceeding to the next class of person entitled ((*d*) below), all members of these classes must be disposed of. Difficulties sometimes arise over the clearing of creditors. Since there is no minimum debt laid down, reference ought to be made to each and every creditor, but this is obviously impossible in many cases. The difficulty is overcome by it being sworn that all debts have been paid, or that the testator died leaving no debts.

When a creditor, or a person who may have a beneficial interest in the event of an accretion to the estate, is applying for a grant, it may be required that the applicant should provide a guarantee by sureties and that the sureties should justify (see head 11.1 and Forms 11.3.1 and 11.3.2) but the registrar has a discretion to dispense with this requirement.

A grant will not be made to the legal personal representative of a deceased legatee, devisee or creditor when there are living members of this class except by direction of the registrar (on application ex parte).

(For the circumstances under which a legacy or devise to a person who has predeceased the testator does not lapse, see p 92.)

(d) Contingent legatees, etc

This class comprises:

(*a*) Contingent legatees and/or devisees.

(*b*) Persons having no interest under the will of the testator who would have been entitled to a grant had the testator died wholly intestate (Probate Rule 19 (vi)).

When all the preceding classes have been disposed of, a member of either of these two classes may apply for a grant.

Adopted persons—The expression 'child' or 'children' in the will of a person who died before 1 January 1950 does not include persons adopted into the testator's family unless a contrary intention appears (Adoption of Children Act 1926, s 5 (2), and see *Re Jebb, decd* [1965] 3 All ER 358). Where the deceased died on or after 1 January 1950 but before 1 April 1959 a reference to 'child' or 'children' in a will executed after the date of the adoption order includes a person adopted into the family, provided that the will was executed, or confirmed by codicil, on or after 1 January 1950 and unless a contrary intention appears. Where the deceased died on or after 1 April 1959 but before 1 January 1976 the word 'child' or 'children' includes any person adopted into the family at any time before the death of the testator, provided the will was executed, or confirmed by codicil, on or after 1 April 1959; failing that, the adopted person will be included only if the will was executed after the date of the adoption order and made, or confirmed by codicil, on or after 1 January 1950 (Adoption Act 1958). In respect of deaths on or after 1 February 1973 those provisions related also to persons adopted overseas by virtue of s 4 of the Adoption Act 1968 (see p 122). But where the deceased has died on or after 1 January 1976, a child adopted into the testator's family is to be treated as if he had been born to the adopters, or to the adopter, in wedlock and has, with minor exceptions, the same rights of succession under a will (unless there is an intention to the contrary expressed therein) or on an intestacy as a natural child born to the adopters or to the adopter in wedlock. Thus the word 'child' or 'children' now includes a person adopted into the family at any time, whether before or after the death of the testator, and irrespective of the date of execution of the will in which the word appears (Children Act 1975, to be replaced and continued in due course by the Adoption Act 1976). (As to the definition of an 'adoption', see p 121.)

Legitimated persons—Under s 3 of the Legitimacy Act 1926, a legitimated person (see p 124), his spouse and his issue were entitled to take any interest under a disposition (by will or codicil) coming into operation after the date of legitimation as if the legitimated person had been born legitimate, subject to certain limitations in respect of property devolving with a dignity or title of honour. Where a disposition had been made on or after 1 January 1970, the word 'child' or 'children' appearing therein included illegitimate children who became legitimated by virtue of the Act of 1926 or who were recognised under that Act (s 8) or at common law as having been legitimated. This applied irrespective of the date of legitimation but only in respect of any interest in relation to which the disposition referred only to persons who were, or whose relationship was deduced through, legitimate persons (s 15 (4) of the Family Law Reform Act 1969). However, where the testator has died on or after 1 January 1976, a legitimated person, and any other person, is entitled to take any interest under a will or codicil as if the legitimated person had been born legitimate (s 5 of the Legitimacy Act 1976). The word 'child' or 'children' therefore now includes a person who is legitimated after the death of the testator.

(As to an intestacy and proof of the legitimation, see pp 124–125.)

Children of void and voidable marriages—See p 125. It is expressly provided that s 2 of the Legitimacy Act 1959, now replaced by s 1 of the Legitimacy Act 1976, is not to affect the operation or construction of any will coming into operation before 29 October 1959.

Illegitimate persons—In any disposition made after 1 January 1970, unless the contrary intention appears a reference to the 'children' of any person includes illegitimate children of that person (s 15 of the Family Law Reform Act 1969). A reference to a person related in some other manner to any person includes, unless the contrary intention appears, anyone who would be so related if he, or some other person through whom the relationship is deduced, had been born legitimate. The Act does not apply in respect of property devolving with a dignity or title of honour. As to the manner in which such illegitimate relationship is to be established, see p 127. 'Disposition' means a disposition of real or personal property made inter vivos or by will or codicil; but a will or codicil made before 1 January 1970 is not to be treated as a disposition made after that date merely by reason that it has been confirmed by a codicil executed on or after 1 January 1970.

Personal representatives—See p 128.

Assignees—See p 128.

Life or minority interest—See head 6.2.

Persons entrusted or entitled under foreign law—See head 15.2(*c*) and (*d*).

4.3 Order of preference—death before 1 January 1926

Probate Rule 67 applied the 1954 Probate Rules (see head 1.1) to all pending proceedings as well as to any proceedings commenced after the date on which the Rules took effect. The proviso to Rule 67 expressly preserved the right to a grant of those persons who would have been entitled thereto at the date of death of a person who died before 1 January 1926. That proviso was specifically revoked as from 20 April 1982. However, the operation of Probate Rules 19 and 21, giving the order of priority for a grant, is still restricted to cases where the deceased died on and after 1 January 1926. In these circumstances, should it become necessary to apply for a grant in respect of the estate of a person who died before 1 January 1926, it is advisable to obtain the opinion of the registrar before the papers to lead the grant are prepared. The persons who were originally entitled to a grant of letters of administration with will annexed, once the executors had been cleared off, were as follows:

Residuary legatees and/or devisees in trust.
Residuary legatees and/or devisees, but a residuary legatee or devisee for life was preferred to his substitute.
The legal personal representatives of deceased residuary legatees and/or devisees.
The husband or widow (or, if they were cleared off, the next of kin) and, if the residue was wholly disposed of, legatees, devisees and creditors.

If the residue was not wholly disposed of, or had lapsed, the following additional classes were entitled:

The heir at law (provided there was real estate and the testator had died after 1897) or, in default, the representative of the husband.
The persons entitled in distribution, who were not next of kin but who took their parents' share.
The representative of the widow, or of the next of kin, or of the persons entitled in distribution not being next of kin, or of a residuary legatee as to an unlapsed moiety, or of the heir at law (provided there was real estate and the testator died after 1897).
Legatees, devisees and creditors.
The Crown, Duchy of Lancaster or Duchy of Cornwall.

Where the residue was not wholly disposed of, or part of a gift of residue had lapsed, the persons entitled under the effective disposition, and those entitled to the lapsed or undisposed of residue, were equally entitled to the grant.

(The order of preference for deaths on and after 1 January 1926 is shown at p 87.)

4.4 Oath for administrators with will annexed

Since the oath is the document which establishes the right of the applicants to the grant, it must be prepared with the greatest care. Errors in its preparation may involve its amendment and reswearing, unless the errors are of a minor nature, when a certificate by the solicitor may be accepted.

Form 4.4 Oath for administrators with will annexed
(For heading and title, see Form 2.11)

1
of
2 make oath and say that believe the paper writing now produced to and marked by to be the true and original last will and testament
3 of
late of
formerly of , deceased, who
4 died on the day of , 19 , aged years, domiciled in
5 and that minority life interest arises in h estate,
6 and that to the best of knowledge, information and belief there was no land vested in the said deceased immediately before h death which was settled previously thereto (and not by h will) and which remained settled land notwithstanding h death.
7
8
9 and that will (i) collect, get in and administer according to the law the real and personal estate ( ) of the said deceased; (ii) when required to do so by the court, exhibit on oath in the court a full inventory of the said estate ( ) and when so required render an account of the administration of the said estate to the court; and (iii) when required to do so by the High Court, deliver up the grant of letters of administration with will annexed to that court;
10 and that to the best of knowledge, information and belief [the gross estate passing under the grant does not exceed £ , and the net estate does not exceed £ , and that this is not a case in which an Inland Revenue Account is required to be delivered]
[the gross estate passing under the grant amounts to £ and the net estate amounts to £].
11
12 Sworn by
at
this day of , 19 .
Before me
A Commissioner for Oaths (or Solicitor).

The name and address of the extracting solicitor should appear in the top right-hand corner of the oath (as to the solicitor's office reference, see p 67).

1 This paragraph should commence 'I' or 'We' followed by the full names, addresses and occupations or descriptions of the deponents (see as to this pp 67–70). The order in which they are set out is determined by the extent of their interests. Unless they all have an equal interest, the order will not be changed even though an express application is made for it. An application by a trust corporation that its name should appear first in the grant will be refused unless its interest under the will so permits or the application is made by all the applicants.

2, 3, and **4** These paragraphs correspond to those of the same numbers in the oath for executors, and the notes thereon should be read (see pp 70–73).

5 It is essential in every application that the existence or non-existence of minority and life interests should be disclosed. The fact that they are apparent from the face of the will does not obviate this requirement. If either such interest exists, the grant must be made to at least two individuals or to a trust corporation unless the circumstances are such that the registrar can be persuaded that it is expedient to allow the grant to be made to one individual (s 114 (2) of the Supreme Court Act 1981; see also head 6.2).

Minority interests—must arise out of the terms of the will, that is to say, they must exist among the beneficiaries named, or where the law of intestacy applies among the persons so entitled (see also head 6.2). (As to the position when the first persons entitled are in their minority, see head 9.1(*b*) and below.) The use of the phrase 'that no beneficiary is a minor' should be avoided. In wills made on or after 1 January 1970 the expressions 'full age', 'infant', 'infancy', 'minor', 'minority' and others of a similar nature are to be construed on the basis that from that date onward a person attains full age on reaching the age of eighteen years instead of twenty-one years (s 1 (2) of the Family Law Reform Act 1969). The fact that a will or codicil executed before 1 January 1970 has been confirmed by a codicil executed on or after that date does not enable the original will or codicil to be treated as having been made after 1 January 1970 (s 1 (7) of the Act of 1969). Although in the case of wills made before 1 January 1970 the vesting of the gift has to be deferred until the beneficiary attains the age of twenty-one years because there is a positive indication to that effect, nevertheless by reason of the reduction of the age of majority that person may acquire a right (as a contingent beneficiary) to prove the will on attaining the age of eighteen years; in those circumstances it is correct to swear to the absence of a minority interest unless other circumstances require it.

Life interests—The extent of the life interest is immaterial. If one exists under the will, no matter how small it may be, there will usually have to be at least two grantees or a trust corporation must take the grant (see head 6.2). In cases where a life interest appears on the face of the will, but in fact does not exist at the date of the application for the grant, it should be sworn that no life interest *now* arises in the estate. The manner in which the life interest has ceased may be shown in para **8** or **11**, eg, 'That the life interest under the terms of the will has ceased by reason of the death of (*or as the case may be*)' (see p 90). Difficulties sometimes arise in ascertaining whether a life interest arises in undisposed of residue (see p 138).

6 This paragraph corresponds with that numbered **5** in the oath for executors, and the notes thereon should be read (see pp 73–74).

7 Interests prior to that of the applicants should be dealt with here. If the will appoints executors, the reason why they do not act must be stated. This involves the recital of their renunciation, death, incapacity, citation or omission. If there are no executors appointed it must be so stated. A suitable wording is as follows: 'That the said deceased did not in his said will name any executor' or 'that *HS* the sole executor named in the said will predeceased the deceased (*or* survived the deceased but has since died without having proved the said will) (*or* has renounced probate thereof) (*or* was cited to accept or refuse probate of the said will and that in default of his appearance to the said citation it was ordered by Mr Registrar of the Principal Registry of the said Division on the day of , 19 , that letters of administration (with the said will annexed) of the estate of the said testator be granted to us) (*or* that the will is to take effect as if the appointment of *HS* as sole executor named in the said will had been omitted by reason of the fact that the marriage of the said deceased with the said *HS* was on the day of 19 dissolved (*or* annulled) by final decree of the High Court of Justice (*or* of the County Court) in England and Wales (*or as the case may be*))'.

Residuary interests should be similarly dealt with, and specific reference made to the manner in which they are disposed of. If the will makes no disposition of the residue of the estate, or if the disposition lapses or is inoperative, it must be so stated (see pp 91–95).

When the interests of the applicants arise out of a partial or complete intestacy as to the residue, any prior interests under the law of intestacy must be cleared off (see p 131).

All interests prior to that of the applicant (see p 87) must be specifically referred to and cleared off. The circumstances will vary but the following will give some idea of the wording to be used: 'That *HS* the sole executor appointed in the said will predeceased the deceased and *BB* the relict of the deceased and the residuary legatee and devisee for life named in the said will has renounced letters of administration with the said will annexed of the estate of the said deceased.'

On an application for a grant in respect of spes successionis (see head 8.4) the fact of the renunciation should be stated here, eg 'That *AS* the universal legatee and devisee named in the said will has renounced letters of administration with the said will annexed of the estate of the said deceased and has consented to the same being granted to the person or persons who would be entitled to her estate were she dead intestate' (see also the note to para **8** at pp 102–103).

8 The relationship of the applicants to the testator no longer needs to be stated in the oath unless it is necessary to do so to establish title or identification. Thus when the relationship given in the will is erroneous, the discrepancy must be explained and the identity of the applicant with the person mentioned in the will proved (see p 74). If the basis of the claim of the applicant is membership of a class, the membership must be strictly proved. If there is an intestacy the relationship (if any) must be given and the title of the applicant should be shown as, 'One of the persons entitled to share in the undisposed of estate of the said deceased' or as the circumstances require (see pp 132–133). The exact capacity in which the applicants claim the grant must be set out (see head 4.2).

Where the person entitled to the grant is a minor and the applicant is taking a grant on his behalf, this should be stated here, eg, 'That *CB* and *DB* are the residuary legatees and devisees named in the said will and are both minors, the said *CB* being of the age of years and the said *DB* being of the age of years'; and it should then be shown how the applicants are authorised to take a grant on the minors' behalf, eg, 'that there is no testamentary or other lawfully appointed guardian of the said minors (see p 153), and that I (*first applicant*) am the lawful father and statutory guardian of the said minor and I (*second applicant*) am the person nominated by an instrument in writing dated the day of , 19 , under the hand of the said (*first applicant*) for the purpose of joining with him in taking a grant of letters of administration with will annexed of the estate of the said deceased' (and see head 9.1).

Similarly, where the person entitled is by reason of mental disorder incapable of managing his affairs, this should be stated here and the applicant is then described as the person authorised by order of the Court of Protection to apply for letters of administration with will annexed of the deceased's estate for his use and benefit during his incapacity, or else it should be stated that there is no person authorised, etc, and the title of the applicant to take a grant for the use and benefit of the person suffering from mental disorder must be given (see head 9.2(*c*)). The following illustrates the wording to be used: 'That *CB* relict of the deceased and the residuary legatee and devisee named in the said will is now by reason of mental incapacity incapable of managing her affairs and that I am the person authorised by order of the Court of Protection dated the day of , 19 , to apply for letters of administration with the said will annexed of the estate of the said deceased (*or,* that there is no person authorised by the Court of Protection to apply for letters of administration with will annexed of the estate of the said deceased and that I am the lawful son of the said *CB* and a person who would be entitled to a grant of letters of administration of her estate were she now dead intestate).'

If the person entitled to the grant is applying through his attorney, this should be stated in this paragraph, eg, 'That *CB*, relict of the said deceased, the residuary legatee and devisee named in the said will, now resides in , and we are the lawful attorneys of the said *CB*.'

If the applicant is claiming the grant by virtue of spes successionis (see head 8.4) his relationship to the renunciant must be given here and, if necessary, he should clear off intermediate kin, eg 'that the said *AS* is a widow without issue or parent or any other person entitled in priority to share in her estate by virtue of any enactment and that I am the lawful brother of the whole blood of the said *AS* and [one of the persons] [the only person] entitled to [share in] her estate were she now dead intestate' (see also the note to para **7**, at p 101).

Where the applicant is applying as legal personal representative of a deceased person entitled, the original of the grant from which he derives his title or an official copy thereof must be lodged for inspection. (For the wording in these circumstances, see, eg, the note to para **7** of Form 5.4, at p 133.)

When the applicants for the grant are also the persons entitled to a grant of administration in respect of settled land (see head 12.2) and the grant is to issue including such settled land, para **7** should clear off the persons entitled in priority, and this paragraph should set out additionally the applicants' title to a settled land grant (for wording, see pp 180–182).

Where the grant is to issue to the 'person entrusted' or 'person entitled' under foreign law, or to his attorney (see head 15.2(*c*), (*d*)), the title should be set out here, viz, 'That on the day of , 19 , letters of administration with the said will annexed of the estate of the said deceased were granted by the Court at to (me) (*CB*) the residuary legatee and devisee named in the said will (who now resides in) and that I am (the lawful attorney of the said *CB*) the person entrusted with the administration of the estate of the said deceased by the court having jurisdiction at the place where the said deceased died domiciled', *or* 'That the said deceased died leaving *CB*, his lawful widow and relict, and *DB*, his lawful child, together the only persons entitled jointly and severally to administer his estate by the law of the place where he died domiciled, and that I am the lawful attorney of the said *CB* and *DB*'. It must be remembered that, unless a separate affidavit of facts is to be filed, the facts concerning the persons entitled upon which an affidavit of law is to be based must be set out in the oath.

If the grant is to issue by virtue of an order under Rule 29 (*c*) (see head 15.2(*e*)), it is sufficient to recite the making of the order, viz, 'That on the day of , 19 , by order of a (District Probate) Registrar of this Division it was ordered that letters of administration with will annexed of the estate of the said deceased do issue to me under and by virtue of Rule 29 (*c*) of the Non-Contentious Probate Rules 1954.' If the application for the order is to be combined with that for the grant, it will generally be sufficient to say 'That I am the person applying for an order of the (District Probate) Registrar authorising me under Rule 29 (*c*) of the Non-Contentious Probate Rules 1954 to apply for and obtain a grant of letters of administration with will annexed of the estate of the said deceased.' The facts leading to the order should be set out in a separate affidavit which should be lodged with the oath and other papers.

9 This corresponds to para **8** of the oath for executors and the notes thereon should be read (see p 76). Where the administration is to be for the use and benefit of some other person, the appropriate limitation should be inserted immediately after the words 'personal representative of the said deceased,' thus, for example:

'for the use and benefit of the said minor and until he shall attain the age of eighteen years', *or*

'for the use and benefit of the said minors and until one of them shall attain the age of eighteen years';

'for the use and benefit of the said   and during his incapacity';

'for the use and benefit of the said   and until he shall apply for and obtain letters of administration with will annexed of the estate of the said deceased', or in foreign domicile cases '   until further representation be granted'.

10, 11 and **12** These correspond to paras **9, 10** and **11** of the oath for executors, and the notes thereon should be read (see pp 77–81).

Estate so far as at present can be ascertained—See p 78.

Permitted deductions—See p 138.

Chapter 5

Letters of Administration

Letters of administration will issue when the deceased died without leaving a valid will and in certain special cases when there is a will (see p 3). Administration will not be granted to more than four persons in respect of the same part of the estate (see p 64). If there is a life or minority interest under the intestacy, the grant will usually be required to be made to at least two individuals or to a trust corporation with or without individuals (see head 6.2). The applicant or applicants may be required in special circumstances to provide a guarantee by sureties for proper administration of the estate (see head 11.1).

To ascertain the persons entitled to a grant of letters of administration of the estate of a person dying wholly intestate, it is necessary to look to the date of death of the deceased, because different rules apply in respect of deaths occurring (*a*) before 1 January 1926, (*b*) between 1 January 1926 and 31 December 1952, (*c*) on and after 1 January 1953. An application for a grant in respect of a person dying before 1926 will rarely have to be made, unless the original administrator has died leaving part of the estate unadministered and a further grant is required, and, therefore, only a general outline of the practice in such cases is given below.

5.1 Deaths before 1 January 1926

(a) Distribution of personal estate

Distribution of the personal estate is governed by the Statute of Distribution 1670, the Statute of Frauds 1677 and the Intestates' Estates Act 1890. A surviving husband is entitled to the whole of the personal estate of his wife dying intestate. A surviving wife is entitled to one-third of her husband's estate, if he leaves descendants, and the latter are entitled to the remainder. If there are no descendants, and the death took place before 2 September 1890 the widow takes half the personal estate and the next of kin the other half. Where the husband dies without issue on or after 2 September 1890 the widow takes the whole of the net real and personal estate if this does not exceed £500; otherwise she is entitled to a charge on the estate for £500, the remainder of the personal estate being divided as before between her and the next of kin. If the deceased dies a bachelor or spinster, or a widower or widow, the personal estate is divided amongst the next of kin and the descendants of deceased next of kin.

(b) Real estate

By virtue of the Land Transfer Act 1897 in the case of deaths on or after 1 January 1898 the grant covers both personal and real estate (excluding copyholds and customary freeholds). After the surviving spouse, who had a prior right to a grant (see below), it was necessary, where the estate comprised real property, to consider the claim of the heir at law as at the date of death, who was equally entitled to a grant with the next of kin. The heir at law is ascertained in accordance with the provisions of the Inheritance Act 1833 and the Law of Property Amendment Act 1859. Proof of heirship must be given either in the form of an affidavit by the applicant, tracing his title from the last purchaser, or by production of a certificate of a Master in Chancery to the effect that the applicant is the heir at law.

(c) Persons entitled to a grant

There is now some doubt as to the order of priority to a grant in respect of the estate of a person who has died intestate before 1 January 1926 (see head 4.3) and it is advisable to obtain the opinion of the registrar before the papers to lead the grant are prepared.

The persons entitled to a grant in respect of the personal estate were originally determined in the following order:

Surviving spouse.
Legal personal representative of the husband.
Next of kin:
- Children.
- Remoter issue.
- Father.
- Mother.
- Brothers or sisters (of the whole or half-blood).
- Grandparents.
- Uncles, aunts, nephews, nieces or great-grandparents.
- Cousins german.

Persons entitled in distribution to the personal estate (not being next of kin).
Legal personal representatives of next of kin, the widow or other persons entitled in distribution.
Creditors.
The Crown.

If there was real estate the heir at law was equally entitled with the next of kin. The grant was then usually made to the person having the greater interest (unless they applied for a joint grant) and would not be made to the person having the lesser interest, unless the other consented or was shown to have received notice of the application. The legal personal representative of the heir at law, where there was real estate, had an equal right to that of the legal personal representative of next of kin.

(d) Life or minority interest

See head 6.2. A surviving husband might have a right of curtesy in his wife's real estate; as this was a life interest, there would usually have to be two grantees, the second grantee usually being the heir at law.

(e) Renunciation or death of surviving spouse

On the renunciation of the husband, the heir at law, if there was any real estate, was entitled to the grant in priority to the next of kin (to whom, however, a grant might issue although there was no interest). On the death of the husband, his personal representative was entitled to the grant in priority to the next of kin but, if there was real estate, the heir at law was preferred to both. On the renunciation of the widow, both the heir at law and the next of kin were equally entitled. On the death of the widow, both the heir at law and the next of kin would be preferred to the widow's personal representative.

(The order of preference for deaths on and after 1 January 1926 is shown at p 114.)

5.2 Deaths between 1 January 1926 and 31 December 1952

(a) Distribution of estate

Where a person has died intestate between 1 January 1926 and 31 December 1952, the distribution of his estate both real and personal is governed by the Administration of Estates Act 1925, which provides that the whole of the deceased's estate shall be held by the personal representatives on trust for the persons entitled in distribution. All the old rules of descent are abolished and real and personal estate are placed on the same footing for the purposes of descent. There is one exception to this rule, namely in respect of a person who, being a person of full age suffering from mental illness on 1 January 1926 and unable by reason of his incapacity to make a will, thereafter dies intestate without having recovered his testamentary capacity and leaving a beneficial interest in real estate; such interest will devolve in accordance with the general law in force before 1926 (see above).

The surviving spouse, whether the husband or the widow, of the intestate is entitled to:

(*a*) the personal chattels absolutely (see pp 112–113 for definition); and

(*b*) the net sum of £1,000 free of death duties and costs, with interest thereon from the date of death at the rate of £6 per cent per annum until paid or appropriated (see Intestate Succession (Interest and Capitalisation) Order 1977 (Amendment) Order 1983); and

(*c*) the residuary estate for life, if there are no issue; or
(*d*) half the residuary estate for life, if there are issue (but if the issue die without attaining a vested interest the surviving spouse becomes entitled to the whole of the residuary estate for life); or
(*e*) the residuary estate absolutely, if the deceased died leaving no kin entitled in distribution.

Where the estate exceeds £1,000 after the permissible deductions have been made (see p 138) and the deceased dies leaving a spouse and issue surviving, the issue are entitled to half the residuary estate, which is to be held on the statutory trusts (see below), and to the reversion in the other half on determination of the spouse's life interest. If there are no issue, the next of kin are entitled to the reversion in the whole of the residuary estate on the death of the spouse.

If the deceased dies intestate without leaving a spouse surviving, the following persons are entitled in distribution in the order shown:

Issue.
Parents.
Brothers and sisters of the whole blood.
Brothers and sisters of the half-blood.
Grandparents.
Uncles and aunts, being brothers and sisters of the whole blood of a parent of the intestate.
Uncles and aunts, being brothers and sisters of the half-blood of a parent of the intestate.
The Crown.

(*b*) *Statutory trusts*

The Act directs that where the estate in part or wholly devolves upon the issue, or brothers and sisters of the whole or half-blood, or uncles and aunts of the whole or half-blood, it shall be held on the statutory trusts for their benefit. Issue of the intestate means any children or child of the intestate, or the issue of any child of the intestate who has predeceased him. Where a brother or sister, or an uncle or aunt, of the intestate has predeceased him, any children or child, or other issue, of such person takes his share. No issue can take whose parent was living at the date of death of the intestate and so was capable of taking. No member of these classes can obtain a vested interest unless he or she attains the age of twenty-one years or marries under that age. If a person dies before obtaining a vested interest he is treated as if he predeceased the deceased and his share is divided amongst such members of his class as do obtain a vested interest. If all the members die before obtaining a vested interest, the residuary estate then devolves upon the next class of persons entitled in distribution.

(*c*) *Right to a grant*

In the case of a person dying wholly intestate on or after 1 January 1926 administration is as a rule granted to one or more persons having a beneficial interest in the estate of the deceased, the priority of right to a grant being determined by Probate Rule 21, the order being as follows:

Surviving spouse.
Children or the issue of any such child who has died during the lifetime of the deceased (see pp 120–127 under Adopted persons, Legitimated persons, Children of void and voidable marriages, Illegitimate persons).
Father or mother.
Brothers and sisters of the whole blood or the issue of any deceased brother or sister of the whole blood.
Brothers and sisters of the half-blood or the issue of any deceased brother or sister of the half-blood.
Grandparents.
Uncles and aunts of the whole blood or the issue of any deceased uncle or aunt of the whole blood.
Uncles and aunts of the half-blood or the issue of any deceased uncle or aunt of the half-blood.
The Treasury Solicitor on behalf of the Crown (including the solicitor for the affairs of the Duchy of Lancaster and the solicitor for the Duchy of Cornwall).

On clearing the persons entitled, a grant may issue to creditors or to persons who, not having an immediate beneficial interest, may have an interest if there is an increase in the amount of the estate (as 'persons interested in the estate in the event of an accretion thereto').

(d) Grant to surviving spouse

Where the value of the estate after the permissible deductions have been made (see p 138) does not exceed £1,000, the surviving spouse is entitled to the whole of the estate and may take a grant of letters of administration alone as 'the only person now entitled to the estate'. Where, however, the value of such estate exceeds £1,000, a life interest arises unless the deceased left no kin within the degrees entitled to share (in which case the spouse takes the whole of the estate absolutely and may take a grant as 'the only person entitled to the estate'). The life interest will usually necessitate the grant being made to a trust corporation, with or without an individual, or to at least two individuals (see head 6.2). For this purpose the spouse may take a grant with one or more of the next of kin entitled to share in the estate. (For the practice where it is sought to join with the spouse a person not next entitled, see head 6.1.)

(e) Renunciation or death of surviving spouse

If the net estate does not exceed £1,000, a grant may be made on the renunciation of the spouse to the next of kin of the deceased, who will take as 'persons interested in the estate in the event of an accretion thereto', or to a trust corporation. Where the surviving spouse dies before taking a grant, his personal representatives are entitled in priority. On the renunciation of the spouse's personal representatives, or of the persons first entitled to constitute themselves the spouse's personal representatives, the next of kin may take a grant as 'persons interested, etc'. Children of both spouses, however, should, if possible, first constitute themselves personal representatives of the surviving spouse before taking a grant.

If the net estate exceeds £1,000, so that a life interest arises, the grant may be made on the renunciation of the surviving spouse to a trust corporation or to at least two of the next of kin as 'persons entitled to share in the estate'. Should the surviving spouse die before taking a grant, the life interest lapses and, so long as there is no minority interest, a grant may issue to one of the next of kin as 'one of the persons entitled to share in the estate'. The spouses's personal representatives may take a grant only on clearing off all the next of kin. If the surviving spouse and the next of kin are all dead, the spouse's personal representatives have a prior right to a grant unless it can be sworn that the spouse's beneficial interest has been wholly satisfied; in that case the grant may issue to the personal representatives of the next of kin without further clearing off the spouse's personal representatives.

(f) Effect of divorce, annulment or separation

See pp 117–119.

(g) Life or minority interest

See head 6.2.

(h) Grant to next of kin

The next of kin may take a grant as 'persons entitled to share in the estate' if there is no spouse surviving, or they may be joined with the surviving spouse if the estate exceeds £1,000 (see p 109). A grant will not issue to a minor even although he may have acquired a vested interest by marrying under the age of twenty-one years; instead, the grant will usually be made to his guardian and a co-grantee, or to his guardians, limited until the minor attains the age of twenty-one years (see p 153). By reason of the reduction of the age of majority from twenty-one years to eighteen years, a beneficiary will now have the right to apply for a grant on attaining the age of eighteen years. But this does not affect the vesting of the estate of an intestate who dies before 1 January 1970 and the vesting will not take place until the beneficiary reaches the age of twenty-one years.

(i) Adopted persons

See p 120.

(j) Legitimated persons

See p 124.

(k) Children of void and voidable marriages

See p 125.

(l) Illegitimate persons

See p 126.

(m) Creditors

See p 127.

(n) Persons entrusted or entitled under foreign law

See head 15.2(*c*), (*d*).

(o) Personal representatives

See p 128.

(p) Assignees

See p 128.

(q) Missing beneficiary

See head 13.6.

5.3 Deaths on or after 1 January 1953

(a) Distribution of estate

The provisions of the Administration of Estates Act 1925 regulating the distribution of the estate of a person dying intestate and leaving a spouse were modified by the Intestates' Estates Act 1952 in respect of persons dying on or after 1 January 1953, the effect being to increase the share of the surviving spouse, to cut down the classes of kin who are entitled to share the estate with the spouse and to avoid the creation of a life interest in favour of the spouse except where there are issue. In addition, the surviving spouse was given certain rights in respect of the matrimonial home designed to allow him or her to continue to reside there should he or she so wish. A further modification was made by the Family Law Reform Act 1969 so that in respect of persons dying on or after 1 January 1970 'issue' of the deceased includes illegitimate children or their issue and 'parents' include the parents of an illegitimate child. The status of adopted and legitimated persons is now for most purposes the same as that of legitimate persons (s 8 (9) of and Sched 1 to the Children Act 1975, as to legitimated persons now repealed and replaced by the Legitimacy Act 1976, and as to adopted persons to be repealed in due course and replaced by the Adoption Act 1976). Moreover the amount of the surviving spouse's statutory legacy has been increased on several occasions in order to keep pace with the change in the value of money; further adjustments to the amount may now be made by order of the Lord Chancellor (s 1 of the Family Provision Act 1966). When considering the rights of a surviving spouse arising out of the statutory legacy, regard must be paid to whether the date of death occurred in one of the following periods:

(i) between 1 January 1953 and 31 December 1966;
(ii) between 1 January 1967 and 30 June 1972 (Family Provision Act 1966);
(iii) from 1 July 1972 to 14 March 1977 (Family Provision (Intestate Succession) Order 1972);
(iv) from 15 March 1977 to 28 February 1981 (Family Provision (Intestate Succession) Order 1977);
(v) from 1 March 1981 onwards (Family Provision (Intestate Succession) Order 1981).

Note—In the text the amount of the statutory legacy has been given as if the deceased had died on or after 1 March 1981; the amounts for the other periods are set out in the table which appears below and to which reference should be made whenever appropriate:

Death	*Statutory legacy of surviving spouse*	
	Issue (see p 113)	*No issue (see p 113)*
on and after 1 March 1981	£40,000	£85,000
between 15 March 1977 and 28 February 1981	£25,000	£55,000
between 1 July 1972 and 14 March 1977	£15,000	£40,000
between 1 January 1967 and 30 June 1972	£ 8,750	£30,000
between 1 January 1953 and 31 December 1966	£ 5,000	£20,000

No alteration has been made in the rights of next of kin to share in the estate if there is no surviving spouse, and the order of entitlement is therefore:

Issue.
Parents.
Brothers and sisters of the whole blood.
Brothers and sisters of the half-blood.
Grandparents.
Uncles and aunts, being brothers and sisters of the whole blood of a parent of the intestate.
Uncles and aunts, being brothers and sisters of the half-blood of a parent of the intestate.
The Crown.

A surviving spouse is entitled to:

(*a*) the personal chattels absolutely; these are defined by s 55 (1) (*x*) of the Administration of Estates Act 1925 as meaning carriages, horses, stable furniture and effects (not used for business purposes), motor cars and accessories (not used for business purposes), garden effects, domestic animals, plate, plated articles, linen, china, glass, books, pictures, prints, furniture, jewellery, articles of household or personal use or ornament, musical and scientific instruments and apparatus, wines, liquors and consumable stores (and see *Re Crispin's Will Trusts* [1975] 1 Ch 245), but do not include any chattels used at the death of the intestate for business purposes nor money or securities for money; **and**

(*b*) the net sum of £40,000 (see table, p 112), free of death duties and costs, with interest thereon from the date of death at the rate of £6 per cent per annum until paid or appropriated (see Intestate Succession (Interest and Capitalisation) Order 1977 (Amendment) Order 1983) together with half the residuary estate for life, if there are issue (but if the issue die without attaining a vested interest the surviving spouse becomes entitled as in (*c*) or (*d*) below); **or**

(*c*) the net sum of £85,000 (see table, p 112), free of death duties and costs, with interest thereon from the date of death at the rate of £6 per cent per annum until paid or appropriated, together with half the residuary estate absolutely, if there are no issue but the deceased dies leaving a parent or parents, or brother or sister of the whole blood or issue of a deceased brother or sister of the whole blood; **or**

(*d*) the residuary estate absolutely if the deceased dies leaving no issue, parent or brother or sister of the whole blood or their issue.

Where the estate exceeds the amount of the spouse's statutory legacy and the deceased dies leaving a spouse and issue surviving, the issue are entitled to half the residuary estate, which is to be held on the statutory trusts (see below), and to the reversion in the other half of the residuary estate on determination of the spouse's life interest. If there are no issue, then the parent or parents, or, if both parents predeceased the deceased, the brothers and sisters of the whole blood and the issue of deceased brothers and sisters of the whole blood, are entitled to half the residuary estate absolutely, which, in the case of brothers and sisters of the whole blood or their issue, is to be held on the statutory trusts (see below). More remote classes of kin have no interest in the estate if the spouse survives.

(b) Statutory trusts

In respect of deaths before 1 January 1970 the statutory trusts are as set out in relation to deaths between 1 January 1926 and 31 December 1952 (see p 108). Sections 3 (2) and 14 (3) of the Family Law Reform Act 1969 made certain alterations and the position in respect of deaths on or after 1 January 1970 is as follows. Where the estate devolves in part or wholly upon the issue, or brothers and sisters of the whole or half-blood, or uncles and aunts of the whole or half-blood, it is to be held on the statutory trusts for their benefit. Issue of the intestate means any children or child of the intestate including his adopted, legitimated and illegitimate children, or the lawful issue of any such child (including an illegitimate child) who has predeceased him. Where a brother or sister, or an uncle or aunt, of the intestate has predeceased him, any lawful children or child, or other issue, of such person take his share. No issue can take whose parent was living at the date of death of the intestate and so was capable of taking. No member of these classes can obtain a vested interest until he or she attains the age of eighteen years or marries under that age. If a person dies before obtaining a vested interest he is treated as if he predeceased the deceased and his share is divided amongst such members of his class as do obtain a vested interest. If all the members die before obtaining a vested interest, the estate then devolves upon the next class of persons entitled in the distribution.

(c) Right to a grant

In the case of persons dying intestate on or after 1 January 1953 administration is granted to one or more persons having a beneficial interest in the estate of the deceased. The order of priority of right to a grant where the deceased died leaving a spouse surviving is as follows (Probate Rule 21):

Surviving spouse.
Children or the issue of any such child who has died during the lifetime of the deceased (see pp 120–127 under Adopted persons, Legitimated persons, Children of void and voidable marriages, Illegitimate persons).
Father or mother.
Brothers and sisters of the whole blood or the issue of any deceased brother or sister of the whole blood.
The Treasury Solicitor on behalf of the Crown (including the solicitor for the affairs of the Duchy of Lancaster and the solicitor for the Duchy of Cornwall).

Where the deceased died without leaving a spouse surviving, certain additional classes have a right to a grant following after brothers and sisters of the whole blood and before the Treasury Solicitor, as follows (Probate Rule 21):

Brothers and sisters of the half-blood or the issue of any deceased brother or sister of the half-blood.
Grandparents.
Uncles and aunts of the whole blood or the issue of any deceased uncle or aunt of the whole blood who has died (see *Re Lockwood* [1958] 1 Ch 231 as to the right of issue of uncles and aunts to share in the estate).
Uncles and aunts of the half-blood or the issue of any deceased uncle or aunt of the half-blood who has died.

On clearing the persons entitled, a grant may issue to creditors or to persons who, not having any immediate beneficial interest, may have an interest if there is an increase in the amount of the estate (as 'persons interested in the estate in the event of an accretion thereto').

As in the case of a beneficiary under a will who has been found guilty of the murder or manslaughter of the testator, a person entitled to, or to share in, the estate of an intestate, and who has been found guilty of the murder or manslaughter of the intestate, is not allowed under the forfeiture rule to take any benefit from the estate, subject in certain circumstances to the right as from 13 October 1982 to apply to the court within three months from the date of conviction for an order modifying the effect of the rule (see p 89). For the procedure to be followed in applying for a grant in such circumstances, see p 90.

(d) Grant to surviving spouse

The surviving spouse is entitled first in priority to a grant. A life interest will arise only if the deceased dies leaving the spouse and issue surviving and the estate, after the permissible deductions have been made (see p 138), exceeds £40,000 (see table, p 112). In such a case, the grant will usually have to be made to a trust corporation, with or without an individual, or to at least two individuals (see head 6.2). For this purpose the spouse may take a grant with one or more of the issue. (For the practice where it is sought to join with the spouse a person other than one of the issue, see head 6.1.) In all other cases, except where there is a minority interest, when the practice is as for a life interest, the spouse may take a grant alone as 'the only person (now) entitled to the estate' or, if there are parents or brothers and sisters of the whole blood or their issue and the net estate amounts to more than £85,000 (see table, p 112), as 'one of the persons entitled to share in the estate'.

Where the deceased dies leaving a widow and child en ventre sa mère and the estate exceeds £40,000 (see table, p 112), a trust corporation or at least two individuals will usually have to take the grant, it being sworn in the oath that a life or minority interest may arise. If the widow proposes to apply for the grant, application will therefore have to be made for the appointment of a second administrator (see head 6.1) unless leave is given for the widow to take the grant alone (see head 6.2).

(e) Polygamous marriage

There does not seem as yet to be clear authority for the proposition that where a person enters into two polygamous marriages, both valid by the law of his domicile at the time, and later dies intestate domiciled in England and Wales, both wives, provided they survive, would be entitled to the statutory share in his estate, and to a grant of letters of administration. Nevertheless this would seem to be the position (see *Coleman* v *Shang* [1961] AC 481 (PC), and the Report of the Law Commission on Polygamous Marriages, Law Com No 42, paras 118–120; see also *Re Sehota, decd* [1978] 3 All ER 385).

(f) Renunciation or death of surviving spouse

If the net estate does not exceed £40,000 (see table, p 112) and the deceased dies leaving issue, a grant may be made on the renunciation of the spouse to a trust corporation or to the issue of the deceased who will take as 'persons who may have a beneficial interest in the estate in the event of an accretion thereto'. Where the deceased dies leaving no issue and the net estate does not exceed £85,000 (see table, p 112), a grant may be made on the renunciation of the spouse to a trust corporation or to the parents or, if there are no parents, to brothers and sisters of the whole blood or their issue as 'persons who may have a beneficial interest, etc'. In both instances, where the surviving spouse dies before taking a grant, his personal representatives are entitled in priority. On the renunciation of the spouse's personal representatives, or of the persons first entitled to constitute themselves the spouse's personal representatives, the parents, or the brothers and sisters of the whole blood or their issue, may take a grant as 'persons who may have a beneficial interest, etc'. Children of both spouses must, if possible, constitute themselves personal representatives of the surviving spouse before taking a grant. Persons applying as 'persons who may have a beneficial interest, etc' may be required to provide a guarantee by sureties with a justification by such sureties (see head 11.1 and Forms 11.3.1 and 11.3.2) but the registrar has a discretion to dispense with this requirement.

Where the deceased dies leaving issue and the net estate exceeds £40,000 (see table, p 112) so that a life interest arises, the grant may be made on the renunciation of the surviving spouse to a trust corporation or to at least two of the children as 'persons entitled to share in the estate'. Should the surviving spouse die before taking a grant, the life interest lapses and, provided no minority interest arises, a grant may issue to one of the children as 'one of the persons entitled to share in the estate'. Where the deceased dies leaving no issue and the net estate exceeds £85,000 (see table, p 112), the grant may be made on the renunciation or death of the surviving spouse to one or both parents or to one of the brothers and sisters of the whole blood or their issue as '(one of the) persons entitled to share in the estate'. The spouse's personal representatives may take a grant only on clearing off the issue, parents or brothers or sisters of the whole blood or their issue. Where the surviving spouse and the next of kin entitled to share are all dead, the spouse's personal representatives have a prior right to the grant unless it can be sworn that the spouse's beneficial interest has been wholly satisfied; in that event the grant will issue to the personal representatives of the next of kin without the need further to clear off the spouse's personal representatives.

(g) Life or minority interest

See head 6.2.

(h) Effect of divorce or annulment

Where the marriage of a person dying intestate has been dissolved or annulled, the former spouse has no claim to the estate of the deceased (save under s 1 (1) of the Inheritance (Provision for Family and Dependants) Act 1975, or under s 26 of the Matrimonial Causes Act 1965 in respect of a person dying before 1 April 1976). On an application for a grant, the oath must recite the fact that a decree of divorce or nullity of marriage has been pronounced and that the deceased did not subsequently marry again. An office copy of the decree absolute must be filed. The doctrine of relation back of a judicial act to the first moment of the day on which it takes place does not apply to making a decree nisi absolute; where a wife lodged the notice of application for decree absolute on the same day on which, but after, the husband died it was held that she remained his widow and was entitled to a grant of representation of his estate in that capacity (*Re Seaford, decd* [1968] P 53).

The recognition of a decree of divorce obtained in another country is now governed by the Recognition of Divorces and Legal Separations Act 1971, as extended by the Domicile and Matrimonial Proceedings Act 1973 and certain common-law rules referred to therein. Where the decree of divorce has been granted on or after 1 January 1972 by a court in Scotland, Northern Ireland, the Channel Islands or the Isle of Man it will be recognised in the same way as a decree granted in England and Wales, irrespective of the domicile of the deceased. However, no proceeding in those countries resulting in a decree being granted on or after 1 January 1974 is to be regarded as validly dissolving a marriage unless it has been instituted in a court of law of one of those countries. Where the decree of divorce was granted before 1 January 1972, the previous practice must be followed and it must be shown that the court of the country in which the decree was obtained exercised jurisdiction on a basis which would have entitled the decree to be recognised as valid in this country. Usually it is sufficient to show that the decree was obtained in the country in which the parties were domiciled at the date of institution of the proceedings (but see *Indyka* v *Indyka* [1967] 2 All ER 689, where it was said that it was enough that one party had a real and substantial connection with the country in question).

In respect of a divorce obtained at any time (that is, before or after 1 January 1972) by means of judicial or other proceedings in any country outside the British Isles which is effective under the law of that country, the combined effect of the Acts of 1971 and 1973 and of the common-law rules as extended by the Act of 1973 is that such a divorce will be recognised as valid provided that at the date of commencement of the proceedings:

(i) either spouse was habitually resident in that country (if the law of the country uses the concept of domicile as a ground of jurisdiction in divorce matters, the reference to habitual residence includes a reference to domicile within the meaning of that law); or
(ii) either spouse was a national of that country; or

(iii) both spouses were domiciled in the country concerned, or the divorce was recognised as valid under the law of their common domicile; or

(iv) one of the spouses was domiciled in the country in which the divorce was obtained and the divorce was recognised as valid under the law of the domicile of the other spouse; or

(v) neither of the spouses having been domiciled in the country in which the divorce was obtained, the divorce was recognised as valid under the law of the domicile of each of the spouses respectively.

There are some limitations on complete recognition. For instance where reasonable notice of the proceedings was not given by one spouse to the other, or where one spouse was not given a reasonable opportunity to take part in the proceedings, or where recognition of the decree would be manifestly contrary to public policy, recognition will be withheld (see *Joyce* v *Joyce and O'Hare* [1972] 2 All ER 156).

A divorce obtained by non-judicial proceedings and entitled to recognition only under paragraphs (iii), (iv) or (v) above will not be so recognised if both parties to the marriage have, throughout the period of one year immediately preceding the commencement of the proceedings, been habitually resident in the United Kingdom. Moreover, the validity of a divorce, wherever granted, will not be recognised if it was obtained at a time when according to English law there was no subsisting marriage between the parties.

When reliance is placed upon a decree of divorce which has been granted by a court in an overseas country, other than the British Isles, it is sufficient in the appropriate circumstances to recite in the oath that at the date of commencement of the proceedings the facts relating to the domicile, habitual residence or nationality of the parties were such as to justify recognition of the validity of the divorce (as indicated in paras (i) to (v) above). Sometimes these facts are set out in the decree itself. In any other case where it is claimed that the deceased was divorced, and, in particular, where the divorce is alleged to have been obtained by extra-judicial proceedings, a full statement of the facts should be submitted for the decision of the registrar, who may call for further evidence of the facts or the law. Whenever possible an official copy of the foreign decree should be filed, with a notarial translation if appropriate; if there is difficulty in obtaining an official copy of the decree and the former spouse died in the deceased's lifetime, the matter should be referred to the registrar.

The Acts of 1971 and 1973 do not apply to decrees of nullity obtained in another country. The test laid down in the case of *Indyka* (see above) in respect of a foreign divorce decree is applicable, namely the court will recognise a decree of nullity granted by the competent court of a foreign country or territory in cases where a real and substantial connection is shown to have existed between that country or territory and the party who had obtained the decree (*Law* v *Gustin* (*formerly Law*) [1976] 1 All ER 113).

An official copy of the decree of nullity should be filed with the papers to lead the grant.

(For the wording in the oath, see p 130.)

(i) Effect of separation

Where a wife who has obtained a decree of judicial separation in the High Court (or divorce county court) or a separation order from a magistrates' court in the exercise of its matrimonial jurisdiction has died intestate before 1 August 1970, property acquired by or devolving upon the wife after the date of the decree or order and whilst the separation continues in force will devolve upon her next of kin as if the husband had predeceased her (Matrimonial Causes Act 1965, s 20 (3)). Property to which a wife who has obtained a decree of judicial separation or a separation order and who has died before 1 August 1970 is entitled for an estate in remainder or reversion at the date of the decree or order is deemed to be property devolving upon the wife after the date of the decree or order. The oath must set out the fact of the making of the decree or order and an official copy must be lodged with the papers. The grant to the next of kin will be limited to the estate acquired after the date of the decree or order. (For the wording to be inserted in the oath, see p 131.) A grant in respect of the wife's remaining estate may issue to the husband. These provisions apply only in the case of the wife dying intestate. A wife who is separated from her husband by decree or order retains her full rights in respect of his estate should he die intestate before 1 August 1970. But where a decree of judicial separation is in force and the separation is continuing and either of the parties whose marriage is the subject of the decree dies on or after 1 August 1970 intestate as respects any or all of his or her real or personal property, irrespective of when the property was acquired, that property devolves as if the other spouse had then been dead (s 18 of the Matrimonial Causes Act 1973). Moreover the fact that a wife, or a husband, who dies intestate on or after 1 August 1970 has obtained a separation order from a magistrates' court now makes no difference to the devolution of her or his estate, which follows the usual rules of succession between husband and wife (s 18 aforesaid).

It would appear that where a husband and wife have been legally separated by the decree of a foreign court which would be accepted as valid in this country and one of them subsequently dies intestate domiciled in England and Wales, the effect of the decree of separation on the devolution of the deceased's estate would depend on the law of the country in which the decree was obtained.

Where under a deed of separation between husband and wife, each has agreed to give up any claim he or she might have to the estate of the other, it would appear that the surviving spouse will retain the right to a grant of letters of administration on an intestacy. If the survivor will not renounce that right, application may be made for a discretionary grant under s 116 of the Supreme Court Act 1981 (see head 13.6).

(j) Grant to next of kin

The next of kin may take a grant as 'persons entitled to share in the estate' where there is no spouse surviving, or when they are to be joined with the surviving spouse, or the spouse renounces or dies, and the net estate exceeds £40,000 or £85,000 as appropriate (see table, p 112); if the net estate does not exceed that figure, they may still be joined with a surviving spouse, or take on renunciation, as 'persons who may have a beneficial interest, etc' (see p 116). A grant will not issue to a minor even although he may have acquired a vested interest by marrying under the age of eighteen years; instead the grant will usually (see head 6.2) be made to his guardian and a co-grantee, or to his guardians, limited until he comes of age (see p 153). The estate of a person who dies intestate before 1 January 1970 will not vest in a beneficiary absolutely until he has attained the age of twenty-one years (or marries under that age) although he acquires the right to obtain the grant on reaching the age of eighteen years.

(k) Adopted persons

Under the provisions of the Adoption Act 1958 where, after the making of an adoption order, the adopter or the adopted person or any other person died intestate on or after 1 January 1950 leaving real and personal property, such property (excluding property subject to an entailed interest under a disposition made before the date of the adoption order) devolved as if the adopted person were the lawful child of the adopter. Since 1 January 1976 the status and right of succession to property following the making of an adoption order have been governed by s 8 (9) of and Sched 1 to the Children Act 1975 (to be repealed in due course and continued by the Adoption Act 1976). Under these Acts an adopted person is to be treated in law (*a*) where the adopters are a married couple, as if he had been born as a child of the marriage, and (*b*) in any other case, as if he had been born to the adopter in wedlock. Moreover an adopted child is to be treated in law as if he were not the child of any person other than the adopters or adopter. When considering, therefore, the right of priority to a grant of letters of administration of the estate of any person dying intestate on or after 1 January 1976, the children of the deceased or of any other person are to be regarded as including not only legitimate children, but also adopted children, and kin of the deceased bear the same relation to such children as they would to a legitimate child.

The oath must show that an adoption order has been made under the Act, the effect of such an order and that it is still subsisting. Where the applicant is applying in person, a certified copy of the entry in the Adopted Children Register will usually have to be produced unless the applicant has available a copy of the adoption order. In respect of deaths before 1 January 1970 there is no need to clear off specifically in the oath adopted persons or persons claiming through such adopted persons unless the oath discloses that an adoption order has been made. Where the deceased died on or after 1 January 1970 adopted children are cleared off by use of the general form of wording (see below and pp 131–132).

Where a person has been adopted by two spouses jointly, the relationship of that person to any child or other adopted child of both spouses is deemed to be that of brother or sister of the whole blood. In any other case, the relationship to any child or other adopted child of the adoptive parent is deemed to be that of brother or sister of the half-blood. The following descriptions should be used in the oath, where appropriate, 'the lawful adoptive son (or daughter)', 'the lawful adoptive father (or mother)', 'the lawful adoptive brother (or sister or as the case may be) of the whole (or half-) blood'.

In the case of deaths before 1 January 1950 the old law applies and neither the adopter nor his adopted child has any right of succession, or right to take a grant, in respect of the estate of the other should that other die intestate.

It may sometimes be necessary, in order to clear down to the person applying for the grant, to refer in the oath to a child having been adopted and thereby taken out of the family of the deceased. Thus, for instance, when the only child of the deceased has been adopted out of the family and application is made by a parent of the deceased, the oath should state that the deceased died 'intestate a widow without issue or any other person entitled in priority to share in her estate by virtue of any enactment. That by an adoption order made under the Adoption Act 1958 (or as the case may be), *CB* the lawful son of the said deceased was duly adopted, and the said estate therefore devolves in all respects as if the said *CB* were the lawful child of the adopter or adopters and not the child of the deceased.' The reference to the adopted child should be by his name previous to the adoption; in no circumstances should a copy of the adoption order be included with the papers to lead the grant.

The Act of 1958 extended to adoption orders made by the English, Scottish or Northern Irish courts, and, by virtue of the Adoption Act 1964, to adoption orders made in the Isle of Man or any of the Channel Islands as respects anything done or any event occurring on or after 16 July 1964. Section 4 of the Adoption Act 1968 provided that adoptions effected overseas, as specified by order, were to be recognised as conferring the same rights (including rights of succession) as adoption orders made by virtue of the Adoption Act 1958. Now Sched 1 to the Children Act 1975 (to be replaced and continued in due course by s 38 (1) of the Adoption Act 1976) defines 'adoption' under the Act as including adoption (i) by an adoption order made under s 8 (1) of the Act of 1975; (ii) by an adoption order made under the Act of 1958 or the Adoption Act 1950 or any enactment repealed by the Act of 1950; (iii) by an order made in Northern Ireland, the Isle of Man or in any of the Channel Islands; (iv) which is an overseas adoption as defined by s 4 (3) of the Adoption Act 1968; (v) which is an adoption recognised by the law of England and Wales and effected under the law of any other country. It would seem therefore that an adoption under a foreign jurisdiction (as well as one coming within the provisions of the Act of 1968) for instance in accordance with the law of the domicile of the adopters, could give the adopted person the status and rights of succession conferred by the Act of 1975 (see *Re Marshall* [1957] 1 Ch 507; *Re Valentine's Settlement* [1965] 2 All ER 226). In *Re Varadi* (1969, unreported motion), an order was made for a grant of letters of administration to issue to the attorney of the adopted daughter of the deceased, who had died intestate, a widower, domiciled in England; at the date of the adoption the adopters were domiciled in and nationals of Czechoslovakia, they and the adopted person were all ordinarily resident there, and the adoption was regarded as valid by Czechoslovak law.

Section 4 of the Adoption Act 1968 was brought into operation by the Adoption Act 1968 (Commencement No 1) Order 1973 so as to be effective in respect of deaths occurring on or after 1 February 1973. The Adoption (Designation of Overseas Adoptions) Order 1973 lists the places adoptions effected in which will be recognised under the Act of 1968 provided they have been made under the law in force (not including customary or common law) in the place in question. Those places are as follows:

Commonwealth Countries and United Kingdom Dependent Territories

Australia
Bahamas
Barbados
Belize (formerly British Honduras)
Bermuda
Botswana
Canada
Cayman Islands
The Republic of Cyprus
Dominica
Fiji
Ghana
Gibraltar
Guyana
Hong Kong
Jamaica
Kenya
Lesotho
Malawi
Malaysia
Malta
Mauritius
Montserrat
New Zealand
Nigeria
Pitcairn
Rhodesia
St Christopher-Nevis-Anguilla
St Vincent
Seychelles (Republic)
Singapore
Sri Lanka
Swaziland
Tanzania
Tonga
Tortola (formerly British Virgin Islands)
Trinidad and Tobago
Uganda
Zambia

Other Countries and Territories

Austria

Belgium
Denmark (including Greenland and the Faroes)
Finland
France (including Réunion, Martinique, Guadeloupe and French Guyana)
The Federal Republic of Germany and Land Berlin (West Berlin)
Greece
Iceland
The Republic of Ireland
Israel
Italy
Luxembourg
The Netherlands (including Surinam and the Antilles)
Norway
Portugal (including the Azores and Madeira)
South Africa and South West Africa (Namibia)
Spain (including the Balearics and the Canary Islands)
Sweden
Switzerland
Turkey
The United States of America
Yugoslavia

Evidence of the overseas adoption order may be given by producing a certified copy of the entry in a public register of the country concerned, or a certificate as to the adoption signed by a person authorised so to do by the law of the country in question, or a certified copy of such a certificate.

By the Adoption Act 1968 (Commencement No 2) Order 1978 and the Children Act 1975 (Commencement No 3) Order 1978 certain provisions of the Adoption Act 1968 and s 24 of the Children Act 1975 were brought into effect from 23 October 1978. Under these sections provision is made for the making, revocation or annulment of Convention adoption orders and the annulment of certain overseas adoption orders, consequent upon the ratification by the United Kingdom of the Hague Convention on Jurisdiction, Applicable Law and Recognition of Decrees Relating to Adoptions of 1965. The general purpose is to allow adoptions to be granted where the adopters and the child are nationals of, or habitually resident in, different countries which have ratified the Convention and to be recognised fully in all such countries. So far it applies only to the United Kingdom, Australia and Switzerland. The application for a Convention adoption order in England and Wales may be made only to the High Court. A child who is the subject of such an order has the same status in England and Wales as that conferred on any other adopted person within the scope of Sched 1 to the Children Act 1975. The relevant provisions will in due course be repealed and continued by the Adoption Act 1976.

(l) Legitimated persons

The Legitimacy Act 1926 provided that children born out of wedlock but whose parents had subsequently married, whether before or after the date of the Act, would be regarded as legitimated persons as from 1 January 1927 or the date of their parents' marriage, whichever was the later. The Act applied where the father was at the date of the marriage domiciled either in England (s 1), in which case legitimation was dependent on the parents being free to marry at the date of the birth of the child, or in a foreign country the law of which allowed legitimation by the subsequent marriage of the parents (s 8). The Act of 1926 was amended by the Legitimacy Act 1959 so as to provide in addition that an illegitimate child was legitimated by the subsequent marriage of its parents where the father was at the time of the marriage domiciled in England, notwithstanding that one or both of the parents were not free to marry at the date of birth of the child. Such a child was legitimated from 29 October 1959, the date on which the Act of 1959 came into operation, or the date of the marriage, whichever was the later. Those sections of the Legitimacy Act 1926 have been repealed and re-enacted by the Legitimacy Act 1976. Apart from these statutory provisions, where a person is born of parents who at the date of his birth and at the date of their subsequent marriage are domiciled in a country which recognises legitimation by subsequent marriage, and he is legitimated under the provisions of the law of that country, English law will accept him as legitimated as from the date from which the law of that country would regard him as legitimated, but subject to any conditions which that law may impose (*Re Hurll* [1952] Ch 722).

In respect of deaths occurring before 1 January 1976 a legitimated person, his spouse and his issue may take any interest in the estate of a person dying intestate after the date of legitimation to which they would be entitled if the legitimated person had been born legitimate subject to certain limitations in respect of property devolving with a dignity or title of honour. Similarly, where a legitimated person or his issue dies intestate before 1 January 1976, he is to be regarded as having been born legitimate for the purpose of ascertaining the persons entitled to share in the estate. The situation since 1 January 1976 is now regulated by the Legitimacy Act 1976. In respect of deaths taking place on or after 1 January 1976 a legitimated person, and any other person, is entitled to take any interest as if the legitimated person had been born legitimate. 'Legitimation' includes legitimation under ss 1 and 8 of the Act of 1926 and legitimation, whether or not by virtue of the subsequent marriage of the parents, recognised by the law of England and Wales and effected under the law of any other country. When considering the right of children of a person who has died intestate to a grant of administration, these will include legitimated children; the parents or other kin of a legitimated child are entitled to a grant as if the child had been born legitimate. The exact rights of legitimated persons and others to take interests in property are explained in ss 5 and 6 of and Sched 1 to the Legitimacy Act 1976.

On an application by, through or in respect of a legitimated person, proof of the legitimation should be given by producing a copy of the declaration, if any, made by the court under s 45 (2) of the Matrimonial Causes Act 1973 (or s 39 (2) of the Matrimonial Causes Act 1965). If the birth has been re-registered under the terms of s 9 of the Legitimacy Act 1976, it is sufficient to produce a copy of the amended birth certificate. The oath must state, if such be the case, that the applicant is the person referred to in the declaration or certificate. In the absence of such proof, an applicant may be required to effect a re-registration of the birth or to obtain a declaration of the court as to the legitimation. If re-registration is not possible in the circumstances and it is not open to the applicant to obtain a declaration or it would impose hardship on him to have to obtain a declaration, the evidence in support of the contention of legitimation should be submitted to the registrar for his decision as to its sufficiency. If he is not satisfied, he may direct that an application be made to the court on motion or to a judge on summons, with notice to the Attorney-General.

If, in the event of the legitimation not being established, the Crown would be beneficially interested in the deceased's estate, notice of the intended application should be given to or served on the Treasury Solicitor (or the solicitor for the Duchy of Lancaster or the Duchy of Cornwall, in appropriate cases). It must be shown that such notice has been given, usually by production of his acknowledgment or his consent to the grant being made to the applicant. A registrar may direct that no grant shall issue within a specified time after the notice has been given, in order to give the Treasury Solicitor (or as the case may be) an opportunity to oppose the making of the grant to the applicant (Probate Rule 37).

Where the title to a grant depends on the legitimation of a person, the applicant may be described in the oath or affidavit as 'the lawful legitimated   ' or 'the lawful   by legitimation'. A person who has obtained a decree of *legitimacy* under s 45 (1) of the Matrimonial Causes Act 1973 is rightfully to be described as a lawful child.

(m) Children of void and voidable marriages

A child of a void marriage (ie, a marriage, not being voidable only, in respect of which the High Court has or had jurisdiction to grant a decree of nullity, or would have or would have had if the parties were domiciled in England), whenever born, is to be treated as the legitimate child of his parents if, at the time of the act of intercourse resulting in his birth or at the time of the celebration of the marriage, whichever is the later, both or either of the parties reasonably believed that the marriage was valid (Legitimacy Act 1976, s 1). The father of the child must have been domiciled in England at the date of the birth, or, if he died before the birth, at the date of his death. Any additional rights under an intestacy conferred by this section of the Act do not operate unless the intestate died on or after 29 October 1959 (see Sched 1 to Legitimacy Act 1976; also as to the succession to a dignity or title of honour). Before an application is made for a grant based on this section, the registrar should be asked for directions as to the supporting evidence he will require.

A voidable marriage annulled by decree after 31 July 1971 is treated as if it had existed up to decree absolute so that a child born during the marriage is legitimate. If the decree was made on or before that date, a child of the marriage is deemed to be a legitimate child of his parents, provided that he would have been a legitimate child of the parties to the marriage had it been dissolved and not annulled.

Such children may be described in the oath as 'lawful' children.

(n) Illegitimate persons (death between 1 January 1927 and 31 December 1969)

By s 9 of the Legitimacy Act 1926 an illegitimate child, not being a legitimated person, may take such interest in the estate of his mother as he would have been entitled to if he had been born legitimate, provided that the mother has died intestate on or after 1 January 1927 (but before 1 January 1970) and has left no legitimate issue surviving her. The issue of an illegitimate child who has predeceased his mother take their parent's interest. The Act also provided that where an illegitimate child, not being a legitimated person, dies intestate on or after 1 January 1927 (but before 1 January 1970) leaving his mother surviving him, she is entitled to such interest in his estate as she would have been entitled to if her child had been born legitimate and she had been the only surviving parent. In such circumstances an illegitimate child takes his place in the order of priority of right to a grant of administration in respect of the estate of his mother, dying intestate, as if he had been born legitimate. The oath must show that the mother left no legitimate children surviving her. If the deceased left a surviving spouse, the illegitimate child may be joined as a co-grantee if the net estate exceeds £8,750 (or £5,000 if the death took place before 1 January 1967, and £1,000, if the death took place before 1953). The applicant should be described in the oath as 'the natural child and the only person (*or as the case may be*) entitled to the estate'.

On the death of an illegitimate child intestate before 1 January 1970 the mother has a right to a grant of administration subject to the prior right of the deceased's spouse and issue, if any. The applicant should be described in the oath as 'the natural mother and the only person entitled to the estate'. Where an illegitimate person has died intestate before 1 January 1970 leaving no spouse, issue or mother his estate devolves on the Crown as bona vacantia.

(o) Illegitimate persons (death on or after 1 January 1970)

Section 9 of the Legitimacy Act 1959 has been repealed by the Family Law Reform Act 1969 in respect of deaths on or after 1 January 1970. From that date on the death intestate of either parent of an illegitimate child, that child, or if he is dead, his issue, is entitled to any interest in the parent's real and personal property to which he, or his issue, would have been entitled if he had been born legitimate. The description 'illegitimate child' does not include for this purpose an illegitimate child who has been legitimated by his parents' subsequent marriage or who has been adopted: the right of succession of such a person derives from his legitimation or adoption. Issue of a deceased illegitimate child does not include illegitimate children of that child. Moreover where an illegitimate child dies intestate in respect of any part of his real or personal property, each parent will be entitled to take any interest in the child's estate to which he or she would have been entitled had the child been born legitimate. An illegitimate child is to be presumed not to have been survived by his father unless the contrary is shown (s 14 (4) of the Family Law Reform Act 1969). In considering the right to a grant of administration references to children of the deceased include references to his illegitimate children, who will rank equally with legitimate, legitimated and adopted children of the deceased; a reference to the father or mother of the deceased will be construed as a reference to the parents of an illegitimate child (Probate Rule 21 (1), (6)). Where the applicant's title to a grant depends upon his establishing an illegitimate relationship (except that with his mother) evidence of the relationship is required to be lodged with the papers to lead the grant. This will usually be in the form of an affidavit unless it is possible to produce a birth certificate showing the name of the father and that he was the informant, or an affiliation order against the father. The applicant may be described in the affidavit or oath as 'the natural son (or daughter) and the only person (*or as the case may be*) entitled to the estate' or as 'the natural father (or mother) and the only person, etc'.

(p) Creditors

A creditor may take a grant only on clearing off all persons entitled thereto. Where the deceased dies leaving a surviving spouse or next of kin, their renunciations must be filed with the other papers to lead the grant or they must be cited to accept or refuse a grant (see head 19.2). It is not necessary to clear off next of kin whose only right to a grant is as 'persons interested in the estate in the event of an accretion thereto' (see p 116). It may be required that the creditor should supply a guarantee by sureties and that the sureties should justify (see head 11.1 and Forms 11.3.1 and 11.3.2) but the registrar has a discretion to dispense with this requirement. Where the deceased died leaving no kin and the creditor can swear definitely to that fact, the grant will issue on his filing the renunciation of the Treasury Solicitor on behalf of the Crown (or of the solicitor for the Duchy of Lancaster or the Duchy of Cornwall, in appropriate cases). However, if it can be sworn only that the deceased died without known kin, the creditor must first issue a citation to accept or refuse a grant, addressed to the kin, if any (see head 19.2), a copy being served on the Treasury Solicitor (or as the case may be). If the amount of the estate is very small, the issue of a citation is often dispensed with and an application may be made to a registrar for an order for a grant under s 116 of the Supreme Court Act 1981 (see head 13.6).

Where funeral expenses are owed to an undertaker who has incurred them on proper authority, and who is unable to recover them by reason of no application having been made for a grant of representation to the deceased's estate, he is not entitled to a grant as of right since he is not strictly a creditor of the deceased. However, he may make application for an order under s 116 of the Supreme Court Act 1981 (see head 13.6).

(q) Personal representatives

The legal personal representative of any next of kin entitled to a grant, or of a creditor (see above), has the same right to a grant as the deceased whom he represents, subject to the proviso that, unless a registrar otherwise directs, a living person will be preferred to the personal representative of a deceased person who, if living, would be entitled in the same degree (Probate Rules 21 (5), 25 (3)). (For the right of the personal representative of a surviving spouse, see p 116.)

When the personal representatives of a deceased person apply for a grant to which that person was entitled, the practice varies according to whether the applicants are executors or administrators. One or more executors may apply for a representative grant without reference to the other executors, but all the administrators should join in an application. Exceptionally, a grant will issue to one or some of the administrators on lodging the renunciation or consent of the others.

Where application has to be made not only for a representative grant but for the leading grant which will give the applicant his title to the representative grant, the two applications will be accepted by the probate registry if lodged at the same time. It will be sufficient for the applicant to describe himself in the oath to lead the representative grant as 'the sole executor (*or as the case may be*) appointed by the will of ' or as 'the proposed administrator of the estate of '.

(r) Assignees

Where all the persons entitled to the estate, whether under a will or under an intestacy, have assigned the whole of their interest in the estate to one or more persons, the assignee or assignees have the same right of priority to a grant as had the assignor with the highest priority (Probate Rule 22 (1)). Where there are two or more assignees, not all of them need apply for the grant, provided that those not applying give their consent to the others making the application. If there is difficulty in obtaining all the consents, reference should be made to the registrar for directions. Assignment to a minor causes a minority interest to arise (see head 6.2). The original deed of assignment and a copy thereof must be lodged with the papers to lead the grant; the original will be handed out after inspection (for the procedure where there is some doubt as to whether the deed is duly stamped, see p 137).

It would appear that where all the members of a class of next of kin disclaim their interest, the estate devolves upon the next class of kin, and not as bona vacantia (*Re Scott, decd* [1975] 1 WLR 1260).

(s) Missing beneficiary

See head 13.6.

(t) Persons entrusted or entitled under foreign law

See head 15.2(*c*), (*d*).

5.4 Oath for administrators

The oath must be prepared with the greatest care as it is the document which establishes the right of the applicants to the grant. Errors will usually necessitate it being amended and re-sworn, except that minor errors may be put right by a certificate by the solicitor.

Form 5.4 Oath for administrators

(For heading and title, see Form 2.11)

1
of
2 make oath and say that
of
3 died on the day of , 19 , aged years
domiciled in
4 intestate
5 and that minority life interest arises under the intestacy
6 and that to the best of knowledge, information and belief there was no land vested in the deceased immediately before his death which was settled previously thereto and which remained settled land notwithstanding his death.
7 And further make oath and say that
of the said deceased
8 and that will (i) collect, get in and administer according to the law the real and personal estate ( ) of the said deceased; (ii) when required to do so by the court, exhibit on oath in the court a full inventory of the said estate ( ) and when so required render an account of the administration of the said estate to the court; and (iii) when required to do so by the High Court, deliver up the grant of letters of administration to that court;
9 and that to the best of knowledge, information and belief [the gross estate passing under the grant does not exceed £ , and the net estate does not exceed £ , and that this is not a case in which an Inland Revenue Account is required to be delivered]
[the gross estate passing under the grant amounts to £ and the net estate amounts to £].
10
11 Sworn by
at
this day of , 19 .
Before me,
A Commissioner for Oaths (or Solicitor)

The name and address of the extracting solicitor should appear in the top right-hand corner of the oath (as to the solicitor's office reference, see p 67).

1 This paragraph should commence 'I' or 'We' followed by the full names, addresses and occupations or descriptions of the deponents (see as to this, pp 67–70). The order in which they are set out determines the order in which they appear in the grant, and should be according to their priority of right to the grant (see pp 109, 114). A trust corporation will be placed first only at the request of both or all the applicants.

2 If the deponents wish to affirm the words 'make oath and say' must be altered to read 'do solemnly and sincerely affirm', and para **7** and the jurat at the foot of the oath must be correspondingly altered.

The full name and address of the deceased must be given in this paragraph. The true and proper name should always be given and then, if it is desired that the grant shall include some other name assumed by the deceased, that name should follow as an alias, eg, 'John Charles Smith, otherwise John Smythe'. The facts justifying the inclusion of an alias must be sworn to in the oath (see pp 72, 134).

The address of the deceased must have been his usual residential address. An accommodation address will only be accepted if it is further sworn that no better address can be given.

If it is desired that several addresses of the deceased shall appear in the grant, these should be set out in the oath and a request for their inclusion in the grant should be made in a letter by the applicant's solicitor. Not more than four addresses will be included.

Ecclesiastical designations, the description 'clerk in Holy Orders', and titles of honour should be stated.

3 This paragraph corresponds to para **4** in the oath for executors and the notes thereon should be read (see pp 72–73).

4 This paragraph must show the manner in which all persons having a right to a grant prior to that of the applicant have been cleared off, whether because they did not survive the deceased or because, having survived, they have renounced their right or have since died without taking a grant or have been cited to take a grant.

Unless the application for the grant is to be made by the spouse of the deceased, it is necessary to indicate first of all the status of the deceased at the date of death, namely, 'a bachelor (*or* spinster)', 'a widower (*or* widow)', 'a single man (*or* single woman)', or 'leaving *AB* her lawful husband her surviving' (*or* his lawful widow and relict him surviving)'.

If the marriage of the deceased has been dissolved or annulled, the following wording should be added: 'That the marriage of the said deceased with   was on the   day of   , 19   , dissolved (*or* annulled) by final decree of the High Court of Justice (*or* of the   County Court) in England and Wales and that the said deceased did not re-marry.' If the decree of divorce or annulment was granted by the court of a foreign country it must be shown in the oath, or if necessary in a separate affidavit of law, that the jurisdiction of that court would be recognised under English law, eg, in the case of a divorce, that at the date of the commencement of the proceedings the parties were domiciled in that country or that either spouse was habitually resident in, or a national of, that country (see pp 117–118), and in the case of an annulment that the decree was granted by a competent court of the country in which the parties were domiciled at the date of institution of the suit (see also p 118).

Where there has been a decree of judicial separation by the High Court (or county court) which affects the right of succession of the surviving spouse of the deceased (see p 119) the following wording should be inserted: 'That on the day of , 19 , by final decree of the High Court of Justice (*or* of the County Court) in England and Wales it was decreed that the said deceased be judicially separated from the said and that the separation under the said decree continued from the making thereof until the date of death of the said deceased'. Where a deceased wife was separated from her husband by a separation order made by a magistrates' court and has died before 1 August 1970 (see p 119), the following wording should be used: 'That on the day of , 19 , by an order made under the Matrimonial Proceedings (Magistrates' Courts) Act 1960 (or under the Summary Jurisdiction (Separation and Maintenance) Acts 1895–1945, as the case may be) by the Justices of the Petty Sessional Division of sitting at in the County of , it was ordered that and that the said deceased be no longer bound to cohabit with the said (which provision had the effect in all respects of a decree of judicial separation). That the separation under the said order continued from the making thereof until the date of death of the said deceased'. Paragraph **8** also requires alteration in these circumstances (see p 134).

Paragraph **4** must then show the manner in which all other persons having a right to a grant prior to that of the applicant have been cleared off. Where the deceased died on or after 1 January 1970 it is necessary to clear off the classes of person given an interest by the Family Law Reform Act 1969: this may be effected by adding after the usual form of clearing the words 'or any other person entitled in priority to share in his estate by virtue of any enactment'. This wording includes legitimated and adopted children as well as illegitimate children. The following table sets out the simpler forms of clearing:

Clearing of	*Wording*
Spouse	Swear that deceased died: a bachelor a spinster a widower a widow a single man a single woman

<table>
<tr><td>Children or other issue</td><td>without issue</td><td rowspan="5">or any other person entitled in priority to share in his (her) estate by virtue of any enactment.</td></tr>
<tr><td>Parents</td><td>(or) parent</td></tr>
<tr><td>Brothers or sisters and their issue</td><td>(or) brother or sister of the whole (or half-) blood or their issue</td></tr>
<tr><td>Grandparents</td><td>(or) grandparent</td></tr>
<tr><td>Uncles and aunts and their issue</td><td>(or) uncle or aunt of the whole (or half-) blood or their issue</td></tr>
</table>

The circumstances will vary from case to case but the following two examples will give some idea of other forms of wording which may be used:

(1) Application by a creditor on the renunciation of the person entitled—

'died... intestate a widower, without issue, parent, brother or sister of the whole or half-blood or their issue, or grandparent or uncle or aunt of the whole blood (or any other person entitled in priority to share in his estate by virtue of any enactment) leaving *AB*, the lawful cousin german of the whole blood of the said deceased, being the lawful son of *DB*, the lawful uncle of the whole blood, who died in the lifetime of the said deceased, and the only person entitled to his estate surviving him, and that the said *AB* has duly renounced letters of administration of the said estate.'

(2) Application by the personal representatives of the widow—

'died... intestate leaving *CD* his lawful widow and relict and the only person now entitled to his estate surviving him, and that the said *CD* has since died without having taken upon herself letters of administration of the said estate.'

Where there has been an assignment of interest (see pp 128, 137), the facts should be recited in this paragraph, eg, 'died... intestate leaving *CD*, his lawful widow and relict, and *DD* and *FD*, his lawful sons, together the only persons entitled to share in his estate, and that the said *DD* and *FD* have by Deed of Assignment dated the day of , 19 , assigned all their right and title to and interest in the said estate to the said *CD*'.

On an application for a grant in respect of spes successionis (see head 8.4) the fact of the renunciation should be stated here, eg 'died... intestate a bachelor, without issue (or any other person entitled in priority to share in his estate by virtue of any enactment) leaving *MD* his lawful mother and the only person entitled to his estate surviving him, and that the said *MD* has renounced letters of administration of the said estate and has consented to the same being granted to the person or persons who would be entitled to her estate were she now dead intestate' (see also the note to para **7** at p 133).

Commorientes—See head 7.2.

Settled land—If the grant is to issue including settled land (see Chapter 12), the persons entitled to such a grant in priority to the applicants must also be cleared off (for wording, see p 181).

5 It must be shown whether or not a minority or life interest arises under the intestacy (see head 6.2). See also the notes to para **5** of the oath for administrators with will annexed (p 100).

Foreign law—See p 214.

6 This paragraph corresponds to para **5** in the oath for executors and the notes thereon should be read (see pp 73–74 and Chapter 12).

7 Here the relationship (if any) of the applicants to the deceased and the exact capacity in which they claim the grant should be set out (see p 102 for incapacity of the person entitled).

Where the death occurred before 1 January 1926 a surviving spouse should be described as 'the lawful husband' or 'the lawful widow and relict', and a relative should be described as 'the lawful father (*or as the case may be*) and (only) (one of the) next of kin'. Where the relative applying is not one of the next of kin, he or she should be described as, for example, 'the lawful child of , a lawful brother of the said deceased who died in his lifetime, and as such one of the persons entitled in distribution to his personal estate'. The heir at law should be described as such.

Where the death occurred on or after 1 January 1926 a surviving spouse should be described as 'the lawful husband (*or* widow and relict) and only person (now) entitled to the estate of the said deceased'. The next of kin should be described as 'the lawful son (*or as the case may be*) and one of the persons entitled to share in the estate of the said deceased (*or* a person who may have a beneficial interest in the estate of the said deceased in the event of an accretion thereto, *or as the case may be*)'. If the applicant is a nephew or niece, a grandchild or a cousin german, it must be shown that the parent through whom the claim to entitlement is made died in the lifetime of the deceased (see note to para **4** above). A creditor applies as 'a creditor of the said deceased'. The personal representative of a deceased person entitled should describe himself as '(one of) the executor(s) of the will (*or as the case may be*) of the said deceased, probate of the said will (*or as the case may be*) having been granted to me out of the Registry on the day of , 19 '; the original grant or a copy thereof must be lodged for inspection.

(As to adopted persons, see pp 120–123, as to legitimated persons, see pp 124–125, and as to illegitimate persons, see pp 126–127.)

If the applicant is claiming the grant by virtue of spes successionis (see head 8.4) his relationship to the renunciant must be given here and, if necessary, he should clear intermediate kin, eg 'that the said *MD* is a widow and that I am the lawful son of the said *MD* and [one of the persons] [the only person] entitled to [share in] her estate were she now dead intestate' (see also the note to para **4**, at p 132).

(For persons 'entrusted' or 'entitled' under foreign law, see the note to para **8** of Form 4.4 at p 103 and pp 211–212.)

If the grant is to issue including settled land (see Chapter 12), this paragraph should set out additionally the applicant's title to such a grant (for wording, see Form 12.4.2).

8 If settled land is vested in the deceased, the words 'save and except settled land', 'limited to settled land', or 'including settled land' should be inserted in the brackets provided, as the circumstances of the case warrant, and also in the brackets in para **9**.

If the deceased was judicially separated from her husband and died before 1 August 1970 and the grant is to issue to her next of kin (see p 119), the following: 'limited to all such estate as the said deceased acquired after the said day of , 19 , and no further or otherwise', should be inserted after 'of the said deceased' in sub-para (i). Further references to the estate in this paragraph and para **9** should be qualified by the words 'limited as aforesaid'.

9 This paragraph corresponds to para **9** in the oath for executors and reference should be made to the notes thereon (see pp 77–79).

Estate so far as at present can be ascertained—See p 78.

10 The purpose of this paragraph is to disclose matters relevant to the application which do not conveniently fall to be dealt with under the previous paragraphs of the oath.

Permitted deductions—When it is desired to make the permitted deductions (see p 138) in order to bring the value of the estate below £40,000 or £85,000 as the case may be (see table, p 112; or £1,000 if the death occurred before 1 January 1953), the following should be inserted in this paragraph:

> 'That after the deduction of the value of the personal chattels, debts, capital transfer tax, costs incurred and to be incurred amounting to £ , the fees payable on application for this grant of representation [and interest (see p 139) at per cent on £ from the date of death of the said deceased to amounting to £] the value of the estate passing under the intestacy amounts to £ '.

Previous grants—If there have been previous grants in the deceased's estate which have been revoked or have ceased to be operative, the relevant circumstances should be recited, eg, 'That the grant of issued out of the Registry on the day of , 19 , was revoked by order dated the day of , 19 '; 'That the grant of letters of administration of the estate of the said deceased issued out of the Registry on the day of , 19 , to for the use of during his minority has ceased and expired by reason of the said having attained the age of eighteen (twenty-one) years' (see also head 13.1). The original or an office copy must accompany the papers when application is made in the Principal Registry, or whenever application is made in a registry other than that from which the previous grant issued.

Alias—If it is desired that the grant should include an alias of the deceased, a paragraph on the following lines should be added to the oath, 'That the true and proper name of the deceased was John Charles Smith, but that certain property, to wit , is vested in him in the name of John Smythe' (see p 130).

Grant issuing by decree or order of the court—When an action has been tried in the High Court an office copy of the judgment or order of the court is sent to the Principal Registry by the Chief Master, together with any testamentary documents pronounced against. When there have been proceedings in a county court, the registrar of that court will endorse any testamentary documents pronounced against and send them together with any order or decree made and his certificate to the registrar of the nearest probate registry. When the grant issues by decree, that fact is recited in the body of the grant; when it issues in accordance with the order of a county court judge, the grant bears a notation 'By Order of the County Court holden at dated the day of , 19 '.

If the grant is to issue by virtue of a court order, details as to the making of the order and its substance must be given in the oath (see p 80).

Nil estate—See p 81.

11 See the note to para **10** of Form 2.11 at p 29.

Chapter 6

Joint Grants and Life or Minority Interests

6.1 Joint grants

A grant may issue to two or more persons but not to more than four persons in respect of the same part of the estate (see p 64). If a life or minority interest arises under the will or intestacy, the grant will usually have to be made to a trust corporation with or without an individual, or to at least two persons (see head 6.2).

No order is necessary if the grant is to be made to two or more persons equally entitled thereto. However, where it is sought to join with a person entitled to a grant a person entitled in a lower degree in the order of priority and there are other persons with a prior claim to be joined as co-administrators, those persons must be cleared off, by renunciation (see head 8.1) or, in default of renunciation, by registrar's order on ex parte application (in the Principal Registry made to the Principal of the Probate Department) (see head 20.1) (Probate Rule 23 (1)).

Subject to three exceptions, a registrar's order obtained by ex parte application (see head 20.1) will also be necessary if it is sought to join with a person entitled to a grant a person who has no right thereto (Probate Rule 23 (2)). The exceptions are as follows:

(*a*) In the case of a trust corporation, provided that the consents of all persons entitled to the grant and of all persons interested in the residuary estate of the deceased are lodged, unless a registrar dispenses with this requirement (see pp 197–198 and Form 14.1.2).

(*b*) In the case of kin of the deceased having no beneficial interest in the estate, in the prescribed order of priority (see p 114), provided that all other persons entitled to join in the grant, including unsatisfied creditors, have renounced their right (see Forms 8.2.2, 8.2.3).

(*c*) In the case of a person nominated by the guardian of a minor (see p 154), unless a registrar directs otherwise.

The application must be supported by an affidavit by the person entitled to the grant together with the consent of the person proposed to be joined. The affidavit in support should show who are the persons having a prior right to that (if any) of the person whom it is sought to join as co-grantee, or otherwise affected, whether they have been notified of the proposed application and, if so, what is their attitude thereto. The registrar may require the application to be made by summons (see head 20.2).

6.2 Life or minority interests

Where under a will or intestacy any beneficiary is a minor or a life interest arises, a grant of administration must be made either to a trust corporation, with or without an individual, or to not less than two individuals unless it appears to the court to be expedient in all the circumstances to appoint an individual as sole administrator (s 114 (2) of the Supreme Court Act 1981). Previous to 1 January 1982 the court had had no discretion to waive this requirement except that it had been established that there was power to make a grant to a single administrator pending suit although there was a possibility of a life or minority interest arising (*In the Estate of Lindley* [1953] P 203; *In the Goods of Haslip decd* [1958] 2 All ER 275).

The application is made ex parte to the registrar (in the Principal Registry through the Probate Department) by lodging an affidavit by the applicant setting out the reasons for the application and the registrar will give his directions accordingly. Alternatively the facts may be recited in the oath to lead the grant and the application made at the time of applying for the grant. The registrar has a complete discretion in the matter but it is suggested that circumstances in which it might be considered appropriate to allow the grant to issue to a single individual in spite of there being a life or minority interest are—

(i) where the proposed grantee is a member of the professional classes, such as a solicitor or accountant, or is the representative of a local authority:

(ii) where the applicant is the surviving spouse and the amount of the estate is only slightly in excess of the statutory legacy:

(iii) where the only minor beneficiary has almost attained his majority:

(iv) where only one individual can be found who is in any way qualified to take the grant on behalf of a minor and the estate is too small to be able to afford the fees of a trust corporation.

Apart from the power now given to the court to dispense with the requirement, a grant may be made to one individual although there is a life interest if (i) the life interest has been cleared off by assignment to the reversioners, or (ii) the reversioners have assigned their interest to the life tenant. In both instances, all the interest, whether at present ascertainable or not, must have been transferred. The deed should be produced for inspection and return; a copy is not required. It is to be noted that where there is any doubt as to whether the deed is duly stamped, the solicitor will be required to present the deed to the Controller of Stamps (Inland Revenue) for adjudication before the grant will issue. To avoid delay it has been arranged that the Adjudication Section will accept the document for noting and indorsement (by stamping it 'Presented') and will return it for submission to the registry provided that the solicitor lodges a written undertaking that he will as soon as the grant issues re-submit the deed for formal adjudication and will pay any stamp duty. Where the surviving spouse of an intestate has transferred his life interest his renunciation of the right to a grant must be filed before a grant will issue to a person with a lower title. Where the reversioners have assigned their interest to the surviving spouse their renunciation is not required on an application for a grant by the spouse. The nature and effect of the assignment should be stated in the oath (see p 132).

Two persons may represent the interests of one individual, whether as guardians (but see p 153), attorneys or otherwise. Where the interest of a person aged between eighteen and twenty-one years does not vest in him until he attains the age of twenty-one years, either under an intestacy (see p 120) or under a will (see p 100), it is correct to swear there is no minority interest.

Foreign law—See p 214.

Ascertainment of life interest—It is sometimes difficult to ascertain whether or not a life interest arises in respect of residue undisposed of by the will or under an intestacy. The rule is that the value of the estate which has ultimately to be distributed by the personal representatives, or which ultimately will come into their possession, determines the matter. It is therefore necessary to take into account certain property of the deceased which does not pass under the grant. Suppose that *A* dies after 1 March 1983 intestate, leaving his spouse and two children surviving him. His estate consists of 'free' estate in Great Britain to the value of £38,000 and property situated in a foreign country to the value of £7,000. The total value of the property to be dealt with by the personal representatives is £45,000. If the permitted deductions (see below) do not reduce this figure to £40,000 or below, a life interest in respect of half the estate in excess of £40,000 arises in favour of the surviving spouse.

The value of the estate for this purpose should strictly be the value at the time of the payment or appropriation in respect of the spouse's statutory charge. The registry will usually accept the value at the date of the deceased's death on an application for a first grant, but regard must be had to any substantial increase in the value of an asset before the date of application for the grant, which would cause a life interest to arise. In any case of doubt the solicitor may be asked by the registry to submit a note showing the basis on which it is claimed that the surviving spouse is entitled to the whole of the estate.

The permitted deductions to arrive at the net value of the estate are:

(1) The value of the personal chattels (see pp 112–113).

(2) Debts.

(3) Capital transfer tax payable out of the estate without a right of recovery from any other person or property.

(4) Costs incurred and to be incurred amounting to £ .
(Costs must be fair and reasonable according to the considerations mentioned in the Rules of the Supreme Court (Non-Contentious Probate

Costs) 1956. Generally, see the notes published by The Law Society for guidance, pp 1005–1006 *Law Society's Gazette*, 15 October 1980; see also reference in *Maltby* v *D J Freeman & Co* [1978] 2 All ER 913, at p 917. A charge based on a higher rate than is usual will only be allowed if the registrar is satisfied that in the circumstances it is fair and reasonable and in this connection it is recognised that the costs may often be higher where the gross estate is quite small. He will determine the matter on the principle that the estimated costs relate to that part of the estate which can be distributed immediately. This would exclude the costs of administration of a trust and of the holding of an estate during the subsistence of a life interest, and costs which cannot be forecast with reasonable certainty.)

(5) The probate fees payable on the application.

[Interest at 6 per cent on £1,000 (see Intestate Succession (Interest and Capitalisation) Order 1977) (Amendment) Order 1983), calculated from the date of death to the end of the week on which the application is lodged, if the death occurred before 1 January 1953. (In the case of deaths on or after 1 January 1953 the interest at 6 per cent on the statutory legacy is payable primarily out of the income of the estate and may not be deducted except in so far as the income is insufficient to pay such interest.)]

For the wording to be inserted in the oath, see p 134.

6.3 Adding a second administrator

If there is only one personal representative (including an executor but not being a trust corporation) administering the estate during the minority of a beneficiary or during the subsistence of a life interest, application may be made to the court by any person interested or by such person's guardian or receiver for an order appointing one or more additional personal representatives to act while the minority or life interest subsists and until the estate is fully administered (s 114 (4) of the Supreme Court Act 1981). The application is made ex parte to the registrar (in the Principal Registry through the Record Keeper) supported by an affidavit by the applicant as to the facts together with the consent of the proposed administrator, the grant if possible and such further evidence as may be deemed necessary or as the registrar may direct (Probate Rule 24). Where the original grantee is not the applicant, it is advisable that the affidavit in support should show whether he has been notified of the proposed application and, if so, what is his attitude thereto. The registrar may require the application to be made by summons (see head 20.2); no fee is payable for the summons. If the grant issued from a district probate registry the application may be made to any district probate registrar or to a registrar of the Principal Registry. It may be directed that the original grant be noted with the appointment of the additional administrator, or that it be impounded or revoked, as the circumstances warrant.

An administration bond is no longer required but it may be necessary to provide a guarantee by sureties (see head 11.1). In the appropriate circumstances the grant will be noted with the appointment of the additional administrator without the need for a further application; no fee is payable for notation of the grant.

An additional personal representative who is appointed in this way to act with an executor does not become an executor so as to form part of any chain of representation (see head 3.1) through the testator in respect of whose estate he has been appointed an administrator (s 114(5) of the Supreme Court Act 1981).

Chapter 7

Death and Presumptions Relating to Death

7.1 Proof of death

Usually the statement in the oath that the deceased died on a particular date will be accepted as sufficient and it will not be necessary to produce a certificate of death.

The following paragraphs deal with those special cases where something further is required, including those cases where it is necessary to presume the death of the deceased.

(a) Service deaths

A notification of death or of the presumed death of a member of the forces issued by the Ministry of Defence on one of the prescribed forms (as distinct from a letter of condolence) is accepted. It should be lodged with the application for the grant and will be returned on request after the grant has issued.

(b) Merchant Navy deaths

The deaths of seamen or officers on ships on the British register are evidenced by the certificate (RBD6 or RBD6A) of the Registrar-General of the General Register and Record Office of Shipping and Seamen, at Llantrisant Road, Llandaff, Cardiff CF5 27S. Where such a certificate cannot be obtained, the Registrar General of Shipping and Seamen may be prepared to issue on request a certified extract from the list of crew (on Form RBD7 for merchant ships and on RBD8 for fishing vessels). This is evidence only that the person named was on board the ship at the time of its loss, although in respect of deaths presumed to have occurred before 1 January 1980, the extract may also contain a certificate that the Registrar-General has no information that the person named survived the loss. If necessary, confirmation of the facts shown on a certificate of presumed death will be obtained by the registrar of the registry in which the application is proceeding. The Registrar-General may also issue on request a form of certificate in respect of a seaman who died on shore or on an unregistered ship.

(c) Offshore installations

When a person dies, or is lost in circumstances such that it is reasonable to believe that he has died, either (i) on or from an offshore installation or a lifeboat, liferaft, etc, belonging to such an installation, or (ii) in the neighbourhood of such an installation whilst engaged in any operation connected therewith, and the death or loss does not require to be registered under the Merchant Shipping Acts, such death or loss has to be notified to the Registrar-General of Shipping and Seamen, and it is then registered by the appropriate registrar of births and deaths, according to the ordinary residence of the deceased, in the Marine Register. A certified copy of the entry may be obtained and will be accepted as proof of death.

(d) Civil aviation

Certificates of death or presumed death issued under any Civil Aviation Act and deposited with the Registrar-General will be accepted without verification.

(e) Other deaths

Certificates of presumed death issued by certain Government departments, such as the Commonwealth Relations Office, in respect of persons who were subject to their jurisdiction, will also be accepted without verification.

A certificate of death or presumed death which does not come within the categories described above may still be accepted at the discretion of the Senior Registrar as sufficient evidence of the death or presumed death of the deceased. The certificate should be submitted to the Senior Registrar for a decision or left with a district registrar for onward transmission.

(f) Leave to swear death

If no sufficient certificate can be produced, an application must be made for an order of the court. It is to be noted:

(*a*) that the Family Division has no power to make orders presuming the death of any person; and

(*b*) that a decree of presumed death and of dissolution of marriage made by the Family Division has no application outside matrimonial matters.

A conclusive order of presumption of death may be obtained only from the Chancery Division. Nevertheless, the Family Division will make an order giving leave to swear that a person who is thought to be dead died 'on or since' a certain date. Such an order will only be made in respect of a deceased person to whose estate a grant of representation is necessary. No order will be made in respect of the presumed death of an executor or beneficiary (see, however, grants under s 116 of the Supreme Court Act 1981 at head 13.6).

The application is made ex parte (see head 20.1), whatever the amount of the estate, to a registrar of the Principal Registry (through the Probate

Department) or, if the application is to be made in a district probate registry, to any district probate registrar. The registrar may require the matter to be brought before a registrar of the Principal Registry or a judge by summons, or before the court on motion. The principal affidavit must be made by the applicant for the grant and must deal with the following matters:

(i) The full name, address, description or status, and age or date of birth of the presumed deceased person.
(ii) Whether he died testate or intestate. (If there is a will, it must be lodged with the affidavit.)
(iii) When the presumed deceased was last seen alive, and the nature and result of the inquiries made to find him since that date. (All relevant letters and advertisements must be exhibited to the affidavit.)
(iv) If the presumed deceased died intestate, or if the residue of his estate is not wholly disposed of by the will, the names and exact relationships of the persons entitled to share in his estate or in the undisposed residue, and whether or not they are sui juris.
(v) Particulars of all policies of insurance on the life of the presumed deceased and the attitude of the insurance companies to the application.
(vi) Particulars of the estate of the presumed deceased including any bank accounts and whether they have been operated since the deceased disappeared.
(vii) That the applicant believes that the presumed deceased is actually dead.

Whenever they can be obtained, affidavits in corroboration of part or the whole of the facts set out in the affidavit of the applicant should be filed. If the presumed deceased was domiciled outside England and Wales and the court of the country of domicile has made an order presuming his death and vesting his estate in the persons entitled thereto, a copy of the order, with a translation if necessary, should be lodged with the other papers.

If the death is presumed to have occurred when a ship disappeared the following additional evidence should be given by an official of the shipping company:

(i) That the presumed deceased was aboard the ship when she left her last port.
(ii) When the ship was last seen from, or was in communication with, the shore or another ship.
(iii) Whether a certificate of the total loss of the ship has been issued by the Registrar-General of Shipping and Seamen or other competent authority.
(iv) Whether the insurers of the ship and cargo have met their liabilities on the basis of a total loss.

Similar details should be supplied, when appropriate, in the case of a lost aircraft.

An official record is now kept at the Principal Registry of disasters resulting in the death of two or more persons in such circumstances that a certificate of (presumed) death has to be submitted to the Senior Registrar (see p 142) or an order for leave to swear death is required. Before applying for a grant or order following the death of a person in such a disaster, inquiry should be made of the Secretary of the Principal Registry as to the nature of the evidence required in the light of any previous application.

The order, if made, is not given out but retained in the registry or, on request, sent to the registry at which application for the grant is to be made. The registrar may direct that any subsequent application for a grant should be supported by a guarantee by sureties (see head 11.1 and Forms 11.3.1 and 11.3.2), particularly where the person concerned has not been heard of for a number of years but there is little or no evidence to show that he might have died (and see pp 192–193).

7.2 Commorientes

Where two or more persons have died on or after 1 January 1926 and in the case of husband and wife before 1 January 1953 in circumstances rendering it uncertain which of them survived the other or others, such deaths are, subject to any order of the court, for all purposes affecting the title to property, presumed to have occurred in order of seniority, and the younger is deemed to have survived the elder (Law of Property Act 1925, s 184). The presumption applies where there is no evidence of survivorship and it is therefore not necessary to show that the deaths occurred consecutively although the order is not known (*Hickman* v *Peacey* [1945] AC 304). The right to obtain a grant in respect of a commoriens is determined according to the usual rules. On an application for a grant in such circumstances, the following wording should be inserted in the oath: 'That all possible inquiries as to survivorship have been made, but it appears that the said deceased and the said   died in circumstances rendering it uncertain which of them survived the other'. The oath should then set out the circumstances under which the deceased and the other person or persons died, the fact that s 184 of the Law of Property Act 1925 is being relied upon to establish the title of the applicant and the manner in which such title arises by reason of the presumption. The presumption does not apply in respect of the estate of a deceased person who had made specific provision in his will for his dying in such circumstances. Where the deceased persons died domiciled outside England and Wales the question of succession and whether a presumption as to the order of their deaths arises depends on the law of their domicile.

In the case of a husband and wife dying on or after 1 January 1953 in the circumstances described it is specifically provided by the Intestates' Estates Act 1952 that the presumption shall not apply in respect of the spouse dying intestate who would otherwise be deemed to have died first, and that his estate shall devolve as if his spouse had predeceased him. On an application for a grant in such circumstances, the oath must contain the wording set out in the previous paragraph and must also state the circumstances under which the deaths occurred; it is unnecessary to refer to the relevant sections of the Acts.

If there is uncertainty as to survivorship, the matter should be referred to the registrar at the earliest opportunity with such evidence as is readily available, for a decision as to whether further inquiries should be made. If possible, there should be an affidavit by the person who found the bodies or an affidavit or statement by the doctor who was called in or both, as the circumstances warrant; a copy of the notes of evidence made at the coroner's inquest may assist the registrar if they are available but the application to the registrar for directions should not be delayed merely to obtain the notes of evidence. (See also p 143 as to the official record now kept at the Principal Registry of disasters resulting in the death, or presumed death, of two or more persons. It may often be possible for the registry to indicate what evidence, if any, as to the survivorship will be required in such cases.) It is helpful if on the application to the registrar details are provided as to the amount of the respective estates and the possible beneficiaries.

No presumption operates in respect of persons dying at the same time before 1 January 1926 in circumstances such that it is uncertain which survived the other, and the estates of such persons usually devolve upon their respective next of kin as on an intestacy subject to the rights of the heir at law.

Chapter 8

Renunciation by Person Entitled

8.1 Renunciations

By executing a formal instrument of renunciation a person abandons any right he may have to a grant of representation. The instrument must be unqualified in its terms. The renunciation of probate by an executor does not operate as a renunciation of any right he may have to a grant of administration (Probate Rule 35 (1)). Thus, an executor who is also a residuary legatee and devisee and who does not wish to take a grant in any capacity must renounce not only his right to probate of the will but also his right to a grant of letters of administration with will annexed before a person with an inferior title can take a grant. A renunciation of administration should be made in the highest capacity in which the renunciant is entitled to the grant. It then acts, subject to a direction to the contrary by a registrar of the Principal Registry, or a district probate registrar if the grant is to be obtained at a district probate registry, as a renunciation of any further right he may have in a lower capacity (Probate Rule 35 (2)); so that where a person entitled to share in the estate of an intestate renounces his right to a grant, he will not be able to obtain a grant as a creditor.

A renunciation operates from the day on which it is made, but it does not become final until the moment the grant passes the seal. It is usual to file the instrument with the papers to lead to the issue of a grant to some other person. An executor, or a residuary legatee and devisee if there is no executor appointed, may renounce his right to prove the will before application is made for a grant; in that case the instrument should be filed in the registry together with the original will, an inclusive fee of £1 being payable for depositing the will. Moreover, an executor to whom power has been reserved may renounce at any time after the grant of probate has issued to the other executor or executors; no fee is payable for noting the record of the grant. A further renunciation will not be required should it become necessary at a later date to obtain a second or subsequent grant. Unnecessary renunciations should never be filed. If lodged, they will be given out. If on receipt of a renunciation and original will it is found that a grant has already issued in respect of the estate of the deceased, consideration will be given to notification being given to the previous grantee and to beneficiaries under the will, as well as to revocation of the grant.

There are important differences between the renunciation of an executor and of a person entitled to a grant of administration:

(*a*) An executor should not renounce if he has intermeddled in the estate (see also pp 242, 246), and the instrument of renunciation must recite the fact that he had not intermeddled; but it has been doubted whether trivial acts of intermeddling will preclude an executor from renouncing (*Holder* v *Holder* [1968] Ch 353). This principle does not apply to a person entitled to a grant of administration, and he may renounce his right notwithstanding that he has intermeddled in the estate of the deceased.

(*b*) An executor by representation cannot renounce his duties as an executor of a testator in the chain (*In the Goods of Perry* (1840) 2 Curt 655; *Brooke* v *Haymes* (1868) LR 6 Eq 25).

(*c*) A minor executor's right to probate cannot be renounced by any person on his behalf, but a minor entitled to a grant of letters of administration may renounce his right to the grant through a guardian assigned to him by order and specially authorised to renounce. (As to minors, see head 9.1.)

A renunciation on behalf of a person suffering from mental disorder will be accepted only if it has been made by the person authorised (if any) by the Court of Protection. A person resident out of England and Wales may renounce his right to a grant by an attorney expressly appointed for that purpose. The personal representative of a person who, not being an executor, is entitled to a grant and who survives the deceased but then dies, is not bound by the renunciation of that person and may take a grant despite it. A personal representative may himself renounce his right to a grant to which he is entitled in his representative capacity but this is not effective to allow another person to take a grant in a lower capacity unless the renunciant is the sole personal representative or unless the other personal representatives have also been cleared off by renunciation or citation.

8.2 The form of renunciation

The appropriate forms of renunciation must be used (see Forms 8.2.1–8.2.3, below). Any number of persons having equal rights may renounce by the same instrument, but each signature must be witnessed by a disinterested person. The document need not be under seal, but if it is it must bear the stamp duty of 50p. This does not apply to the renunciation of a corporation, for the sealing is equivalent to signature by an individual. It must be dated.

A renunciation written in a foreign language must be accompanied by a properly authenticated translation. If it is written in English but was given in a non-English speaking country, it will not be accepted unless it was witnessed by a notary or British consul or it is apparent that the renunciant understood English; the solicitor may certify as to this fact.

(For renunciations by corporations, see pp 202, 204.)

Form 8.2.1 Renunciation of probate

(For heading and title, see Form 2.11)

1 Whereas *AB*, of , deceased, died on the day of , 19 , having made and duly executed his last Will and Testament bearing date the day of , 19 , and in the said Will appointed the sole executor thereof

2 Now I the said do hereby declare that I have not intermeddled in the estate of the said deceased and will not hereafter intermeddle therein with intent to defraud creditors

3 and I hereby renounce all my right and title to the probate and execution of the said Will

4 Signed by the said
this day of , 19 ,
in the presence of

1 If the appointment of the executor has been made in a codicil to the will, this paragraph should be altered so as to set out the correct position. Should several executors have been appointed, all the names should be given. If the renunciation is by an executor to whom power has been reserved, the fact of the issue of a grant of probate in which power has been reserved to him should be recited.

When the renunciant is also giving up his right to a grant of letters of administration with will annexed, the capacity in which he is entitled to such a grant should be set out, viz, by adding at the end of the paragraph 'and named the said as residuary legatee and devisee in trust' (see also note to para **3**, below).

2 If the name of the renunciant differs from the name by which he is called in the will an explanation should be given. Usually it will be sufficient to insert 'in the will called ' after the renunciant's name in this paragraph. A corresponding statement should appear in the oath of the applicant for the grant; if the discrepancy between the names is great, a further explanation may have to be given (see p 68 et seq). The renunciant does not have to make an affidavit to prove his identity.

3 When the renunciant is also renouncing his right to a grant in a lower capacity, the following should be added at the end of the paragraph: 'and to letters of administration with the said will annexed of the estate of the said deceased'.

4 The renunciation should be signed before a disinterested witness who should then add his signature, address and occupation or status.

Form 8.2.2 Renunciation of administration with will
(For heading and title, see Form 2.11)

1 Whereas *AB*, of , deceased, died on the day of , 19 , having made and duly executed his last Will and Testament bearing date the day of , 19 , and in the said Will appointed *DE* the sole executor thereof, who predeceased the said deceased,
2 and named his wife *CB* as residuary legatee and devisee.
3 Now I the said *CB* do hereby renounce all my right and title to letters of administration with the said Will annexed of the estate of the said deceased.
4 Signed by the said
this day of , 19 ,
in the presence of

1 This paragraph should set out the names of all the persons who have a right to a grant in respect of the deceased's estate prior to that of the renunciant and the manner in which they have been cleared off If no executor was appointed, this should be stated, viz, 'and did not thereof appoint any executor'.

2 The name and the title to the grant of the renunciant should be stated. It is no longer necessary to state the relationship, if any, of the renunciant to the testator unless this must be done to establish title or identification. Thus, if the relationship given in the will is erroneous, a short explanation should be given, viz, 'in the will erroneously described as the of the deceased' and a corresponding explanation given in the oath of the applicant for the grant (see the note to para 2 of Form 8.2.1, above, and the note to para 8 of Form 4.4, at pp 101–102).

3 If the renunciant is also an executor, Form 8.2.1 should be used. When the renunciation is being given to enable a spes grant to issue (see head 8.4), the following should be added at the end of the paragraph: 'and consent to letters of administration with the said Will annexed being granted to the person or persons entitled to my estate were I now dead intestate'; the persons entitled should not be expressly named but the oath must show the relationship of the applicant for the grant to the person renouncing and, if appropriate, clear off persons with a higher degree of relationship (see pp 101, 130).

4 See the note to para 4 of Form 8.2.1, above.

Form 8.2.3 Renunciation of administration
(For heading and title, see Form 2.11)

1 Whereas *AB*, of , deceased, died on the day of , 19 , intestate leaving *CB* his lawful widow and relict and the only person now entitled to his estate.
2 Now I the said *CB* do hereby renounce all my right and title to letters of administration of the estate of the said deceased.
3 Signed by the said
this day of , 19 ,
in the presence of

1 This paragraph should indicate how the renunciant is entitled to a grant to the deceased's estate by giving the usual clearing on an intestacy (see the note to para **4** of Form 5.4, at pp 130–133), followed by the relationship of the renunciant to the deceased and the capacity by which he derives title to a grant (see the note to para **7** of Form 5.4, at p 133).

2 When the renunciation is being given to enable a spes grant to issue (see below), the following should be added at the end of the paragraph: 'and consent to letters of administration being granted to the person or persons entitled to my estate were I now dead intestate'; the persons entitled should not be expressly named but the oath must show the relationship of the applicant for the grant to the person renouncing and, if appropriate, clear off persons with a higher degree of relationship (see p 131).

3 See the note to para **4** of Form 8.2.1, at p 148.

8.3 Retractation

In special circumstances a renunciant will be allowed to retract his renunciation; an ex parte application (see head 20.1) supported by an affidavit as to the facts must be made to a registrar of the Principal Registry or to the district registrar of the registry in which the renunciation was filed for his order (Probate Rule 35 (4)). Only in exceptional circumstances will leave be given to an executor to retract his renunciation of probate after a grant has issued to some other person entitled in a lower degree.

8.4 Spes successionis

Where a will leaves the whole estate to one person and contains no other bequests or devises or where on an intestacy the beneficial interest in the whole of the deceased's estate devolves upon one person only, that person may request that the grant be made to the person or persons who would be entitled to his estate were he then dead intestate, in virtue of spes successionis (Probate Rule 27). A spes grant will not issue unless:

(*a*) the whole estate, both real and personal, vests finally and absolutely in one person (who, if he takes under a will, is described as 'the universal legatee and devisee');

(*b*) that person renounces his right to a grant and consents to it being made to the person or persons entitled to the renunciant's estate were he then dead intestate (see Forms 8.2.2 and 8.2.3);

(*c*) the applicant is a person who would be entitled to the renunciant's estate were he then dead intestate. When there is more than one such person, it is not necessary that all should apply for the grant; instead one or more may apply.

When there is an intestacy, whether under a will or not, as to the whole of the estate, which thereupon passes to the surviving spouse, a spes grant will not be made to a child of that spouse if he is also a child of the deceased. Instead, such a child, on the renunciation of the surviving spouse, may take the grant as a 'person who may have a beneficial interest in the estate in the event of an accretion thereto'. A surviving spouse is unable to consent to a spes grant unless he is entitled to the whole of the estate of whatever amount.

It may be required that the applicant lodge a guarantee by sureties and that the sureties should justify (see head 11.1, and Forms 11.3.1 and 11.3.2), but the registrar has a discretion to dispense with this requirement.

Chapter 9

Incapacity of Person Entitled

Incapacity may arise from various causes. The following are the most common:

9.1 Minority (Probate Rules 31 and 32)

A minor now means a person who has not attained the age of eighteen years, the age of majority having been reduced from twenty-one years as from 1 January 1970 (s 1 of the Family Law Reform Act 1969). A grant may not issue to a minor but instead will usually be made to his guardian for the use and benefit of the minor. Such guardian may be the statutory guardian (see p 155), a testamentary guardian (see p 155), a guardian duly appointed by a court of competent jurisdiction (see p 156), both parents of the minor jointly (see p 156), a nominated guardian (see p 158), or an assigned guardian (see p 160). Subject to the direction of a registrar, a grant will issue to a person not under disability in preference to the guardian of a minor entitled in the same degree (Probate Rule 25 (3)).

(a) Minor executors

The appointment of a minor as an executor of a will does not vest in the minor the testator's estate, or any part of it, nor does it constitute him a personal representative for any purpose unless and until probate is granted to him in accordance with the Probate Rules (s 118 of the Supreme Court Act 1981). Where a minor is sole executor, a grant of letters of administration with will annexed will be made to his guardian, or to such other person as the court thinks fit, limited until the minor attains his majority (Probate Rule 31). If the minor has no interest in the residuary estate of the deceased, a grant for his use and benefit and until he attains the age of eighteen years will, unless a registrar of the Principal Registry, or the district probate registrar of the registry in which application for the grant is to be made, directs otherwise, be made to the person entitled to the residuary estate. The grant will usually be made to a single individual only if no life interest or beneficial minority interest arises but in exceptional circumstances leave may be given for the grant to issue to a single individual when there is a life interest or a beneficial minority interest (see head 6.2).

If one of several executors is a minor, probate may be granted to the other executor or executors not under disability, and power will be reserved to the minor executor to prove the will when he attains the age of eighteen years. He may then take a grant of double probate (see head 3.4) or renounce his executorship. If the executors who are not under disability are cleared off by renunciation or citation, the position is the same as when a minor is the sole executor (see above).

A minor executor cannot renounce the right he will have to probate on attaining his majority through any person acting on his behalf.

(b) Minors beneficially interested in the estate

If a minor, not being an executor having no beneficial interest in the residuary estate of the deceased, is the sole or sole surviving person entitled to a grant, or is the only person entitled of his class who can take a grant, the grant of administration to his guardian or guardians will be expressed to be for the use and benefit of the minor and until he shall attain the age of eighteen years unless otherwise directed. As a minority interest arises in these circumstances, usually at least two persons (or a trust corporation: see p 197) must take the grant (see head 6.2). When the minor comes of age the grant ceases, and if there is estate still remaining to be administered a direct grant may be made to him (see head 13.1). If there are several persons entitled to a grant, all of whom are minors, the grant to their guardians will be limited for their use and benefit and until one of them attains the age of eighteen years. On the happening of that event any further grant required may be made to the person who has come of age and to the guardian of those who are still in their minority; in such a case, the subsequent grant will not be limited.

When there are several branches of a family all the members of which are incapable through minority, the grantees should represent each branch so far as it is practicable. In such a case, guardians representing as many branches of the family as possible should join in taking the grant.

The right of a minor to a grant of administration may be renounced only through a person assigned as guardian to the minor by order of a registrar (see p 160) and authorised so to renounce.

Of the various types of guardian, statutory guardians, testamentary guardians, guardians appointed by the High Court or other competent court and both parents of the minor are of equal standing, and the oath to lead the grant must show whether or not any such guardians exist. Members of any one of these classes may not take a grant unless all the members of the other classes which may exist renounce their right to it. Similarly, when a class consists of more than one guardian, the grant will not be made to one of them without the consent of the others of the same class. In the absence of guardians of any of the above classes, recourse must be had to nomination or assignment.

When a nominated or assigned guardian is applying for a grant, the oath should state, if appropriate, '...that there is no statutory, testamentary or other lawfully appointed guardian...' and, if it is not otherwise apparent, clear off both parents. When a person has been nominated to act as co-administrator with a statutory or testamentary guardian or with a guardian appointed by the High Court, the oath must show that there are no other guardians of the same standing available, eg, '... that there is no testamentary or other lawfully appointed guardian...', or as the case may be.

When an application is made for a grant of administration to a guardian or to both parents for the use and benefit of a minor, it may be a requirement that the applicants supply a guarantee by sureties and that the sureties should justify (see head 11.1, and Forms 11.3.1 and 11.3.2), but the registrar has a discretion to dispense with this requirement. For the special form of wording to be used in the oath, see p 102.

(c) Nomination of co-administrator

If there is only one guardian willing and competent to take a grant, it will usually be necessary for some other person or persons to be joined with him, unless the circumstances are such that the registrar is prepared to allow the grant to be made to a single individual (see head 6.2). This may be effected by the guardian nominating some fit and proper person or persons, or a trust corporation, to act as co-administrator. The person or persons nominated need not be related to the infants, but should be intimate with the family or conversant with the deceased's affairs. The nomination, containing a statement as to the nominee's fitness, should be signed by the guardian in the presence of a disinterested witness and should accompany the papers to lead the grant (see Form 9.1.1, below).

Form 9.1.1 Nomination of co-administrator
(For heading and title, see Form 2.11)

1 Whereas *AB*, of , deceased, died on the day of , 19 , having made and duly executed his last Will and Testament bearing date the day of , 19 , whereof he did not appoint an executor and wherein he named his wife *CB* as residuary legatee and devisee for life and *DB* and *EB* his children as residuary legatees and devisees substituted.

2 And whereas the said *DB* and *EB* are both minors being of the age of years and years respectively.

3 And whereas there is no testamentary or other lawfully appointed guardian of the said minors but the said *CB* is the lawful surviving parent and the statutory guardian of the said minors.

4 Now I the said *CB* do hereby nominate *PR*, of , to be my co-administrator for the purpose of joining with me to obtain a grant of letters of administration with the said Will annexed of the estate of the said deceased.

And I hereby certify that the said *PR* is a fit and proper person to act in that capacity.

5 Signed by the said
this day of , 19 ,
in the presence of

1 Set out in this paragraph the circumstances by reason of which a nomination is required. In the case of an intestacy, substitute after the date of death: 'intestate leaving *CB* his lawful widow and relict and *DB* and *EB* his lawful children together the only persons entitled to share his estate' or as the case may be.

2 The names and ages of the minors must be stated.

3 Show here how the person making the nomination derives his right so to do; thus, if the guardian has himself been nominated, this paragraph should read:

> 'And whereas there is no statutory, testamentary or other lawfully appointed guardian of the said minor, and both his parents are dead, and *GH* the lawful uncle of the whole blood and next of kin of the said minor has been duly nominated by him as his guardian for the purpose of obtaining letters of administration (with will annexed) of the estate of the said deceased to be granted to him and to his co-administrator' or as the case may be.

4 Give the occupation or description of the nominee. If the deceased died intestate, omit the reference to a will. Two or more persons may be nominated.

5 See the note to para **4** of Form 8.2.1, at p 148.

(d) Statutory guardian

A statutory guardian is the surviving parent (either lawful or adoptive) of a minor (Guardianship of Minors Act 1971, s 3) and that fact must be deposed to in the oath to lead the grant. It therefore follows that there can be only one statutory guardian, and if there is no other guardian, he or she must nominate a co-administrator (see above). The mother of an unborn child is not its statutory guardian, although she may be assigned its guardian. On the death of the other parent, the mother of an illegitimate child does not become its statutory guardian; but the natural father of such a child may become its statutory guardian, provided he is entitled to its custody under an order made by virtue of s 9 of the Guardianship of Minors Act 1971, as extended by s 14 thereof. Where a child has been adopted by one person only, that person is not the statutory guardian, but may be nominated as guardian if the circumstances are appropriate (see below).

A registrar has discretion, upon good cause being shown by affidavit, to make an order passing over a statutory guardian. Such an application may be necessary when the statutory guardian is a person suffering from mental illness. The incapacity of the statutory guardian must be proved by the usual medical evidence (see p 161) on an application for an order of the court assigning a guardian or guardians (see p 160).

(e) Testamentary guardians

Either parent (whether lawful or adoptive) may appoint a guardian to children in their minority by deed or will (Guardianship of Minors Act 1971, s 4). A guardian so appointed is termed a testamentary guardian and must act with the surviving parent, or, if there is none, with any guardian similarly appointed by that other parent. The mother of an illegitimate child may appoint a guardian by her will (*Re A, S* v *A* (1940) 164 LT 230); so may the natural father in certain circumstances (Guardianship of Minors Act 1971, ss 9 and 14).

The appointment of the guardian is proved by production of the deed or probate of the will.

(f) Guardians appointed by the High Court

The High Court has the fullest power to appoint guardians to persons in their minority who are in need of protection (Guardianship of Minors Act 1971, s 5), and may even exercise such power in respect of children in Great Britain whose parents are abroad, whether they are possessed of property within the jurisdiction or not (*Re D* (*Infants*) [1943] Ch 305). This jurisdiction is now exercised by the Family Division, except where the sole question is the appointment of a guardian of a minor's estate, which is still dealt with by the Chancery Division (Administration of Justice Act 1970, s 1 and Sched 1); it may also be exercised by county courts and magistrates' courts.

The appointment of the guardian is proved by production of an office copy of the order. If the order has been made by a county court, a certificate of the order should be produced, and in the case of an order of a magistrates' court, the original should be produced and a copy lodged with the papers.

It has to be borne in mind that where a minor is a ward of court, important decisions relating to his person or to his property should not be taken without the concurrence of the judge or the registrar to whom the ward has been assigned. Therefore, when application has to be made for a grant for the use and benefit of a ward, including, if appropriate, the assignment of guardians for that purpose, the directions of the judge or registrar should be obtained. If the wardship proceedings are inactive, an informal reference through the probate registry may be sufficient.

(g) Both parents taking a joint grant

Where both parents of a minor are alive, a grant for the use and benefit of the minor may issue to them jointly, without the need for the minor to nominate them or for them to make a prior application to be assigned as guardians of the minor. Adoptive parents, having taken over all the rights, duties and liabilities of the natural parents, have a similar right to a joint grant.

(h) Guardians appointed under foreign law

A grant of representation in respect of the estate of a deceased who died domiciled in England and Wales will be made to the guardians of a minor who is domiciled in another country if it can be shown by an official document issued by the foreign court or by an affidavit of foreign law that they are the guardians entrusted with the care of the property of the minor. The domicile of the minor should be sworn to in the oath. If the deceased died domiciled elsewhere than in England and Wales, it must be shown that the guardians of the minor, determined in accordance with the law of the country of the minor's domicile, are in the circumstances the persons 'entitled' or 'entrusted' under the law of the country of the deceased's domicile (see head 15.2(*c*), (*d*)).

(i) Local authority

A homeless or delinquent child may be received into, or committed to, the care of a local authority. Where the local authority has by resolution taken over the rights and duties of the parents (under s 3 (1) of the Child Care Act 1980, replacing s 2 of the Children Act 1948) in respect of such child, or where the local authority has the care of a child under a 'care order' made under the Children and Young Persons Act 1969, a grant may issue to the nominees of the local authority for the child's use and benefit. There must first of all be an application by the local authority for a registrar's order assigning the authority itself as guardian of the child for the purpose of taking the grant. Provided that the oath contains all the necessary information it will not usually be necessary for a separate affidavit to be filed in support of the application for the order, and the documents in support of the application may be lodged with the documents to lead the subsequent grant at either the Principal Registry or a district probate registry. If the child in care is the sole beneficiary the local authority is for this purpose a custodian trustee (see pp 195–196) and takes the grant in its own name as a trust corporation. If, however, there are other beneficiaries who are not also in the care of the authority, the application for the grant must be made by nominees of the authority and the grant will issue to them for the use and benefit of the authority. In all cases, the grant also issues for the use and benefit of the child in care and is limited until he attains the age of eighteen years or until further representation is granted.

Where a separate affidavit is not to be filed in support of the application for the order assigning the authority as guardian, the oath should state in addition to the usual particulars:

(i) that a resolution has been passed by the local authority under s 3 (1) of the Child Care Act 1980 (replacing s 2 of the Children Act 1948) vesting all parental rights and powers over the child in that authority and that it is still in force; a copy of the resolution, authenticated by the certificate of the Town Clerk, Chief Executive Officer, Director of Administration or other appropriate officer of the local authority, must be lodged; alternatively

(ii) that a care order has been made under the Children and Young Persons Act 1969 and that it is still in force; a copy of the order should be lodged;

(iii) that the persons applying on behalf of the local authority have been authorised so to apply by a further resolution of the authority; a copy similarly authenticated must also be lodged;

(iv) in appropriate cases that the local authority is entitled to act as a custodian trustee under the Public Trustee Act 1906 and thereby as a trust corporation by virtue of s 128 of the Supreme Court Act 1981 and that it has power to take a grant;

(v) that the child in care is the sole beneficiary, or as the case may be setting out the names of the other beneficiaries and whether they are consenting to the application for a grant; any consents should be lodged with the other papers.

No guarantee is required. For the form of oath for a grant to a trust corporation see Form 14.1.1 and for a grant to a corporation which is not a trust corporation see Form 14.2.

Where a local authority is acting as a custodian trustee, namely where the child in care is the sole beneficiary, the authority is entitled to continue so to act after the child ceases to be in care and thus to continue to administer the estate until a further grant issues.

However where such a child is transferred into the care of another authority, it would seem that the grant expires on the transfer in as much as a new custodian trustee has been appointed (see p 196) whereupon the first local authority ceases to be a custodian trustee and thereby a trust corporation. A further grant must then be obtained by the new custodian trustee in order to continue the administration of the deceased's estate.

(j) Nominated guardians

If there is no statutory, testamentary or other lawfully appointed guardian or no such guardian willing and competent to act, and it is not possible for both parents to apply jointly for a grant, a minor who has attained the age of sixteen years may nominate a guardian provided that guardian is his or her next of kin; alternatively, a female minor may nominate her husband (see Form 9.1.2, below). If only one guardian is nominated, a second administrator will usually have to be nominated by him (see p 154). If the spouse of a female minor is also a minor, the next of kin should be nominated. If the spouse is capable of acting and there is also a statutory guardian, the spouse should be nominated to act with the statutory guardian; otherwise the statutory guardian will be preferred. When there is objection to the nomination of any of this class, an application must be made to a registrar for an order assigning some other person as guardian. If the next of kin are incapable of acting as guardians, application may be made for the next nearest of kin to be assigned as guardians.

It would appear that by reason of the status conferred on adopted persons by the Children Act 1975 (to be repealed and continued in due course by the Adoption Act 1976) (see p 120), relationship by adoption is now sufficient to constitute all persons sufficiently related 'next of kin' so as to enable them to be nominated as a guardian, without the need to apply for them to be assigned by registrar's order.

Remote relations and strangers in blood may not be nominated by a minor as guardians but may be assigned (see p 160). When it is desired that a trust corporation should take a grant, it is usually preferable that it should take the grant in its own right (see pp 197–198) without an order assigning it as guardian.

All the minors who have attained the age of sixteen years must join in the nomination of guardians. When any of such minors refuse or are unable to join in the nomination, the opinion of a registrar should be taken, and he may require the facts to be set out in an affidavit. If in these circumstances nomination by some of the minors is allowed, they will nominate guardians for all the minors, and the grant will issue for the use of them all. A nominated guardian may also act for other minors who are below the age of sixteen years, provided that he is also the next of kin of such minors; otherwise it may be necessary to apply for a guardian to be assigned to the other minors.

A nomination of guardians by minors is not binding on the court and may be set aside when good cause is shown.

The instrument of nomination in the prescribed form (see below) must be lodged with the papers to lead the grant.

Form 9.1.2 Nomination of guardian by minor
(For heading and title, see Form 2.11)

1 Whereas *AB*, of , deceased, died on the day of , 19 , having made and duly executed his last Will and Testament bearing date the day of , 19 , whereof he did not appoint an executor and wherein he named *EB* and *FB* as residuary legatees and devisees .

2 And whereas the said *FB* is now a minor of the age of seventeen years.

3 Now I the said *FB* do hereby nominate *EB* my lawful brother of the whole blood and my only next of kin to be my guardian for the purpose of obtaining letters of administration with the said Will annexed of the estate of the said deceased to be granted to him and to his co-administrator.

4 Signed by the said
this day of , 19 ,
in the presence of

1 Set out in this paragraph the circumstances by reason of which the minor is entitled to a grant, clearing off the persons with a prior right and detailing the persons if any with equal right. In the case of an intestacy, substitute after the date of death 'intestate a widower leaving *EB* and *FB* his lawful children and the only persons entitled to share his estate' or as the case may be.

2 Insert the name and age of the person making the nomination together with the names and ages of any other minors under the age of sixteen years for whom the nominee may act as guardian (see above).

3 The minor may nominate only his next of kin. In the example given, there is only one next of kin, who must in turn nominate another person to join with him in taking a grant (see Form 9.1.1). If two or more persons are nominated, the words 'him and his co-administrator' should be replaced by 'them'.

In the example given, the nominee has a right to a full grant, and there is no limitation; where none of the applicants has a right to a full grant, add at the end of the paragraph, 'for my use and benefit and until I shall attain the age of eighteen years'. When there is another minor who by reason of his age is unable to join in the nomination, the limitation should read 'for my use and benefit and for the use and benefit of the said and until one of us shall attain the age of eighteen years'.

When the nominee is required to join in taking a grant with a person entitled to a full grant, this paragraph should read '...for the purpose of joining with the said in obtaining letters of administration (with the said Will annexed) of the estate of the said deceased'.

4 See the note to para **4** of Form 8.2.1 at p 148.

(k) Assigned guardians

The assignment of a guardian to a minor is made by order of a registrar of the Principal Registry or, if the application for a grant is to be made in a district probate registry, any district probate registrar. The application is made ex parte (in the Principal Registry to the Principal of the Probate Department) (see head 20.1) by lodging an affidavit as to the facts by the proposed guardian and, if the registrar so requires, an affidavit as to the fitness of the proposed guardian made by some responsible person. The affidavit in support should contain information as to the age of the minor, where he is now living, who is looking after and maintaining him and what arrangements are to be made in future for his care and maintenance, and as to the amount of the estate; it should also state whether or not the minor has been the subject of wardship proceedings (see p 156). If application is made for the appointment of only one guardian, the nomination of the proposed co-administrator and his consent to act must be referred to in the affidavit of facts. In selecting persons to be assigned as guardians to minors, preference is given to the next of kin; if the proposed guardians are not the next of kin, it should be explained in the affidavit in support why they are to be passed over, and any consents or renunciations by them should be lodged with the papers. It must be shown whether or not there are statutory, testamentary or other guardians, or both parents are alive. A guardian may be assigned to a minor notwithstanding that there are statutory, testamentary or other guardians, or that both parents are alive, but notice of the application for the registrar's order may have to be given to such persons.

(See also Trust corporation as guardian, at p 198.)

(l) Concurrent administration

When the guardians of a minor or minors, having obtained a grant for the latter's use and benefit, become entitled to a further grant in respect of the estate of some other deceased by virtue of their representative capacity, there is no need for them to be re-appointed guardians for that purpose. It is only necessary to produce the first grant to prove their title. The second grant will be limited in the same way as the first.

9.2 Mental incapacity (Probate Rule 33)

When a person entitled to a grant is by reason of mental disorder incapable of managing his affairs, a grant may be made for his use and benefit and will usually be expressed to be limited during his incapacity.

Unless otherwise directed by a registrar, all other persons having an equal right with him must first be cleared off. Mental incapacity for this purpose may range from the extreme cases of mental illness down to the milder cases of senility or incapacity to manage ordinary affairs.

(a) Proof of mental incapacity

Incapacity must be proved by medical evidence unless the Court of Protection has authorised the applicant to apply for a grant under Pt VIII of the Mental Health Act 1959. Where the incapable person is resident in a hospital or other institution, a certificate will usually be accepted from the responsible medical officer if it is in the following terms: 'I certify that— 1 The above-named patient, who is now resident in this institution, is in my opinion by reason of mental disorder incapable of managing and administering his property and affairs. 2 In my opinion, the above-named patient is unlikely to be fit to manage and administer his property and affairs within a period of three months. (Signed) Responsible Medical Officer.' The certificate should bear the name of the institution and of the patient, and should be dated. The registrar should be asked for his directions if such a certificate cannot be obtained. In other cases, evidence of incapacity should be tendered in the form of a certificate by the doctor of the person who is incapable certifying the period during which he has attended the patient in respect of the disability and that, in his opinion, the patient is incapable of managing and administering his property and affairs and is unlikely to become capable within a period of three months. In the absence of such a certificate the registrar's directions should be obtained.

Notice of intended application for a grant must be given at the earliest possible time to the Court of Protection (at 25 Store Street, London WC1E 7BP), except where the person incapable is an executor with no beneficial interest in the estate, and the acknowledgment by that department of such notice should be filed with the papers to lead the grant. The applicant (including a person authorised by the Court of Protection) may be required to provide a guarantee by sureties (see head 11.1) and the latter may have to justify (see Forms 11.3.1 and 11.3.2), although the registrar has a discretion to dispense with this requirement in any particular case. A person authorised by the Court of Protection should lodge a copy of the order under seal with the papers to lead to the grant. For the special form of wording used in the oath, see p 102.

(b) Probate

When one of several executors is suffering from mental illness, probate will be granted to the competent executors, power being reserved to the person who is mentally ill to prove the will when he regains his mental capacity. On the occurrence of that event he may obtain a grant of double probate (see head 3.4).

When a sole or sole surviving executor is suffering from mental illness, a grant of letters of administration with will annexed may be made to the person authorised by the Court of Protection to apply for the grant, for his use and benefit and until he regains his mental capacity. If there is no person so authorised and the executor has no interest in the residuary estate of the deceased, the grant may be made for the executor's use and benefit to the residuary legatee and devisee named in the will, or, if the residuary estate is not disposed of, to the person entitled to the residuary estate as on an intestacy. If the executor has an interest in the residuary estate, the grant may be made to the person who would be entitled to a grant in his estate if he were then dead intestate. However, if the will has provided for an executor to be substituted by another (see p 75) if the first-named is unable or unwilling to act, and he is suffering from mental illness, a grant of probate will issue to the substituted executor, the mental incapacity being proved in the usual way (see head 9.2(*a*)).

(c) Administration

When the person entitled to a grant, not being an executor, is suffering from mental illness, a grant for his use and benefit and until he regains his mental capacity will be made, in the first place, to the person authorised by the Court of Protection to apply for the grant. If there is no person so authorised, the grant will usually be made to the person or persons who would be entitled to a grant in his estate if he were then dead intestate. Any other person who wishes to obtain the grant may apply ex parte (see head 20.1) to a registrar of the Principal Registry, or to any district probate registrar if the application for the grant is to be made in a district probate registry, for an order for such a grant to issue; the application should be supported by an affidavit as to the facts and the renunciations, if any, of persons with a prior right. Where the surviving spouse of an intestate is suffering from mental illness and the next of kin take a vested interest in the estate because it exceeds the amount of the spouse's statutory legacy (see p 113) after making the permitted deductions, any grant made to the next of kin will be for the use and benefit of the spouse and limited during his or her incapacity.

Where application for a grant is to be made by the person authorised to apply by the Court of Protection, and two grantees would usually be necessary by reason of a life or minority interest (see head 6.2), the co-grantee should be the next person entitled to be joined. A registrar's order for a joint grant (see head 6.1) will be necessary if it is sought to join any other person. The person authorised by the Court of Protection has no power to nominate a co-administrator.

(d) Mental disorder supervening after the issue of a grant

If a grantee becomes mentally ill after the issue of the grant, the procedure is dependent upon whether he is the sole or one of several grantees.

Where a sole or sole surviving grantee becomes mentally ill a new grant may be made without revocation of the existing grant, which must, however, be impounded unless the subsequent grant is to be made to the person authorised by the Court of Protection, in which case the original grant remains at large. Impounding is effected by an order. The original grant, together with an affidavit of the facts that call for impounding and medical evidence of the incapacity (see head 9.2(*a*)), must be filed in the registry from which the grant issued. An order will then be made by the registrar and the grant retained in the registry until the grantee regains his mental capacity, when it will be handed out on the limited grant being brought into the registry, together with medical evidence of capacity and the consent of the second grantee, or proof that notice has been given to him; the limited grant is noted with the fact that it has ceased and is also handed out. No fee is charged either for impounding a grant or for releasing it after impounding. If the original grant cannot be produced, the applicant may be required to give an undertaking to bring it into the registry should it be discovered later. The affidavit in support of the application for impounding may also serve as the oath to lead a new grant. Any subsequent grant which may issue will be of the nature of de bonis non, and the practice relating to such grants (see head 13.2), with the necessary adaptations, must be followed; an Inland Revenue account is required (see p 231). Such a grant will be made to any other person equally entitled to take it. If there is none, it will be made to the person authorised by the Court of Protection, or, if none, to the person who would have been entitled to it had the grantee been suffering from mental illness at the date of application for the first grant (see above). A grant to an executor to whom power has been reserved will be one of double probate (see head 3.4) with a note showing that the earlier grant has been impounded. A grant of administration will be for the use and benefit of the incapable grantee, limited during his incapacity.

When one of several grantees has become mentally ill, the grant must be revoked (see head 16.2). A further grant may then be made to the persons entitled thereto. If the applicants have a right equal to that of the incapable grantee (whether or not they are original grantees) the grant will be general in its terms, but if any of them has an inferior title, the grant will be for the use and benefit of the incapable grantee and limited during his incapacity. If the original grant was one of probate and it is proposed that the capable executors should apply for a new grant, the affidavit to lead the order for revocation may also serve as the oath to lead the new grant; the will may there be referred to as that which has already been proved and need not be marked, nor need a copy be annexed; also, in these circumstances it is not necessary to lodge a fresh Inland Revenue account and the values of the estate to be quoted in the affidavit should be those appearing in the original grant.

9.3 Physical incapacity (Probate Rule 33)

Where an application is to be made for a grant for the use and benefit of a person entitled who is incapable of managing his own affairs by reason of physical incapacity, the same considerations and procedure apply as if he were suffering from mental incapacity (see above), except that notice of the intended application does not have to be given to the Court of Protection nor can there be a person authorised by the Court of Protection to apply for a grant. The incapacity must be severe and strictly proved to the satisfaction of a registrar, to whom reference should be made. Unless the person alleged to be incapable consents to the application, notice thereof must be given to him unless the registrar is prepared to dispense with this requirement. The applicant may be required to provide a guarantee by sureties (see head 11.1) and the sureties to justify (see Forms 11.3.1, 11.3.2) but the registrar has a discretion to dispense with these requirements.

Where the incapacity is not so severe as to justify recourse to this procedure, it may be possible to apply for a direction that the grant issue to an attorney of the incapable person although the latter resides in England (see head 10.7).

Chapter 10

Attorney Grants

If the person entitled to a grant resides out of England and Wales, he may swear the papers to lead to a direct grant being made to him in the country where he resides, or, alternatively, he may appoint an attorney or attorneys to act on his behalf (Probate Rule 30 (1)). The latter is the more common and convenient course.

The attorney need not be resident in England and Wales; it is no longer a bar to an application by an attorney that he resides in the same country as the donor of the power.

When an application is made for a grant of administration to an attorney it may be required that the applicant should supply a guarantee by sureties and that the sureties should justify (see head 11.1, and Forms 11.3.1 and 11.3.2), but the registrar has a discretion to dispense with this requirement.

10.1 Attorney of executors

Where the person applying for a grant through his attorney is an executor, notice of the intended application must be given to any other executors, unless the registrar dispenses with the giving of such notice.

When all the executors reside out of England and Wales and application for a grant is made by the attorney or attorneys of them all, the grant will be limited for the use of them all, and until all of them apply for and obtain probate of the will (provided usually that there are not more than four of them; see pp 64, 81, 168). If the attorney of one of several executors applies, the grant will be limited for his use and benefit, and until he or all or any of the executors apply for and obtain probate of the will.

A grant to the attorney of an executor will be one of letters of administration with will annexed.

10.2 Attorney of administrators

A person entitled to a grant of administration may apply through his attorney without reference to any other persons equally entitled with him. The grant will be made to the attorney for the use and benefit of the donor of the power and will usually be limited until the donor shall obtain a grant in a direct capacity. If the donor's title is that of guardian of children in their minority, the grant to his attorneys will be further limited for the use and benefit of the minors and until one of them shall attain the age of eighteen years, whichever event shall first happen.

10.3 Number of attorneys

Two attorneys will usually have to be appointed when a life or minority interest arises under the will or intestacy (see head 6.2). This is so even when the donor of the power is an executor. Exceptionally, when only one attorney has been appointed and two grantees are required, application may be made to a registrar for an order giving leave for some other person having no title to the grant to be joined as co-administrator with the attorney (see head 6.1).

Where there are only two persons entitled to the grant and one of them resides out of England and Wales, a grant may be made to the person resident in England and Wales and the attorney of the other person entitled, but it will be limited until the donor of the power applies for a grant himself, and the person resident in England and Wales will be required expressly to consent to such limitation. If he refuses to consent the attorney of the person resident abroad may be joined only by order of a registrar (see head 6.1). The registrar will require the consent of the donor of the power to the issue of an unlimited grant to his attorney which may exclude him from taking a direct grant during the lives of the grantees.

10.4 The instrument of attorney

Generally the instrument should specifically authorise the attorney to take out a grant, and it must set out the full name, address and date of death of the deceased (see Form 10.4, below). However, a general power of attorney giving the donee various wide and detailed powers will be accepted, as will also the short form of general power of attorney contained in Sched 1 to the Powers of Attorney Act 1971, and which appoints the donee to be the attorney in accordance with s 10 of the Act. A formal document should be executed though there is discretion in the registrar to accept an informal one. A power of attorney may be executed in anticipation of departure from England and Wales, but it does not become effective until the donor is out of the country. The oath must state in all cases that the donor of the power is 'now resident in ' (*or* 'on the high seas').

The instrument of attorney should be signed by the donor in the presence of a disinterested witness; alternatively, it may be signed and sealed by another person by direction, and in the presence of the donor, in which case there must be two witnesses to the execution who must attest the instrument (Powers of Attorney Act 1971, s 1). It should be under seal, although the court has a discretion to accept a power not under seal (*In the*

Goods of Elderton (1832) 4 Hag Ecc 210; see also *In the Goods of Boyle* (1864) 3 Sw & Tr 426). If it consists simply of a power to extract a grant of representation, no stamp duty is payable; otherwise it must bear a duty stamp of 50p. (As to proof of instruments creating powers of attorney, see s 3 of the Powers of Attorney Act 1971.)

Powers of attorney written in a foreign language must be accompanied by a translation certified by a competent authority. A power written in English, although given in a non-English-speaking country, will be accepted if witnessed by a notary or a British consul or if there is sufficient information that the donor understood English; the solicitor will be allowed to certify as to this latter fact. Doubtful cases should be referred to a registrar.

A general power of attorney which may be required for other purposes will be handed out with the grant at the solicitor's request in return for a copy, or the copy may be lodged with the papers to lead the grant. No fee is payable for examination of the copy with the original.

Form 10.4 Power of attorney

(For heading and title, see Form 2.11)

1 Whereas *AB*, of , deceased, died on the day of , 19 , having made and duly executed his last Will and Testament bearing date the day of , 19 , and in the said Will appointed *CB* the sole executrix thereof.

2

3 Now I the said *CB* at present residing at

4 do hereby nominate, constitute and appoint *ST*, of

5 to be my lawful attorney for the purpose of obtaining letters of administration with the said Will annexed of the estate of the said deceased to be granted to him for my use and benefit, and until I shall duly apply for and obtain probate of the said Will to be granted to me and I hereby promise to ratify and confirm whatever my said Attorney shall lawfully do or cause to be done in the premises.

6 In Witness whereof I have hereunto set my hand and seal this day of , 19 .

Signed, sealed and delivered by the said *CB* in the presence of } LS

1 Set out in this paragraph the circumstances by reason of which the donor of the power is entitled to a grant, clearing off the persons with a prior right or, if the donor is an executor, detailing the other executors, if any.

In the case of an intestacy, substitute after the date of death: 'intestate leaving *CB* his lawful widow and relict and the only person now entitled to his estate', or as the case may be.

If the deceased died domiciled out of England and Wales his domicile should be stated here.

2 When a grant in respect of the estate of a deceased person who died domiciled out of England and Wales has already issued in another country and the grantee is giving the power to enable a further grant to be obtained in England and Wales, or the foreign grant to be resealed, this should be recited here, eg, 'And whereas a grant of probate of the said Will (*or* of letters of administration of the estate of the said deceased) issued out of the Court at on the day of , 19 , to the said *CB*'. If the donor is the 'person entitled' (see head 15.2(*d*)) by the law of the deceased's domicile at the date of death, this should be shown here, eg, 'And whereas the said *CB* is the only person entitled to administer the estate of the said deceased by the law of the place where he died domiciled'.

3 It must be stated where the donor of the power is residing. Generally an attorney grant will not issue when the donor is resident in England and Wales but the registrar has a discretion to direct a grant to issue to the attorney of a person so resident in special circumstances (see head 10.7).

4 Insert the address and occupation, or description, of the attorney (see note to para **1**, Form 3.2, at pp 69–70).

5 In the case of an intestacy, omit the words 'with the said Will annexed'. Similarly, 'probate of the said Will' should be replaced by 'letters of administration with the said Will annexed of the estate of the said deceased' or 'letters of administration of the estate of the said deceased' as the circumstances warrant.

For the form of limitation where there are several executors, see under Attorney of executors, head 10.1, and where the donor is the guardian of minors, see under Attorney of administrators, head 10.2. Any other corresponding limitation should be set out in this paragraph.

If the deceased died domiciled out of England and Wales, substitute 'until further representation be granted' for 'until I shall ... to be granted to me'. When the power has been given by more than four persons, it should contain the limitation '...until any of us, not exceeding four in number, shall apply ...' (but see p 64).

If the power is to be given for the purpose of resealing a colonial grant, this paragraph should read '... for the purpose of applying to the High Court of Justice in England to have the said grant of probate (*or* administration) resealed in England under the provisions of the Colonial Probates Acts 1892 and 1927 ...'.

6 The power should be signed before a disinterested witness who should then add his signature, address and occupation or description. If the power is signed by another person on behalf of the donor (see p 166), substitute 'Signed, sealed and delivered by *ST* by direction, and in the presence, of the said *CB*, all in the presence of '; there must be two witnesses. It should normally be under seal (see p 166).

10.5 Application by attorney administrator

On an application by an attorney administrator for a grant in respect of another deceased in his capacity as legal personal representative of a person entitled, it is unnecessary for him to produce the original power or a copy thereof.

10.6 Death of donor of power or of his attorney

A grant made to an attorney comes to an end with the death of the donor of the power. The subsequent grant will be of the nature de bonis non (see head 13.2). On the death of the attorney the grant ceases to be operative. The subsequent grant is a cessate grant (see head 13.1) to be made to the donor of the power in a direct capacity, or to any other attorney appointed by him.

10.7 Attorney of a person resident in England

In special circumstances a grant may issue to the attorney of a person who is entitled to a grant of administration with or without will annexed (*not* probate) and who is resident in England and Wales (Probate Rule 30 (2)). For instance, when the person who would normally make application for the grant and thereafter administer the estate is unable to do so by reason of age or infirmity, not amounting to mental or physical incapacity (see heads 9.2, 9.3), and there is no other way of obtaining a grant without causing the estate unnecessary expense, application supported by an affidavit of facts may be made ex parte (see head 20.1) to a registrar (in the Principal Registry to the Principal of the Probate Department) for his direction that an attorney grant should issue. The grant will be limited until the donor of the power obtains a grant himself or in such other way as the registrar directs. The application should generally be made before the papers to lead the grant are prepared.

10.8 Foreign law

See pp 210, 214.

10.9 Grant to consular officer

If the person entitled is a national of a foreign State with which a Convention, applied by Order in Council, has been concluded under the Consular Conventions Act 1949 and he has not appointed an attorney, application for a grant may be made by the consular officer of the foreign State. The grant will issue to the consul and his successors in office for the use and benefit of the national and will be limited until further representation be granted. Application may also be made to the consular officer on behalf of a foreign charitable or other organisation. Conventions have to date been concluded with Norway, Sweden, France, Greece, Mexico, Federal Republic of Germany, Italy, Denmark, Spain, Austria, Belgium, Japan, Yugoslavia, USSR, Bulgaria, Poland, Hungary, Mongolia and Czechoslovakia.

Chapter 11

Guarantees

Since 1 January 1972 it has not been necessary on an application for a grant of administration, whether with will annexed or based on an intestacy, to give a bond for the due administration of the estate. Instead, as from that date the court may require as a condition of granting administration to any person that one or more sureties should guarantee that they will make good, within prescribed limits, any loss which any person interested in the administration of the deceased's estate may suffer in consequence of a breach by the administrator of his duties as such (s 120 (1) of the Supreme Court Act 1981).

11.1 When guarantee may be required

By virtue of Probate Rule 38 (1), a guarantee will not be required as a condition of granting administration except where the grant is to issue:

(i) to a creditor or the personal representative of a creditor, or to a person who has no immediate beneficial interest in the estate but who may have such an interest in the event of an accretion thereto;

(ii) to the applicant for a spes grant (see head 8.4);

(iii) to the attorney of a person entitled to a grant (see p 165);

(iv) for the use and benefit of a minor (see p 154);

(v) for the use and benefit of a person who is by reason of mental or physical incapacity incapable of managing his affairs (see pp 161, 164);

(vi) to a person who appears to the registrar to be resident elsewhere than in the United Kingdom.

Additionally the registrar may require a guarantee in other cases where he considers that there are special circumstances which make it desirable to do so, for instance when there is a special risk to beneficiaries or to other persons who might have an interest in the estate. Whenever the registrar considers that a guarantee would be necessary, he must cause notice to be given to the applicant, or to his solicitor, to give him the opportunity of being heard with respect to the requirement (Probate Rule 5 (4)).

Where the grant is to issue in the circumstances listed in (i) to (vi) above, and none of the applicants belongs to any of the classes of person excepted from the requirement to give a guarantee (see below), it is advisable so as to avoid delay either to lodge a guarantee with the papers to lead the grant in anticipation that this will be called for, or to make a pre-lodgment inquiry as to whether a guarantee will be called for to the registrar (in the Principal Registry to the Principal of the Probate Department). If, when the papers to lead the grant are lodged, neither of these courses has been adopted, or if in any case the special circumstances appear to call for it, the matter will be referred to the registrar and, where he considers that a guarantee ought to be provided, notice of this requirement will be sent to the solicitor. He must then file the guarantee or, if he considers this unnecessary, attend before the registrar to make representations to this effect. On the making of an order on an ex parte application the registrar will usually indicate whether or not he requires a guarantee.

11.2 Exceptions

A guarantee is never required when a grant of administration is to issue to the Treasury Solicitor, the Official Solicitor, the Public Trustee, the Solicitor for the affairs of the Duchy of Lancaster or the Duchy of Cornwall or the Crown Solicitor for Northern Ireland, or to the consular officer of a foreign State to which s 1 of the Consular Conventions Act 1949 applies (see head 10.9) (s 120 (5) of the Supreme Court Act 1981).

Probate Rule 38 (2) further provides that a guarantee is not to be required except in special circumstances where the applicant, or one of the applicants, is:

(*a*) a trust corporation;
(*b*) a solicitor holding a current practising certificate under the Solicitors Act 1974;
(*c*) a servant of the Crown acting in his official capacity;
(*d*) a nominee of a public department or of a local authority within the meaning of the Local Government Act 1972.

11.3 Form of guarantee

Every guarantee by a surety has to be in accordance with Form 1 in the Schedule to the Non-Contentious Probate Rules (see below).

Form 11.3.1 Surety's guarantee
(For heading and title, see Form 2.11)

1 Whereas of , died on the day of , 19 , and
2
and
(hereinafter called 'the administrator(s)') is/are the intended administrator(s) of his estate. Now therefore:
3 1 I/We of
and of hereby [jointly and severally] guarantee that I/we will, when lawfully required to do so, make good any loss which any

person interested in the administration of the estate of the deceased may suffer in consequence of the breach by the administrator(s) of his/her/their duty:—

(*a*) to collect and get in the estate of the deceased and administer it according to law;

(*b*) when required to do so by the court, to exhibit on oath in the court a full inventory of the estate and, when so required, to render an account of the estate; or

(*c*) when so required by the court, to deliver up the grant to the court.

2 The giving of time to the administrator(s) or any other forbearance or indulgence shall not in any way affect my/our liability under this guarantee.

4 3 The liability under this guarantee shall be continuing and shall be for the whole amount of the loss mentioned in paragraph 1 above, but (my) (our aggregate) total liability shall not in any event exceed the sum of £ .

5 Dated this day of , 19 .

Signed, sealed and delivered by the above-named
in the presence of

LS

A Commissioner for Oaths (or Solicitor).

1 The name and address of the deceased and the date of death are inserted here.

2 The full names, addresses and descriptions of the applicants for the grant must be inserted here. The applicants do not themselves subscribe to the guarantee.

3 The full names, addresses and descriptions of the sureties must be inserted here. An insurance or other guarantee company or a trust corporation enters into the guarantee in its corporate capacity and its name should be given, not that of the officer authorised to act on behalf of the company or corporation.

Sureties—The sureties must be responsible persons over the age of eighteen years and resident in the United Kingdom; an application supported if necessary by an affidavit as to the facts may be made to the registrar for his direction accepting a surety resident elsewhere. In the place of individual sureties a corporation will be accepted (see below). It is no objection to an individual surety that he is related to the deceased or to any of the proposed grantees.

Addresses—Addresses must be the residential addresses of the sureties; accommodation addresses will not be accepted.

Descriptions—Each description must be clear and certain, and of such a character that it can reasonably be inferred that the surety is capable of meeting his or her obligations under the guarantee. Vague descriptions will not be accepted and the actual occupation (if any) by which the surety makes his or her living must be shown. If he is retired from business, he must be described as having retired from some stated occupation. If he has no occupation, it must be stated. (See also pp 69–70.)

One surety is sufficient if:

(*a*) the gross value of the estate does not exceed £500; or

(*b*) a corporation is a surety (see below).

Two sureties are required in all other cases, although the registrar may in a proper case exercise a discretion to reduce their number.

Any substitution of sureties appearing on the face of the guarantee must be referred to in the delivery clause as having been made before the guarantee was executed by the sureties.

Corporation as surety—An insurance or other guarantee company or a corporation whose articles of association allow it to act as surety will be accepted provided it files an affidavit by its proper officer setting out:

(*a*) that it is empowered by its articles of association to act as surety;

(*b*) that the guarantee is executed in the manner required by the articles of association;

(*c*) sufficient information as to its financial position to satisfy the registrar that its assets are sufficient to satisfy all claims which may be made against it under any guarantee which it has given or is likely to give for this purpose.

To avoid having to file an affidavit in each case in which it acts as surety, a corporation which undertakes such probate business may apply to the Senior Registrar for permission to file each year in the Principal Registry an affidavit as to these particulars, upon undertaking to file a further affidavit immediately should there be any alteration during the course of the year in the articles of association affecting the giving of guarantees. A list of approved companies and corporations is supplied to each probate registry and any one of them is accepted without further evidence.

Justification—Every surety, other than a corporation, must justify, that is to say, the surety must make an affidavit to the effect that he or she is worth a sum corresponding to the gross value of the estate or such other sum as may have been directed by the registrar (see Form 11.3.2, below). It is no longer necessary that a declaration on oath by the applicant setting out particulars of the estate should accompany the justification by sureties.

4 The liability of each surety does not exceed the gross value of the estate as sworn in the oath. In the case of an 'excepted estate' (see pp 77 and 228) the exact value of the estate will not usually be given in the oath. If, however, the liability is to be limited to the value of the estate, that value should be sworn to in the oath, otherwise the liability will have to be based on the upper limit stated in the oath, namely £10,000, or £25,000, or £40,000, as the case may be, unless other evidence as to the amount of the gross estate can be produced. If the deceased died domiciled in England and Wales this will be the estate in the United Kingdom, or if the domicile of the deceased at the date of death was elsewhere, the estate in England and Wales. It follows that on an application for a second grant if the value of the unadministered estate only has to be given in the oath, the liability will be correspondingly reduced. In exceptional circumstances application may be made to the registrar to reduce or increase the limit of liability.

Where community of property existed between the deceased and his spouse under the law of their domicile, the limit of liability will be half (or as the case may be) the gross value of the estate.

5 The guarantee must be executed before any person authorised by law to administer an oath, a description which includes besides a commissioner for oaths, any solicitor who holds a current practising certificate, provided that he is not acting for a party to the proceedings, or is not himself interested in such proceedings. It is sufficient to use the description 'Solicitor'. The guarantee does not have to be delivered before the same person before whom the oath was sworn. Alterations should be initialled by the commissioner or other authorised person except that any alteration to the limit of liability made before delivery must be recited in the attestation clause.

A guarantee given by a corporation does not have to be attested by a commissioner for oaths or other person authorised to administer oaths but is delivered by the seal of the corporation being affixed in the presence of the officers authorised by the articles of association to affix the seal.

Form 11.3.2 Affidavit of justification
(For heading and title, see Form 2.11)

1 We, *GH*, of , and *LM*, of , jointly and severally make oath and say

2 that we are the proposed sureties on behalf of *DE* the intended administrator of the estate of *AB*, of , deceased, in the sum of £ ;

3 And I the said *GH* for myself further make oath and say that I am, after payment of all my just debts, well and truly worth in real and personal estate the sum of £ ; and I the said *LM*, for myself further make oath and say that I am, after payment of all my just debts, well and truly worth in real and personal estate the sum of £

4 Sworn by both the above-named deponents
at
this day of , 19 .
Before me
A Commissioner for Oaths (or Solicitor).

1 The full name, address and description of each deponent should be given. If either or both wish to affirm, this should be shown, viz, by inserting 'do solemnly and sincerely affirm' after the name of the affirmant or by substituting those words for 'make oath and say' as the situation demands.

Paragraphs **3** and **4** should be correspondingly altered.

2 Insert the full amount of the liability.

3 Insert the amount of the liability in each case.

4 See the note to para **10** of Form 2.11, at p 29.

(*Note*—This form may be adapted for use when only one surety is required.)

11.4 Further security

There would seem to be no authority for the court to require an additional guarantee when further estate is discovered after the grant has issued; a guarantee may be required only as a condition of granting administration.

The new practice does not apply to grants of administration made before 1 January 1972 (s 12 (4) of the Administration of Estates Act 1971). In respect of such grants it may be necessary for bond to be given for the increased estate unless the original bond was given in a penal sum sufficient to cover the increase (eg, see s 42 of the Stamp Act 1815). If the circumstances are such that under the current practice a guarantee by sureties would not normally be required, it may be that the registrar would be prepared to exercise his discretion (under s 82 of the Court of Probate Act 1857) to dispense with further security. Otherwise the administrators must file an affidavit declaring the value of the increased estate and, if necessary, give bond to cover it. In the Principal Registry, the grant, affidavit and bond should be lodged with the Record Keeper. The registrar will then issue his certificate that sufficient security to cover the new value has been given.

11.5 Enforcement

The guarantee enures for the benefit of any person interested in the administration of the estate as if it had been contained in a contract under seal between that person and the surety or sureties. Where there are two or more sureties, each surety will be treated as having bound himself jointly and severally. No action on the guarantee may be brought without first obtaining the leave of the High Court (s 120 (3) of the Supreme Court Act 1981). The application for leave is usually made on summons (see head 20.2) to a registrar, notice being served on the administrator the surety and any co-surety (Probate Rule 41A). The registrar has a discretion (under Probate Rule 60) to require the application to be made by summons to a judge or to the court on motion (see head 20.3). It is not necessary to assign the guarantee, as was the case with a bond.

An administration bond given before 1 January 1972 may be enforced and assigned under the old practice (para 10, Sched 6 to Supreme Court Act 1981). If it is sought to sue on the bond for a breach of the conditions thereof, application should be made by summons to a registrar (see head 20.2) for an order assigning the bond to a named person. The summons must be served (see p 251) on the administrator and on every surety. The application should be supported by an affidavit setting out the alleged breach of condition, a copy of which should be served with the summons. The person to whom the bond is ordered to be assigned is entitled by virtue of the order to sue thereon in his own name as trustee for all persons interested in the estate.

Chapter 12

Settled Land Grants

Where in the case of a person dying on or after 1 January 1926 there was land vested in him at the date of his death which was settled previously to his death and not by his will and which remained settled land notwithstanding his death, there must be a grant of representation to enable such land to be dealt with in accordance with the terms of the settlement. The grant may be limited to the settled land or it may be a general grant specifically including the settled land, but in either case the person or persons entitled thereto are determined in accordance with special rules (see below). A general grant including settled land will not issue if the general grant to which the applicants are entitled is of a different nature from the settled land grant. Thus, where the executors named in the deceased's will, although trustees of the settlement, were not such at the date of death, a separate grant of probate in respect of the deceased's free estate will issue to them and they may then apply for a further grant of letters of administration with will annexed limited to the settled land.

A settled land grant to the estate of a deceased tenant for life in whom settled land was vested is still necessary even although the settlement may have come to an end since the date of his death by reason of the subsequent death of the next and last tenant for life. But when the land ceases to be settled land on the death of the last tenant for life, in whom it was vested, his legal personal representatives may vest the land in the remainderman, and no settled land grant is necessary.

Land which is the subject of a settlement and which has been converted into capital money is not regarded as settled land and a settled land grant will not be made in respect of such capital money.

12.1 Probate

A grant of probate limited to or including settled land may only be made to the persons who are trustees of the settlement at the date of the death of the tenant for life (as to who are 'trustees of the settlement' see s 30 (1) of the Settled Land Act 1925). These may have been appointed special executors as to the settled land by the will of the tenant for life, but if they have not been appointed they will be deemed to have been so appointed. In either case they will be special executors as to the settled land (Administration of Estates Act 1925, s 22).

When a settlement arises under a will or an intestacy, and there are no trustees thereof at the date of death of the tenant for life, the settlor's legal personal representatives are to be regarded as trustees of the settlement until other trustees are appointed (s 30 (3) of the Settled Land Act 1925). It is the practice to look upon such personal representatives, if acting as such at the date of death, as special executors and entitled to a grant of probate in respect of the settled land.

Special executors have most of the privileges which attach to the office of general executors. They may renounce their right to take a grant in respect of the settled land, or they may have power reserved to them to do so at a later date (see head 3.3). A right which does not attach is that of a chain of representation through the survivor of them. When a special executor dies, whether testate or intestate, his interest in the settled land, so far as the extraction of a grant is concerned, ceases entirely.

12.2 Letters of administration with will annexed

When there were no trustees of the settlement at the date of death of the tenant for life, or if there were and they are now dead or have renounced probate limited to the settled land, it will be necessary to obtain a grant of letters of administration with will annexed to deal with it.

It is possible for grants of probate and letters of administration with will annexed limited to settled land to issue in respect of the estate of the same tenant for life, eg, probate save and except settled land to the general executors; probate limited to a certain parcel of settled land to the special executors; and letters of administration with will annexed limited to another parcel of settled land to the trustees of the settlement at the time of application for the grant.

Letters of administration with will annexed 'limited to settled land' may be granted to the following classes of persons, who are preferred in the order in which they are set out. Each member of the preceding class must be cleared off before a member of the lower class will be considered.

(*a*) Trustees of the settlement appointed since the death of the tenant for life.

(*b*) The general personal representatives of the deceased tenant for life. In practice the person entitled to a general grant of representation in respect of the estate of a deceased tenant for life will be allowed to combine his application for that grant with the application in respect of the settled land and so obtain a grant of administration including settled land without having to make two separate applications, provided that if separate grants were to be issued they would be of the same nature.

Before 3 July 1967 Probate Rule 28 (3) listed an additional class, namely the personal representative of the settlor when there were no trustees of the settlement at the time of application for the grant and the settlement arose under a will or an intestacy. However, it is now accepted that, if there are no trustees, members of this class may take a grant of probate as special executors if in office at the date of death (see above under Probate), or, if appointed after the date of death, a grant of letters of administration with will annexed as trustees of the settlement (class (*a*)).

Other persons interested in the conveyance of the property, whether this remains or has ceased to be settled land on the death of the testator, may obtain a grant if none of the classes set out above is in existence or if they are unwilling or incompetent to take the grant. Such a grant is made under the discretionary power conferred on the court by s 116 of the Supreme Court Act 1981 and may be general or limited in such manner as the court thinks fit (*Re Bridgett & Hayes' Contract* [1928] Ch 163; *Re Bordass' Estate* [1929] P 107; *Re Birch's Estate* [1929] P 164). The production of an order under the section is necessary to the issue of the grant (see head 13.6).

12.3 Letters of administration

The same classes of person are entitled to the settled land grant as those entitled to a grant of letters of administration with will annexed except that the first class consists of trustees of the settlement at the time of application for the grant and thus includes persons who were trustees at the date of death of the deceased tenant for life.

12.4 Procedure

A grant limited to settled land may be made to a single individual in spite of the existence of a life or minority interest in the land in respect of which the grant is to issue because such interest does not arise under the will or intestacy but instead under the settlement.

It is essential to show not only that the land remained settled land after the death of the deceased but also that the land was actually vested in the deceased and that the persons applying for the grant are entitled thereto. For this purpose it is necessary to lodge in the registry all the relevant documents, in particular the instrument or instruments which created the settlement (the original deed or the probate copy of the will), together with any amending deeds, the vesting deed or assent, if any, and any appointments of fresh trustees. These will be returned after inspection.

Where a previous grant has issued, eg, save and except settled land, the application may be made at the Principal Registry or at any district probate registry. If the application is to be made at the Principal Registry or at a district probate registry other than the registry from which the first grant issued, an office copy of that grant must be lodged with the papers.

There is no specific requirement that on an application for a grant of administration limited to settled land a guarantee by sureties should be lodged (see head 11.1).

Form 12.4.1 Oath for special executors
(For heading and title, see Form 2.11)

1
of
2 make oath and say that we believe the paper writing now produced to and marked by us to be the true and original last Will and Testament
3 of
late of
formerly of , deceased, who
4 died on the day of , 19 , aged years, domiciled in
5 and that there was land vested in the said deceased immediately before his death which was settled previously thereto (and not by his will) and which remained settled land notwithstanding his death, namely, under the will of *ST*, deceased, proved in the
registry on the day of , 19 .
6 And we further make oath and say that we were the trustees of the said settled land at the date of death of the said deceased, and as such the special executors as to the said settled land
7 and that we will (i) collect, get in and administer according to the law all the estate (limited to the said settled land) of the said deceased; (ii) when required to do so by the court, exhibit on oath in the court a full inventory of the said estate (limited to the said settled land) and when so required render an account of the administration of the said estate to the court; and (iii) when required to do so by the High Court, deliver up the grant of probate to that court; and that the whole of the said estate, limited to the said settled land, amounts in value to the sum of £ and no more, to the best of our knowledge, information and belief.
8 Sworn by the above-named deponents
at
this day of , 19 .
Before me
A Commissioner for Oaths (or Solicitor).

(*Note*—For the form of oath for a general grant including settled land, see Form 3.2.)

1 See note to para **1** of Form 3.2, at pp 67–70.

2 See the note to para **2** of Form 3.2, at pp 70–71. If the deceased's will has already been proved the will does not have to be identified and marked again on an application for a grant limited to settled land. In that event, the following details of the former grant should be substituted for paras **2**, **3** and **4**: '...make oath and say that , of , formerly of , deceased, died on the day of , 19 , domiciled in , having made and duly executed his last will and testament, and that on the day of , 19 , probate of the said will save and except settled land was (*or* letters of administration with will annexed of the estate, save and except settled land, of the said deceased were) granted out of the Registry to (*recite the names of the grantees and their title if stated in the previous grant*)'. Where the will has not already been proved, or where application is being made for a general grant including a parcel of settled land and a grant limited to another parcel of settled land has already issued, the will must be identified and marked in the usual manner and, if appropriate and necessary, its validity established.

3 and **4** See the notes to paras **3** and **4** of Form 3.2, at pp 72–73.

5 Details of the settlement must be set out in this paragraph. If the settlement was made by deed, substitute 'under an indenture of settlement dated the day of , 19 ', or if a compound settlement 'under a compound settlement arising out of an indenture of settlement dated the day of , 19 , and the will of proved in the Registry on the day of , 19 ' (or such documents as constitute the compound settlement) (see *Re Taylor's Estate* [1929] P 260; *Re Sharpe's Deed of Release* [1939] Ch 51).

If there was other settled land in respect of which the applicants are not entitled to a grant, this fact must be stated.

6 The title of special executors is usually described as set out in this paragraph. Note the special position of the settlor's legal personal representatives (see p 177); when application is made in that capacity, it must be stated that there are no trustees of the settlement and the facts relating to the issue of a grant in respect of the settlor's estate to the applicants must be recited, the original grant or an official copy thereof being lodged with the papers to lead the grant for inspection.

7 The value of the estate to be inserted in respect of a grant limited to settled land is that of the settled land only.

See also the note to para **10** of Form 3.2.

8 See the note to para **10** of Form 2.11, at p 29.

Form 12.4.2 Oath for administrators (settled land)
(For heading and title, see Form 2.11)

1
of
2 make oath and say that
of
3 died on the day of , 19 , aged years domiciled in
,
4 having made and duly executed his last Will and Testament and we believe the paper writing now produced to and marked by us to be the said true and original last will and testament.
5 And we further make oath and say that there was land vested in the said deceased immediately before his death which was settled previously thereto (and not by his will) and which remained settled land notwithstanding his death, namely, under the will of *ST*, deceased, proved in the Registry on the day of , 19 ,
6 that
7 and that we are the present trustees of the said settled land
8 and that we will (i) collect, get in and administer according to the law all the estate (limited to the said settled land) of the said deceased; (ii) when required to do so by the court, exhibit on oath in the court a full inventory of the said estate (limited to the said settled land) and when so required render an account of the administration of the said estate to the court; and (iii) when required to do so by the High Court, deliver up the grant of letters of administration (with will annexed) to that court; and that the whole of the said estate, limited to the

said settled land, amounts in value to the sum of £
and no more, to the best of our knowledge, information and belief.

9 Sworn by the above-
named deponents
at
this day of , 19 .
Before me
A Commissioner for Oaths (or Solicitor)

(*Note*—For the oath for a general grant of administration, with or without will annexed and including settled land, see Form 4.4 and Form 5.4).

1 See the notes to para **1** of Forms 4.4 and 5.4, at pp 99 and 130 respectively.

2 See the notes to para **3** of Form 3.2, at p 72, and to para **2** of Form 5.4, at p 130.

3 See the note to para **4** of Form 3.2, at pp 72–73.

4 See the note to para **2** of Form 3.2, at pp 70–71, as to the identification of the documents put forward for proof, and where the will has already been proved see the note to para **2** of Form 12.4.1, at p 179, as to the necessity for marking.

In the case of an intestacy, replace the whole paragraph by the word 'intestate'.

If a grant has already issued in respect of the deceased's estate, this paragraph should read as follows: 'having made and duly executed his last will and testament, and that on the day of , 19 , probate of the said will save and except settled land was (*or* letters of administration with will annexed of the estate, save and except settled land, of the said deceased were) granted out of the Registry to (*recite the names of the grantees and their title if stated in the previous grant*)'; or in the case of an intestacy 'intestate, and that on the day of , 19 , letters of administration of the estate of the said deceased save and except settled land were granted out of the Registry to , etc'.

5 See the note to para **5** of Form 12.4.1, at p 180. In the case of an intestacy, delete '(and not by his will)'.

6 The applicants must clear off all persons having a prior right to a grant in respect of the settled land, eg, if they claim the grant as personal representatives of the tenant for life, they must clear off trustees at the death of the tenant for life and any trustees who have since been appointed. Thus, 'there were no trustees of the said settled land at the date of death of the said deceased', or '*RS* the surviving trustee of the said settled land at the date of death of the said deceased and as such the special executor as to the said settled land has duly renounced probate of the said will limited to settled land', or 'there were no trustees of the said settled land at the date of death of the said deceased and there are now no trustees of the said settled land', etc.

7 Here the exact capacity in which the applicants claim the grant should be set out. Note the special position of the settlor's legal personal representatives (see p 177 and the note to para **6** of Form 12.4.1, at p 180).

8 See the note to para **7** of Form 12.4.1, at p 180.
9 See the note to para **10** of Form 2.11, at p 29.

Chapter 13

Other Special Grants

13.1 Cessate grants

A cessate grant is one which issues as the result of a previous grant having ceased to be operative either by reason of the fulfilment of the condition or limitation contained in it (eg, the attainment of his majority by a minor, the recovery of mental capacity, the finding and proving of a will after a copy of it has been admitted to proof) or because the original grantee has died leaving the condition or limitation in the original grant unfulfilled (eg, the death of a sole or sole surviving attorney or guardian).

The application for the grant may be made at the Principal Registry or at a district probate registry, which need not be the registry from which the first grant issued.

Form 13.1 Oath for cessate grant of administration
(*For heading and title, see Form 2.11*)

1
of
2 make oath and say that ,
of ,
formerly of , deceased, died on the day of , 19 , aged years, domiciled in , having made and duly executed his last Will and Testament
3 wherein he did not name any executor
4 and wherein he named me, the said , residuary legatee and devisee;
5 And that on the day of , 19 , letters of administration with the said will annexed of the estate of the said deceased were granted out of the Registry to *GH* and *KL* my lawful uncles of the whole blood and nearest of kin, and the guardians nominated by me, for my use and benefit and until I should attain the age of eighteen years
6 and that on the day of , 19 , I attained the age of eighteen years by reason of which the said grant has ceased and expired.
7 And I further make oath and say that minority life interest (now) arises in h estate, and that to the best of my knowledge, information and belief there was no land vested in the said deceased immediately before his death which was settled previously thereto (and not by h will) and which remained settled land notwithstanding his death;

8 and that I believe the paper writing now produced to and marked by me to contain the last Will and Testament as contained in a true and official copy thereof of the said deceased,
9 and that I am the residuary legatee and devisee named in the said will,
10 and that I will (i) collect, get in and administer according to the law the real and personal estate ( ) of the said deceased; (ii) when required to do so by the court, exhibit on oath in the court a full inventory of the said estate ( ) and when so required render an account of the administration of the said estate to the court; and (iii) when required to do so by the High Court, deliver up the grant of letters of administration with will annexed to that court; and that to the best of my knowledge, information and belief the gross unadministered estate passing under the grant amounts to £ and the net unadministered estate amounts to £ .
11 Sworn by the above-named deponent
at
this day of , 19 .
Before me
A Commissioner for Oaths (or Solicitor).

1 See the note to para **1** of Form 3.2, at pp 67–70.

2 If the deponent wishes to affirm, the words 'make oath and say' must be altered to read 'do solemnly and sincerely affirm' and a corresponding alteration made in para **7** and the jurat. See also the notes to paras **3** and **4** of Form 3.2, at pp 72–73. As to the references to the will and other testamentary documents, see the note to para **2** of Form 3.2, at pp 70–71. If the deceased died intestate, substitute for the words 'having made and duly executed his last will and testament' the word 'intestate'.

3 In this paragraph, show how the persons with a prior right to that of the applicant have been cleared off, thus:

> 'Wherein he named *ST* the sole executor, who has renounced probate thereof (*or* who predeceased the said deceased, *or* who survived the said deceased but has since died without having proved the said will)'; see also the note to para **7** of Form 4.4, at p 101. If the deceased died intestate, see the note to para **4** of Form 5.4, at pp 130–133, as to clearing off.

4 Set out in this paragraph the title of the applicant; see the notes to para **8** of Form 4.4, at pp 101–103 (administration with will) and to para **7** of Form 5.4, at pp 133–134 (administration).

5 Give details of the previous grant, reciting the names of the grantees, stating their title and the limitation on the grant, as set out therein; thus, where the previous grant was to an attorney, 'to *GH* the lawful attorney of (me) the said for (my) (his) use and benefit and until (I) (he) should apply for and obtain letters of administration with will annexed of the estate of the said deceased'.

The original or an office copy of the first grant must be lodged with the papers when application is made in the Principal Registry or in a district probate registry other than that from which the first grant issued. It will be returned, unless the original grant has been marked by the applicant (see note to para **8**).

6 Show in this paragraph, if necessary, the reason why the previous grant has ceased to operate; thus, where the first grant was made to an attorney who has since died and the further grant is to be made to another attorney, 'and that the said *GH* has since died, whereby the said grant has ceased and expired'.

7 As to minority and life interests, see the note to para **5** of Form 4.4, at p 100; omit the word 'now' if there has never been a minority or life interest in the deceased's estate. As to settled land, see the notes to paras **5** and **8** of Form 3.2, at pp 73, 76; omit the words '(and not by h [illegible] will)' if the deceased died intestate.

8 The applicant may mark (i) the original will, in which case he must attend and swear the papers in the registry where the will is filed, *or* (ii) the probate copy of the will contained in the original grant, which must then be filed in the registry, or (iii) an office copy of the will (or, if this is not available, a sealed and certified copy of the will) which must be lodged with the papers to lead the grant. If the original will is being marked, the words 'true and original' should be inserted before 'last will' and the reference to a copy deleted. Where an order has been made under s 2 of the Inheritance (Provision for Family and Dependants) Act 1975, the will marked by the applicant will include the memorandum of the order, and the notation relating thereto will be placed on the new grant. Where an order has been made for rectification of the will under s 20 of the Administration of Justice Act 1982 and a memorandum of the order has been annexed to the original grant (see head 2.16), it would seem that a further copy of the memorandum will be included with the will or copy engrossment to be marked, and the new grant will be noted.

9 Insert the title of the applicant to the grant. The relationship of the applicant to the deceased no longer needs to be stated in the oath unless it is necessary to do so to establish title or identification (see note to para **4** above).

10 The applicant swears to administer the whole of the estate, but the value shown in the oath will be that of the gross and net estate remaining unadministered, valued as at the date of the Inland Revenue account. The appropriate form of Inland Revenue account is at present CAP Form A-5C (see p 231).

11 See the note to para **10** of Form 2.11, at p 29.

Note—This form may be adapted for use when application is to be made for a cessate grant of probate, eg, on application by an executor after a grant of administration with will annexed to his attorney or guardians (see also Form 3.2, p 66 et seq).

13.2 Grants de bonis non

A grant de bonis non is necessary on the death or mental incapacity of a previous grantee, or on the death of the donor of a power of attorney or of a minor or person suffering from mental illness for whose use and benefit the previous grant issued, if there is estate remaining unadministered. The application for the grant may be made at the Principal Registry or at any district probate registry, irrespective of the registry from which the first grant issued.

The usual rules apply to the ascertainment of the person entitled to the grant. Normally, he is the person equally entitled with, or next entitled to, the previous grantee, or if the whole estate vested in the previous grantee, his personal representative. The personal representatives of a person equally entitled have the same right as the deceased whom they represent, but will not be preferred to a living interest unless a registrar otherwise directs (see p 128).

Where the deceased died intestate and a grant issued to his spouse who has since died leaving part of his estate unadministered, the respective rights of the spouse's legal personal representative and of the deceased's next of kin to a grant de bonis non must be considered by reference to the value of the estate as at the date of payment or appropriation in respect of the spouse's statutory legacy (see p 138). The discovery of further assets or an increase in the value of an asset before appropriation may be sufficient to give the next of kin a right to the grant in preference to the spouse's legal personal representative.

Where the first grant was probate and the chain of representation (see head 3.1) is broken, the title to the new grant will be traced through the disposition of the residue of the estate (see p 87); similarly, if the first grant was letters of administration with will annexed made to a residuary legatee and devisee, some other member of that class, or if there is none, the personal representative of the previous grantee, will take the grant. Whenever application is made by a devisee, legatee or creditor or by the legal personal representative of such person, it must be sworn that the legacy, devise or debt still remains unsatisfied.

Form 13.2 Oath for de bonis non grant of administration

(*For heading and title, see Form* 2.11)

1

of

2 make oath and say that

of ,

formerly of , deceased, died on the day of , 19 , aged years, domiciled in , having made and duly executed his last Will and Testament

3 wherein he did not name any executor;

4 that on the day of , 19 , letters of administration with the said will annexed of the estate of the said deceased were granted out of the Registry to *ST* the residuary legatee and devisee in trust named therein

5 and that the said *ST* died on the day of , 19 , leaving part of the estate of the said deceased unadministered;

6 And I further make oath and say that minority life interest arises in h estate, and that to the best of my knowledge, information and belief there was no land vested in the said deceased immediately before his death which was settled previously thereto (and not by h will) and which remained settled land notwithstanding his death;

7 and that I believe the paper writing now produced to and marked by me to contain the last will and testament as contained in a true and official copy thereof of the said deceased

8 and that I am and the residuary legatee and devisee named in the said will,

9 and that I will (i) collect, get in and administer according to the law the real and personal estate ( ) of the said deceased; (ii) when required to do so by the court, exhibit on oath a full inventory of the said estate ( ) and when so required render an account of the administration of the said estate to the court; and (iii) when required to do so by the High Court, deliver up the grant of letters of administration with will annexed to that court; and that to the best of my knowledge, information and belief the gross unadministered estate passing under the grant amounts to £ and the net unadministered estate amounts to £ .

10 Sworn by the above-named deponent
at
this day of , 19 .
Before me
A Commissioner for Oaths (or Solicitor).

1 See the note to para **1** of Form 3.2, at pp 67–70.

2 See the note to para **2** of Form 13.1, at p 184.

3 Set out in this paragraph how the persons with a prior right to the original grantee have been cleared off (see also the note to para **3** of Form 13.1, at p 184).

4 Give details of the previous grant, reciting the names of the grantees and state their title. The original or an office copy of the grant must be lodged with the papers when application is made in the Principal Registry or in a district probate registry other than that from which the first grant issued. It will be returned, unless the original grant has been marked by the applicant (see note to para **8** of Form 13.1, at p 185).

5 This paragraph should recite the death or incapacity of the previous grantee by reason of which a further grant is required. When there is no estate unadministered and the grant de bonis non is to issue for a nil estate for the purpose of making title to trust property, it should be sworn that the previous grantee died 'without having completed administration of the estate'. If the first grant was one of probate, the chain of representation must be broken by the recital of the death intestate of the last proving executor to die, or by the recital of the reason why his executor, if one has been appointed by his will, cannot take the grant to his estate (see head 3.1).

6 and **7** See the notes to paras **7** and **8** of Form 13.1, at p 185.

8 Insert the title of the applicant to the grant; the relationship of the applicant to the deceased no longer needs to be stated in the oath unless it is necessary to do so to establish title or identification (see the notes to para **8** of Form 4.4, at pp 101–103 (administration with will), and to para **7** of Form 5.4, at pp 133–134 (administration)). If necessary, first show how persons with a prior right to that of the applicant have been cleared off, in so far as they have not been cleared off in previous paragraphs.

9 The applicant swears to administer the unadministered estate only, and the value shown in the oath will be that of the gross and net unadministered estate, valued as at the date of the Inland Revenue account form. The appropriate form of Inland Revenue account is at present CAP Form A-5C (see p 231).

10 See the note to para **10** of Form 2.11, at p 29.

13.3 Grants durante absentia

Up to 1 January 1982, s 164 of the Supreme Court of Judicature (Consolidation) Act 1925 gave a creditor or any other person interested in the estate the right to apply to the court for a grant of special administration of the deceased's estate on the ground that after the expiration of twelve months from the death of the deceased, a personal representative of the deceased to whom a grant had been made was residing out of the jurisdiction of the High Court. That section of the Act has been repealed and is not reproduced in the Supreme Court Act 1981. Where it is now considered that a personal representative of the deceased is neglecting his duty to administer the estate by reason of residence abroad, the appropriate course is to apply in the Chancery Division for the appointment of a judicial trustee under the Judicial Trustees Act 1896.

13.4 Grants ad colligenda bona (Probate Rule 51)

If it becomes urgently necessary to obtain a grant of representation in order to prevent loss being caused to the estate through lack of someone authorised to administer it, application may be made to the court for an order for a grant of letters of administration ad colligenda bona. The application, whatever the amount of the estate, is made ex parte to a registrar of the Principal Registry (through the Probate Department), or, if the application for a grant is to be made in a district probate registry, to any district probate registrar; he may direct that the application be made on summons to a registrar of the Principal Registry or a judge (see head 20.2), or to the court on motion (see head 20.3). It must be supported by an affidavit or affidavits setting out the facts necessitating the issue of a grant. The order will limit the grant for the purpose of collecting, getting in and receiving the deceased's estate and doing such acts as may be necessary to preserve it, and until further representation has been granted. There is a discretion to require a guarantee by sureties (see head 11.1). The grant ceases when the object for which it has issued has been attained or when a full grant has issued.

Anyone who can satisfy the court as to his bona fide interest in protecting the estate may apply for a grant ad colligenda bona. The grant is one of administration although there may be a will in existence. If appropriate the executors may be passed over (*Re Clore decd, IRC* v *Stype Investments (Jersey) Ltd* [1982] 3 WLR 228). If there is a minority or life interest, the grant will usually have to be made to at least two individuals or to a trust corporation (see head 6.2).

The ordinary form of oath may be adapted (see Form 5.4). The following points of difference should be noted:

(*a*) The oath need not state whether there is a will in existence or whether the deceased died intestate, nor does it have to contain the usual clearings (compare Form 4.4, and note 7 thereto), but it must deal with the existence of life or minority interests.

(*b*) The making of an order by the court should be recited, eg, 'That on the day of , 19 , it was ordered by that letters of administration of the estate of the said deceased be granted to me'. The applicant then swears to administer the estate as limited by the terms of the order.

If it is desired to obtain further powers to administer the estate, it is usual to apply for an order for a grant under s 116 of the Supreme Court Act 1981 (see head 13.6), which may be either a full grant or limited in such manner as is desired or as the court thinks fit.

13.5 Pending suit grants

The need to obtain a grant of representation as a matter of urgency in order to prevent loss to the estate may arise when there is a dispute giving rise to legal proceedings to determine the validity of a testator's will or the title to a grant or to recall or revoke a grant. In such circumstances, a limited grant of letters of administration pending suit may issue by order of the court under s 117 of the Supreme Court Act 1981 to a person agreed upon by the parties to the action or nominated by the court in default of agreement. Such an administrator has all the rights, duties and powers of a general administrator except that he is subject to the immediate control of the court and must act under its direction. In the exercise of its discretion the court may give him power to distribute any part of the estate or the whole of it, but he may not do so in the absence of any such direction (s 117 (2) of the Supreme Court Act 1981). The grant may issue to a single administrator although a life or minority interest arises or could arise (see head 6.2).

The application for an order appointing an administrator pending suit is now made in the Chancery Division by summons before a master (RSC, Ord 76, r 15 (1)). Thereafter application for a grant of administration pending suit is made by lodging the papers, including an office copy of the order of appointment and an Inland Revenue account, at the Principal Registry; the grant cannot issue from a district probate registry. There is a discretion to ask for a guarantee by sureties (see head 11.1), but if the administrator pending suit has been directed by the order of the Chancery Division to give security as a condition of his appointment, it is unlikely that the guarantee will be required. The ordinary form of oath may be adapted (see Form 5.4). The following points of difference are to be noted:

(*a*) The oath should set out the existence and nature of the contentious proceedings, eg, 'That there is now depending in the Chancery Division of the High Court of Justice an action entitled concerning the validity of the will dated of the said deceased (*or as the case may be*)'.

(*b*) The making of the order appointing the administrator pending suit should be recited, eg, 'That on the day of , 19 , it was ordered in the said Chancery Division that letters of administration of the estate of the said deceased be granted to me pending the said action'. If there is any special limitation contained in the order, this should be mentioned, and the applicant then swears to collect, get in and administer the estate save as to the distribution thereof or in accordance with any special direction in the order.

(*c*) The practice with regard to 'excepted estates' (see p 77) does not apply and the values of the gross and net estate passing under the grant must be shown.

A grant of administration pending suit ceases to be effective on the making of a decree in the action, unless there is an appeal, when it revives until the appeal is finally determined. An application for a full grant afterwards proceeds as if it were an application for a first grant in respect of the deceased's estate save that the probate fee payable will usually be £2 for a second or subsequent grant (see p 266) and an Inland Revenue account is required to be lodged (see p 231), the Capital Taxes Office being asked to transfer the receipt for any tax paid on the previous application. The value shown in the oath will be based on that of the whole estate. An office copy of the decree pronounced in the action, obtainable from the Central Office, must accompany the papers to lead the grant. The application for the grant may be made at the Principal Registry or at any one of the district probate registries.

13.6 Discretionary grants

Section 162 of the Supreme Court of Judicature (Consolidation) Act 1925, as amended by s 9 of the Administration of Justice Act 1928, gave the court a general discretion in respect of persons dying on or after 1 January 1926 to pass over the persons interested in the residuary estate if by reason of the estate's insolvency or other special circumstances the court thought it expedient to grant administration to some other person. In the case of deaths before 1 January 1926 somewhat similar powers were conferred on the court by s 73 of the Court of Probate Act 1857.

On and after 1 January 1982 both these provisions have been repealed and replaced by s 116 of the Supreme Court Act 1981 which gives the court a general discretionary power to appoint as administrator some person other than the person who would normally in accordance with the probate rules have been entitled to the grant when the court considers that, by reason of the special circumstances, it is necessary or expedient so to do. The power is exercisable irrespective of the date of death of the person whose estate is to be administered, and the grant may be general in its scope or limited in any way the court thinks fit. An executor may be passed over as well as a person entitled to a grant of administration. The section in combination with s 114 (2) of the Supreme Court Act 1981 (see head 6.2) gives the court power to appoint a sole administrator even if there is a life or minority interest.

The special circumstances which, in the past, the court has taken into account in making an order for a discretionary grant include the following—

(1) Where the persons entitled are shown to be unfit to administer the estate, for instance by reason of their bankruptcy or general bad character, or where the person entitled has been found guilty of the murder or manslaughter of the deceased (see pp 89–90, 115).

(2) Where the persons entitled are missing and their whereabouts are unknown.

(3) Where a grant is required by a remainderman in order to pass title to an estate of which the deceased was tenant for life (see p 178).

(4) Where it is necessary for a grant to issue as a matter of urgency in order to preserve the estate from loss, and wider powers are required than are conferred by a grant ad colligenda bona (see pp 188–189).

(5) Where a grant is required for the purpose of an action under s 1 of the Law Reform (Miscellaneous Provisions) Act 1934 (*In the Estate of Simpson; In the Estate of Gunning* [1936] P 40) (the order will specify the action which is to be brought against the deceased's estate and the grant will be limited for the purpose of the grantee being a party to the action so specified and for a 'nil' estate, see p 81). A special instance arises where the deceased lost his life in an accident, the person entitled was injured in the same accident and has a possible claim against the deceased's estate and a grant is required to be made to some other person limited to taking or defending on behalf of the deceased's estate any proceedings arising out of the accident, leaving the person entitled free to apply in due course as of right for a grant in respect of the remainder of the estate (see also *Re Newsham, decd* [1966] 3 All ER 681). (There is special provision for an application to be made to the court for an order for the appointment of a person to represent the estate of a deceased person in the absence of legal personal representatives so as to enable proceedings to be taken (or continued) against the estate (see

Proceedings Against Estates Act 1970 as amended by s 27 of the Administration of Justice Act 1977, and RSC, Ord 15, r 6A).)

(6) Where a person wishes to bring a claim under the Inheritance (Provision for Family and Dependants) Act 1975 for financial provision to be made for him out of the deceased's estate and there is no person either entitled or willing to apply for a grant. The Official Solicitor has agreed that in such cases he would be prepared to consider applying under the section for an order for a grant to himself to enable such proceedings under the Act of 1975 to be taken.

(7) Where a trustee in bankruptcy of a beneficiary under the will or on an intestacy requires a grant (the order and grant will be limited to such period as he shall remain trustee of the property of the beneficiary). A similar order will be made in favour of the trustee under a deed of arrangement, if he cannot establish that the entire interest of the beneficiary has been assigned to him.

(8) Where a local authority is applying as custodian trustee (see p 196) on behalf of a person who by reason of age, infirmity or otherwise is in need of care and attention and occupies residential accommodation provided by the authority under s 21 (1) (*a*) of the National Assistance Act 1948, and that person is solely entitled to the deceased's estate.

An application for an order under the section, whatever the amount of the estate, should be made ex parte to a registrar of the Principal Registry (through the Probate Department), or, if the application for a grant is to be made in a district probate registry, to any district probate registrar. The registrar may direct that the application be made on summons to a registrar of the Principal Registry or a judge (see head 20.2), or by motion (see head 20.3). An affidavit, or affidavits, as to the facts will be required in support of the application and should be filed in the registry together with any other material documents. If two grantees are considered to be necessary because of a life or minority interest (see head 6.2), the affidavit should recite the names of both grantees. The order when made may require a guarantee by sureties to be filed (see head 11.1 and Forms 11.3.1 and 11.3.2).

When application is made under (8) above, the oath may be used as the affidavit in support of the application for an order provided all the requisite details are stated therein, and the written consent of the person in care should be lodged. The grant will usually issue to the local authority for the use and benefit of the person in care, limited until further representation be granted. This procedure is an alternative to an application being made by the attorney of the person in care (see p 169) or based on the mental or physical incapacity of the person in care (see heads 9.2, 9.3).

When the applicant's interest in the deceased's estate depends entirely on whether or not the person beneficially entitled thereto is dead, the proper procedure is to apply for an order under the section, and not by way of citation. Unless there are special reasons rendering this course unnecessary, the registrar will require an advertisement for the missing person to be inserted in an appropriate newspaper. The practice whereby the registrar might also require the applicant to take out a special indemnity bond with a guarantee society or an insurance company in place of the usual guarantee by sureties has been discontinued. Those companies which used to supply an indemnity bond in these circumstances have agreed to provide a surety guarantee. Therefore, where the registrar now considers that there should be some form of protection, whether for the administrator or the missing person or persons, he will usually ask for a guarantee by a company surety instead of an indemnity bond. In such a case a copy of the affidavit used to lead the registrar's order should be supplied to the guarantee society or insurance company along with the request for a guarantee. In special circumstances, for instance, where the estate is very small, the registrar may be prepared to allow this procedure to be adopted in respect of an application which should normally be made by way of citation (see head 19.2) and it is the usual procedure when an estate is claimed as bona vacantia by the Treasury Solicitor, or the solicitor for the Duchy of Lancaster, or the solicitor for the Duchy of Cornwall, and it is not possible to clear off the next of kin.

The subsequent application for a grant is made in the usual manner. The oath should recite the making of the order in favour of the applicants and need not clear off persons with prior interests.

13.7 Grants limited as to property (Probate Rule 50)

Under s 155 of the Supreme Court of Judicature (Consolidation) Act 1925 probate or administration in respect of the real estate, or any part thereof, could have been granted either separately or together with probate or administration of the personal estate. It could also have been granted in respect of real estate only, where there was no personal estate, or in respect of a trust estate only. Where a deceased died insolvent, severance of representation would not have been allowed except as regards a trust estate. That section has now been repealed and replaced on and after 1 January 1982 by s 113 of the Supreme Court Act 1981. The court now has a general discretion given by this section to grant probate or administration in respect of any part of a deceased's estate and limited in any way the court thinks fit. However, where the estate of the deceased is known to be insolvent, severance of representation will not be allowed save in respect of a trust estate in which the deceased had no beneficial interest.

Where an applicant is entitled only to a grant limited to part of the estate, a limited grant will issue without an order of the court, eg, where a limited grant has already issued by order and a grant is required in respect of the remaining estate. Moreover, if a will is specifically limited to personal estate, the powers of any executor appointed will be regarded as similarly limited, and the grant of probate will be limited to personal estate. If application to prove such a will is made by someone other than an executor, the grant will be similarly limited unless it is shown that there is no will dealing with real estate in England, Scotland, Northern Ireland or any country in which the grant could be re-sealed. No order is required in these circumstances, provided that it is sworn in the oath that the deceased died solvent and the renunciation of anyone having a prior right to a general grant is filed.

In all other cases application must first be made to the court for an order for the limited grant to issue. Any person entitled to a grant in respect of the whole estate in priority to the applicant must be cleared off by renunciation or citation. The application, whatever the amount of the estate, is made ex parte to a registrar of the Principal Registry (through the Probate Department), or, if the application for a grant is to be made in a district probate registry, to any district probate registrar, by lodging an affidavit by the applicant as to the facts. The affidavit should set out the extent of the estate which the grant is to cover, whether the estate is known to be insolvent, and the manner in which the persons entitled to a general grant in priority have been cleared off. If the registrar so directs, the application must be made on summons to a registrar of the Principal Registry or a judge (see head 20.2) or by motion (see head 20.3), supported by an affidavit in similar terms.

When it is necessary to obtain a grant limited to trust property, application for an order may be made, where the trust was not created by will, by the trustees or the legal personal representative of the last surviving trustee, or, on clearing those persons, by a beneficiary under the trust, with the consent of the other beneficiaries. If the trust was created by will, it has been the practice to make an order in favour of the legal personal representative of the settlor. The persons entitled to a general grant must be cleared off in the usual way.

An application for an order for a grant in respect of part of the free estate of the deceased, excluding trust property, by a person who has no right thereto under the rules should be made under s 116 of the Supreme Court Act 1981 (see head 13.6). The court has power under that section to limit a grant of administration in any way it thinks fit.

Chapter 14

Corporations

14.1 Trust corporations (Probate Rule 34)

There is statutory authority to make grants of representation to trust corporations constituted under the law of the United Kingdom and empowered to undertake trust business (s 161 of the Supreme Court of Judicature (Consolidation) Act 1925, replaced as from 1 January 1982 by s 115 of the Supreme Court Act 1981). In all cases the registered office of the trust corporation must be situated in the United Kingdom. A trust corporation is defined now by s 128 of the Supreme Court Act 1981 as being the Public Trustee or a corporation either appointed by the court in any particular case to be a trustee or authorised by rules made under s 4 (3) of the Public Trustee Act 1906 to act as custodian trustee. The definition was extended (by s 3 (1) of the Law of Property (Amendment) Act 1926, as amended by Sched 5 to the Supreme Court Act 1981) to include the Treasury Solicitor, including the Solicitor for the affairs of the Duchy of Lancaster; the Official Solicitor; any person holding any other official position prescribed by the Lord Chancellor; in relation to the property of a bankrupt and property subject to a deed of arrangement, the trustee in bankruptcy and the trustee under the deed respectively; in relation to charitable, ecclesiastical and public trusts, any local or public authority so prescribed, and any other corporation constituted under the laws of the United Kingdom which satisfies the Lord Chancellor that it undertakes the administration of any such trusts without remuneration, or that by its constitution it is required to apply the whole of its net income after payment of outgoings, for charitable, ecclesiastical or public purposes, and is prohibited from distributing any part thereof by way of profits among any of its members, and is authorised by the Lord Chancellor to act in relation to such trusts as a trust corporation. The corporations which may act as custodian trustees under the Public Trustee Act 1906 and thus as trust corporations are now specified in r 30 of the Public Trustee Rules 1912, as amended by the Public Trustee (Custodian Trustee) Rules 1975 and 1976. In cases of doubt reference should be made to the detailed rules, but it is to be noted that a corporation constituted under the law of any member State of the European Economic Community may now act as custodian trustee provided that it is empowered by its constitution to undertake trust business in England and Wales, has a place of business in the United Kingdom and complies with certain regulations as to registration and the amount of capital available. For instance an Irish bank constituted under the law of the Republic of Ireland may now take a grant as an executor, although it would not have qualified previously as a trust corporation (*Re Bigger decd* [1977] 2 All ER 644). Any Regional Health Authority, Area Health Authority or special health authority may act as a trust corporation in relation to trusts which it is allowed to accept under the National Health Service Reorganisation Act 1973. The British Gas Corporation and the London Transport Executive are custodian trustees in respect of certain pension schemes. Moreover the Greater London Council, the Common Council of the City of London, the corporation of a London borough (acting by the council) and a county council, district council, parish council or community council have power to act as trust corporations in respect of property held upon charitable or public trusts (but not trusts for an ecclesiastical charity or for a charity for the relief of poverty) for the benefit of the inhabitants of their areas and their neighbourhoods. The most recent amendment allows certain local authorities, namely a metropolitan district council or a non-metropolitan county council, the corporation of any London borough (acting by the council), the Common Council of the City of London and the Council of the Isles of Scilly, to act as a custodian trustee limited to any trust under which property devolves for the sole benefit of (i) a person who occupies residential accommodation provided under s 21 (1) (*a*) of the National Assistance Act 1948 by the local authority concerned; or (ii) a person who is in the care of that authority. Where such a corporation is acting as custodian trustee in this way, it is entitled to continue to act as such until a new custodian trustee is appointed, although the person concerned has ceased to occupy the accommodation or to be in the care of that authority. If a local or public authority is a trust corporation by virtue of prescription by the Lord Chancellor under s 3 (1) of the Law of Property (Amendment) Act 1926, it may act as a trust corporation with regard to administration only in relation to charitable, ecclesiastical or public trusts. For all other purposes (for example, an application for a grant as a creditor) such authorities are treated as other than trust corporations and an application for a grant must be made through a nominee (see p 202).

A trust corporation is now defined by the Probate Rules (Probate Rule 2 (2)) as meaning a corporation within the meaning of s 128 of the Supreme Court Act 1981 as extended by s 3 of the Law of Property (Amendment) Act 1926.

A trust corporation takes a grant in its corporate capacity although the intervention of its nominee is necessary for the purpose of executing documents on its behalf.

(a) Probate

A trust corporation may be appointed the executor of a will, either to act alone or in conjunction with other persons appointed as executors. The appointment of a branch office of a bank which is also a trust corporation amounts to the appointment of the bank (*Re J C White*, unreported motion, July 1924).

(b) Administration

A trust corporation may take or join in taking a grant of letters of administration with will annexed in its own right, eg, as the residuary legatee and devisee in trust named in the will. It may also take or join in taking a grant of administration, whether with will annexed or based on an intestacy, on behalf of the person or persons entitled. If there is a minority or life interest arising under the will or the intestacy, administration will usually have to be granted to a trust corporation, with or without an individual, or to not less than two individuals (see head 6.2).

When a will appoints individuals as executors and, being of age, they wish a trust corporation to act on their behalf, they must renounce probate of the will (see Form 8.2.1) and, if they are also entitled to the residue under the will, they must file their consents; all other persons entitled to the residue must also consent (see Form 14.1.2, below). If one of the executors is a minor, and the trust corporation is applying alone, the grant will be limited until the minor applies for and obtains a grant.

If the executors are all under age, a grant may issue to a trust corporation on the consents of all the persons entitled to the residue (see Form 14.1.2, below). If any of these latter, not being executors, are not sui juris the question must be referred to a registrar. If some of or all the executors are also entitled to the residue, consents on their behalf will be accepted if given by their statutory, testamentary or other lawfully appointed guardian, if any. If none, then on the written refusal of the next of kin to act, the grant may issue to the trust corporation but the registrar will give consideration to any claim by the next nearest of kin to be assigned guardians of the minor to take a grant for the use and benefit of the minor (see p 160). The grant to the trust corporation is limited until one of the executors comes of age but is made to the corporation in its own right and not for the use and benefit of the minor executors.

The consents of individuals who are of age and entitled to take a grant of administration, whether under the will or an intestacy, must be filed when a trust corporation applies on their behalf. The consents of all other persons interested in the residuary estate must also be filed (see Form 14.1.2, below). If some of the persons entitled to a grant refuse to consent, they should exercise their right of taking or being joined in taking the grant; if they will neither consent nor renounce their right, the matter must be referred to a registrar for decision. The registrar may dispense with the necessity for lodging consents to such extent and on such conditions as he may think fit. In particular, the appointment of a trust corporation by a spouse entitled to a life interest, or by a residuary legatee and devisee for life, requires the consent of all persons, if any, of the same class and of all persons ultimately entitled to the residuary estate, unless the registrar directs otherwise. A consent on behalf of a minor will not be accepted.

When some of the persons entitled to a grant of administration are under age, and provided that all persons of age renounce their right to the grant and consent, it will be made to a trust corporation limited until one of the minors applies for and obtains a grant on coming of age, except that the limitation will be 'until further representation be granted' where a minor is a contingent beneficiary. If any such person of full age will neither join in taking the grant nor renounce, the matter should be referred to a registrar, who, it is considered, has a discretion to dispense with the renunciation on such terms as he may think fit.

When all the persons entitled to a grant of administration are under age, a grant may issue as of right to a trust corporation on the consent of the statutory, testamentary or other lawfully appointed guardian, if any. If none, then on the written refusal of the nearest of kin to act as guardian the grant may issue to the trust corporation but the claim of the next nearest of kin, if willing to be assigned as guardian to take a grant, will be considered (see p 160). The grant will not be made for the use and benefit of the minors but will be limited until one of them shall apply for and obtain a grant.

On the appointment of a trust corporation as administrator or at any time thereafter, the court may be asked to order reasonable remuneration to be paid to the corporation (see *Re Masters* [1953] 1 All ER 19). If made before the issue of a grant the application should be by way of summons to a registrar (see head 20.2).

(c) Trust corporation as guardian

On the consent of all statutory, testamentary or other lawfully appointed guardians and, if appropriate, of both parents, of a minor who is entitled to take a grant, a trust corporation may be assigned as guardian by registrar's order (see p 160) to take a grant for the use and benefit of the minor and until he becomes of age. A grant may also issue to a trust corporation by registrar's order for the use and benefit of a person who is suffering from mental disorder limited during his incapacity (see p 162). For the procedure where a local authority as custodian trustee (see p 196) is applying for a grant on behalf of a child in its care, see pp 157–158, and for a grant on behalf of a person occupying residential property provided by the authority, see p 192.

(d) Oath to lead a grant to a trust corporation

The papers to lead a grant to a trust corporation must be executed by a nominee appointed for that purpose, and his acts are binding on the corporation (s 115 (3) of the Supreme Court Act 1981). Generally, trust corporations have standing resolutions appointing certain officials to take out grants of representation on their behalf, and papers executed by any one of these officials will be accepted.

Form 14.1.1 Oath for grant of administration by consent to trust corporation
(*For heading and title, see Form* 2.11)

1 I, ,
of ,
a of the Bank plc, whose (registered) office is at

2 make oath and say that ,
of ,
formerly of ,
deceased, died on the day of , 19 , aged years, domiciled in , having made and duly executed his last Will and Testament
3 wherein he did not name any executor;
4 that *DB* widow, the relict of the said deceased and the residuary legatee and devisee for life named in the said will, and *EB* and *FB*, children of the said deceased and the residuary legatees and devisees substituted in the said will, have consented that a grant of letters of administration with will annexed be granted to Bank plc;
5 that the said Bank plc is a trust corporation as defined by Rule 2 (2) of the Non-Contentious Probate Rules 1954 and has power under its constitution to accept the grant now sought;
6 and that by virtue of a resolution of the said Bank plc passed on the day of , 19 (a certified copy of which is annexed hereunto), I was authorised for and on behalf of the said Bank plc to apply for letters of administration with the said will annexed of the estate of the said deceased.
7 And I further make oath and say that minority life interest arises in the estate of the said deceased, and that to the best of my knowledge, information and belief there was no land vested in the said deceased immediately before his death which was settled previously thereto (and not by h will) and which remained settled land notwithstanding his death;
8 that I believe the paper writing now produced to and marked by me to contain the true and original last Will and Testament of the said deceased;
9 and that the said Bank plc will (i) collect, get in and administer according to the law the real and personal estate of the said deceased; (ii) when required to do so by the court, exhibit on oath in the court a full inventory of the said estate and when so required render an account of the administration of the said estate to the court; and (iii) when required to do so by the High Court, deliver up the grant of letters of administration with will annexed to that court; and that to the best of my knowledge, information and belief
[the gross estate passing under the grant does not exceed £ , and the net estate does not exceed £ , and that this is not a case in which an Inland Revenue Account is required to be delivered]
[the gross estate passing under the grant amounts to £ and the net estate amounts to £].
10 Sworn by the above-
named deponent
at
this day of , 19 .
Before me
A Commissioner for Oaths (or Solicitor).

1 The full names, addresses and occupations of the deponents should be given. The nominee may give his official address, and should state his

official position with the trust corporation and the address of the corporation which is usually, but may not necessarily be, its registered office address. Account or other reference numbers should not be included unless this has been specially agreed (on application made through the Secretary of the Principal Registry). If the corporation is taking a grant with a person entitled to the grant, the name of the individual will be placed first in the grant, if entitled thereto, unless both applicants request that the trust corporation should be placed first. See also the notes to para **1** of Form 3.2, at pp 67–70.

2 See the notes to para **2** of Form 13.1, at p 184. If the deceased died intestate, substitute for the words 'having made and duly executed his last will and testament' the word 'intestate'.

3 In this paragraph clear off the persons with a prior right to the persons who have consented to the trust corporation taking the grant; see the note to para **3** of Form 13.1, at p 184.

4 Set out in this paragraph the manner in which the corporation claims the grant. If the deceased died intestate, substitute 'that *DB*, the lawful widow and relict, and *EB* and *FB*, the lawful children, of the said deceased, and together the only persons entitled to share in his estate, have consented, etc', or as the case may be.

5 It must be stated that the corporation is a trust corporation as defined by the Probate Rules, and that it has power to accept the grant.

6 It must be shown that the person executing the papers is empowered to do so, by reciting the making of the resolution. If the resolution is general in its terms, substitute for 'letters of administration . . . said deceased' the words 'all grants of representation to which it may be entitled'.

A certified copy of the resolution should be lodged with the papers to lead the grant, unless the trust corporation is a person holding an official position and the person through whom the application is made is included in a list filed with the Senior Registrar of persons authorised to make such applications.

Omit 'with will annexed' if the deceased died intestate.

7 As to minority and life interests, see the note to para **5** of Form 4.4, at p 100. As to settled land, see the notes to paras **5** and **8** of Form 3.2, at pp 73 and 76; omit the words '(and not by h will)' if the deceased died intestate.

8 See the note to para **2** of Form 3.2, at p 70, as to marking and the description of the will. Omit this paragraph if the deceased died intestate.

9 The corporation, and not its nominee, undertakes duly to administer the deceased's estate, etc. Omit 'with will annexed' if the deceased died intestate. As to the value of the estate, see the note to para **9** of Form 3.2, at pp 77–79.

10 See the note to para **10** of Form 2.11, at p 29.

Note—Where the trust corporation is taking a grant as executor, or residuary legatee and devisee in trust, or residuary legatee and devisee, the oath takes the usual form (see Forms 3.2 and 4.4) subject to the modifications explained in the notes above to paras **1**, **5**, **6**, and **9**. When the appointment of a trust corporation as executor of a will is expressed to be made on terms and conditions specifically referred to as being in existence at the date of the will, or of its republication, it must be stated in the oath that nothing in the terms and conditions limits the corporation's power to take a full grant. Otherwise it may be necessary to produce the terms and conditions when applying for the grant. In the special situation where by operation of law, usually a private Act of Parliament, the appointment of a trust corporation as executor is to be treated as the appointment of another trust corporation by reason of a takeover or merger, the grantee should be described in the oath as '   Company Limited (or as the case may be), in the events which have happened the sole executor (or as the case may be) named in the said will'. Details of the specific provision by which the change of executorship was effected should be given in the oath (see also p 64).

(e) Form of consent

Form 14.1.2 Consent to grant to trust corporation
(*For heading and title, see Form* 2.11)

1 Whereas *AB*, of   , deceased, died on the   day of   , 19   , having made and duly executed his last Will and Testament, bearing date the   day of   , 19   ,

2 whereof he did not appoint any executor but wherein he named *DB*, widow, the relict of the said deceased, the residuary legatee and devisee for life, and *EB* and *FB*, his children, the residuary legatees and devisees substituted

3 Now we, the said *DB*, *EB* and *FB* do hereby consent to letters of administration with the said will annexed of the estate of the said deceased being granted to the   Bank plc of

4 Signed by the said *DB*,
EB and *FB*
this   day of   , 19   .
in the presence of

1 As to the reference to the will, see the note to para **2** of Form 3.2, at p 70. If the deceased died intestate, substitute 'intestate' for 'having made and duly executed his last will and testament, etc'.

2 Set out in this paragraph the position with regard to executors (see also the note to para **3** of Form 13.1, at p 184) and persons, if any, with a prior right to the persons consenting, and give the title of the persons consenting.

If the deceased died intestate, substitute 'leaving *DB* his lawful widow and relict and *EB* and *FB* his lawful children, together the only persons entitled to share in his estate' or as the case may be. If necessary, clear down to the persons consenting (see the note to para **4** of Form 5.4, pp 130–133).

3 If the deceased died intestate, omit 'with the said will annexed'. Give the full title and address of the trust corporation.

4 The consent should be signed in the presence of a disinterested witness who should then sign his name and give his address.

(f) Guarantee

When a trust corporation is applying for a grant of administration, whether alone or with some other person, a guarantee by sureties will not be required except in special circumstances (see head 11.1).

(g) Renunciation by a trust corporation

A trust corporation may renounce its right to a grant either by special resolution under seal or through one of its officials appointed for the purpose by special or general resolution (see Forms 8.2.1 and 8.2.2).

14.2 Corporations other than trust corporations (Probate Rule 34)

A company, association or corporation which is not a trust corporation may take a grant only through its nominee, or if it has its principal place of business out of England and Wales, through its nominee or its lawfully constituted attorney (see p 165). All papers are executed by the nominee or attorney personally, and the grant will issue in his name for the use and benefit of the company and until further representation be granted. A nominee must be expressly appointed to obtain the grant by a resolution of the board of management or other body most completely representing the company or association. The nominee, being an agent of the corporation, is precluded from making a personal application for a grant of representation. A certified copy of the resolution under seal or otherwise authenticated to the registrar's satisfaction must be lodged with the papers. Likewise, where application for the grant is being made through an attorney, the power of attorney under seal or otherwise authenticated must be lodged with the other papers (see Form 10.4). If a life or minority interest arises under the will or intestacy, there will usually have to be at least two nominees or two attorneys, or a trust corporation must apply on behalf of the company (see head 6.2).

A corporation which is not a trust corporation and which has been appointed the executor of a will cannot take a grant of probate through its nominee. Instead, a grant of letters of administration with will annexed will issue to its nominee or attorney. Where the corporation is named as executor, it must be established that it has power under its constitution to take a grant through its nominee; this may usually be accomplished by lodging a copy of the memorandum and articles of association or other document incorporating the constitution with the papers. The requirement is not necessary where the corporation is applying as a beneficiary under the will or as a creditor. Where the corporation has been appointed executor together with an individual, a grant cannot issue to them jointly, because the individual is entitled to a grant of probate, but letters of administration with will annexed may issue to their jointly constituted attorney, provided they are both out of England. If the corporation applies alone, the renunciation of the individual will be required. For the procedure on an application by the individual alone for a grant of probate, see p 76.

(a) Form of oath

Form 14.2 Oath for grant of administration to corporation (not a trust corporation)

(*For heading and title, see Form* 2.11)

1 I, ,
of ,
2 make oath and say that ,
of ,
formerly of , deceased, died on the day of , 19 , aged years, domiciled in , having made and duly executed his last Will and Testament
3 whereof he appointed Company sole executor;
4 that the said Company is not a trust corporation as defined by Rule 2 (2) of the Non-Contentious Probate Rules 1954,
5 but that it has power under its constitution to accept the grant now sought;
6 and that by a resolution of the said Company passed on the day of , 19 (a certified copy of which is annexed hereunto) I was appointed the nominee of the said Company for the purpose of applying for letters of administration with the will annexed of the estate of the said deceased on its behalf.
7 And I further make oath and say that minority life interest arises in the estate of the said deceased, and that to the best of my knowledge, information and belief there was no land vested in the said deceased immediately before his death which was settled previously thereto (and not by h will) and which remained settled land notwithstanding his death;
8 and that I believe the paper writing now produced to and marked by me to contain the true original last Will and Testament of the said deceased;
9 and that I am the duly appointed nominee of the said Company and will (i) collect, get in and administer according to the law the real and personal estate of the said deceased for the use and benefit of the said Company and until further representation be granted; (ii) when required to do so by the court, exhibit on oath in the court a full inventory of the said estate and when so required render an account of the administration of the said estate to the court; and (iii) when required to do so by the High Court, deliver up the grant of letters of administration with will annexed to that court; and that to the best of my knowledge, information and belief
[the gross estate passing under the grant does not exceed £ , and the net estate does not exceed £ , and that this is not a case in which an Inland Revenue Account is required to be delivered]
[the gross estate passing under the grant amounts to £ and the net estate amounts to £].

10 Sworn by the above-
named deponent
at
this day of , 19 .
Before me
A Commissioner for Oaths (or Solicitor).

1 See the note to para **1** of Form 3.2, at pp 67–70.

2 See the note to para **2** of Form 13.1, at p 184.

3 Set out in this paragraph how the corporation claims the grant, whether under the terms of the will or as a creditor, if necessary clearing off the persons with a prior right to the grant (see the note to para **3** of Form 13.1, at p 184).

4 It must be stated that the corporation is not a trust corporation as defined by the Probate Rules.

5 Omit this paragraph if the corporation is not applying by reason of its appointment as executor.

6 It should be shown that the person executing the papers has been expressly empowered to do so, by reciting the making of the resolution. There is a discretion in the registrar to accept a general resolution in a proper case, for instance where a foreign corporation is frequently called upon to take an English grant and the resolution is not limited to taking a grant in the country of origin. A certified copy of the resolution should be lodged with the papers to lead the grant. If the application is by an attorney, substitute 'and that the said Company has its principal place of business out of England and I am the lawful attorney of the said Company'.

7 and **8** See the notes to paras **7** and **8** of Form 14.1.1, at p 200.

9 The nominee, or attorney, undertakes to administer the estate for the use and benefit of the corporation and until further representation is granted. If application is by an attorney, omit the reference to nominee. Omit 'with will annexed' if the deceased died intestate.

10 See the note to para **10** of Form 2.11, at p 29.

(b) Guarantee

There is a discretion to require a guarantee to be given by sureties (see head 11.1). However, where on an application for a grant of administration the applicant or one of the applicants is a nominee of a local authority within the meaning of the Local Government Act 1933 (now superseded by the Local Government Act 1972), a guarantee will be required only in special circumstances.

(c) Renunciation by a corporation other than a trust corporation

A corporation which is not a trust corporation may renounce its right to a grant in the same way that it applies for a grant, namely, through its nominee appointed to renounce on its behalf. A certified copy of the resolution, under seal or otherwise duly authenticated, should be lodged with the renunciation signed by the nominee. A form of renunciation by the corporation under seal may be accepted by the registrar.

Chapter 15

Foreign Law

In the process of obtaining a grant of representation in England and Wales it may be necessary to refer to the law of a foreign country in order:

(*a*) to establish the validity of the will; or
(*b*) to show that the applicants are entitled to the grant

15.1 Validity of the will

The circumstances which govern the choice of a law system by which to establish the validity of a will are dealt with in Chapter 2, at p 13 et seq. The facts determining the choice of law must be proved by filing a statement thereof on oath thus: 'the said will was executed at in '; *or* 'the said deceased was domiciled in (*or* had his habitual residence in) (*or* was a national of) at the time of execution of the said will (*or* at the date of his said death)'. When the testator's domicile at the time of his death is sworn in the oath in the normal course (see p 73) and reference is to be made to the law of the country of domicile at that time to establish the validity of the will, no extra wording is needed. Should it be necessary to establish that the testator was the most closely connected with one particular law system out of several, the facts relied upon to establish such a connection must be included in the statement. It is generally preferred in an application proceeding in the Principal Registry that the facts necessary to be deposed to should be set out in a separate affidavit and not in the oath, so that such affidavit may be filed with the will after the grant has issued. In an application proceeding in a district registry, they may be included in the oath, unless they are of such length as to make it inconvenient so to do, or they have been omitted from the oath, or they have to be given by a person other than the applicant, when a supplementary affidavit should be filed.

If the will is to be set up under Lord Kingsdown's Act (see head 2.1(*a*)), the essential facts bringing the will within the Act must be set out in a supplementary affidavit, or in the oath (see above), thus: 'The said deceased was a British subject at the date of the said will, and the said will is valid by the laws and constitutions of where the same was made (*or* where the said deceased was domiciled at the date of executing the same) (*or* where the said deceased had his domicile of origin) (*or* by the laws and constitutions of Scotland (*or* Northern Ireland), in which country the same was made).' Evidence as to the validity of the will under the law applicable may, of course, be necessary (see below).

(a) Proof of validity

The acceptance of a will as a valid testamentary document by a court of the country in which the deceased died domiciled is alone sufficient to establish its validity (*In the Estate of Yahuda* [1956] P 388). Proof of a will in a foreign court may be a process similar to that followed by the courts of England and Wales, which is usually the case in the United States of America and in the countries constituting the Commonwealth. It is rarely found in Latin or Germanic countries, although there are occasions when the courts of those countries formally pronounce for the validity of a will. In all these circumstances the copy of the will must be accompanied by documents (the act of probate, or a copy of the decree or judgment of the foreign court) fully establishing that the original has been accepted by the foreign court which has made a grant in respect of it, or which has formally pronounced for its validity. These documents should if possible be under the seal of the court. The more common form of proof in Latin and Germanic countries is by the formal lodgment of the original will with a notary. In such cases it is necessary to obtain a copy of the will and of the proceedings before the notary under his seal. If the documents show that the will was executed in the presence of a notary outside England and Wales and was recorded in his archives at the time of execution, it will usually be assumed to be valid as to form by the internal law of the place where it was made, unless the application is contested or there are unusual features. If it is not clear from the documents that the will has been accepted as valid, the production of the official copy is not enough and an affidavit of law (see Form 15.1) must also be provided, in order to establish that the will is valid according to the *internal* law of the country in question.

When, however, the validity of the will is to be established by reference to the law of a country other than that in which the testator died domiciled, and the will has already been proved in that country, the production of an official copy thereof may not be sufficient and an affidavit of law (see below) may also have to be provided, in order to establish that the will is valid according to the *internal* law of the country in question. But a will lodged with a notary in the circumstances described above will usually be taken to be valid without the necessity of filing an affidavit of law.

In the above instances it is not necessary to obtain an order of the court before a duly authenticated copy of the will may be admitted to proof (Probate Rule 53 (1)).

Where the original will is presented for proof, its validity has to be established by an affidavit of law (see below and Form 15.1). However, a will in the English language and in English form will usually be accepted as valid without further inquiry when the law to which reference is to be made is that of Northern Ireland, the Republic of Ireland, Australia, Canada, New Zealand or Tasmania. The fact that a will has been recorded or registered by the appropriate authority in Scotland is no indication that it is valid by Scottish law, but before proving its validity by an affidavit of law it is advisable to ask the registrar whether he would be prepared to accept other evidence. If it has been registered in Scotland and the copy is clearly marked to that effect, there is no need to account for the non-production of the original.

(b) Affidavit of law

Evidence as to the law of a foreign country will be accepted in the form of an affidavit made by any person who is suitably qualified to do so on account of his knowledge or experience, irrespective of whether he has acted or is entitled to act as a legal practitioner there (s 4 (1) of the Civil Evidence Act 1972; Probate Rule 18) (see Form 15.1, below). Usually such a person will be a barrister, advocate, or solicitor who practises, or who has practised, in the courts of the country in question. The affidavits of other persons will be accepted if the registrar is satisfied that by reason of their official position, eg, a diplomatic or consular officer, or otherwise, they have a reliable knowledge of the foreign law. The affidavit must set out particulars of the knowledge and experience claimed by the deponent to make him competent to give expert evidence of the law of the country in question. Thus the evidence of a lawyer who is qualified in the laws of one of the States of the United States of America may be accepted in respect of the laws of another State if he swears that he is fully conversant with the laws of the latter State. The evidence of a fully qualified French lawyer may be accepted as to the law of Belgium if the affidavit shows that he is entitled to practise and has practised in the Belgian courts and is conversant with the law of Belgium.

There is no ban on the acceptance of an affidavit of law made by the person claiming to be entitled or his attorney or the spouse of such person or attorney; it is within the discretion of the registrar to accept such an affidavit in the light of the particular circumstances.

Form 15.1 Affidavit of law

(For heading and title, see Form 2.11)

1 I, ,
of ,
advocate, make oath and say that
2 I am a and have practised as such for the last years in ,
and as such I am fully conversant with the laws and constitutions of ;
3 that I am informed and verily believe that *AB*, of
, deceased, died on the day of , 19 , domiciled in
, having made his last Will and Testament bearing date the day
of , 19 ;
4 that I have referred to the said Will, as contained in a notarial copy thereof, which is now produced to me and marked ' ' and I say that the said

Will is made in conformity with and is valid by the aforesaid laws and constitutions;

5 and that in accordance with the aforesaid laws and constitutions the original will of the said deceased has been deposited amongst the records of *NP*, of , and must remain so deposited forever, but that the said *NP* is authorised to deliver out copies thereof under his hand and seal which are to be accepted as true and authentic copies of the original in all courts in .

6 And I further make oath and say that the said deceased in his said will named *MN* and *ST* as his universal heirs and accordingly I say that the said *MN* and *ST* are the persons entitled jointly and severally to administer the estate of the said deceased by the laws and constitutions of , the place where the deceased died domiciled, without the necessity of obtaining a grant of representation or an order of the court authorising them to administer the said estate.

7 Sworn by the above-named deponent at
this day of , 19 .
Before me
A Commissioner for Oaths (or Solicitor).

1 The full name, address and description should be given (see also note to para **2**). If the person giving evidence wishes to affirm, the words 'make oath and say' should be altered to 'do solemnly and sincerely affirm'. The words 'make oath' in para **6** should be replaced by 'affirm' and 'Sworn' in the jurat (para **7**) by 'Affirmed'.

2 Set out in this paragraph the qualifications of the deponent entitling him to claim to be an expert in the laws of the country concerned, including, if appropriate, the fact that he is practising and/or has practised as a barrister, advocate or solicitor as the case may be, for some time past in the country concerned (see also p 207).

3 If the deceased died intestate, the affidavit being required to establish the title of the applicant for the grant, substitute 'intestate' for the words 'having made his last will and testament, etc'; paras **4** and **5** are then unnecessary.

When the validity of the deceased's will is to be established by reference to the law of a country other than that in which he died domiciled, eg, under the Wills Act 1963, in respect of a testator who died on or after 1 January 1964, the affidavit must recite the facts which are being relied upon to establish a connection between the deceased and the country in question; these facts must of course be proved separately (see pp 205–206). In such a case, add at the end of this paragraph: 'and I am further informed and verily believe that the said will was executed at in [*or* the said deceased was domiciled in at the date of execution of the said will] [*or* the said deceased was habitually resident at in (*or* was a national of) at the date of execution of the said will (*or* at the date of his death)].'

If there are two or more law systems in force in the country to which reference is to be made, it should be stated in this paragraph whether there is any rule in force which governs the choice of law and, if so, how the rule is to be applied, or, if not, that there is no such rule (see p 14).

4 If the original will is being proved, delete the reference to a notarial copy, or alter as appropriate.

Note that where the validity of the will of a testator dying on or after 1 January 1964 is to be established under the Wills Act 1963, the reference is to the internal law of the country in question (see p 13).

5 Where the original will is not available, this paragraph should give the reason for its non-production.

6 If it is necessary to establish the applicant's title to an English grant, this paragraph should be included to show who are the persons (including the applicant) entitled to administer the deceased's estate under the foreign law. Any relevant act of notariety should be referred to and a copy lodged for inspection; a translation is not usually required. If the deceased died intestate, delete the reference to the deceased's will and substitute 'that the said deceased died a widower leaving *MN* and *ST* his lawful children, *or as the case may be*'. If there are several persons entitled to administer, it must be shown whether they are entitled to administer jointly or severally or both. If they are entitled only jointly, all must apply or join in giving a power of attorney. Note that it is with the applicant's power to administer the deceased's estate that the court is usually concerned, not his right to benefit; however the right to benefit may be a material fact on an application under Probate Rule 29 (*c*) (see head 15.2(*e*)).

The words 'the place where the deceased died domiciled' should be altered as appropriate.

7 See the note to para **10** of Form 2.11, at p 29.

(c) Translations

Wills and other documents in a foreign language must be accompanied by translations. These should be prepared by an English notary and authenticated by his seal or by any British consular official. When it is not possible to obtain a notarial or consular translation, a translation made by some other person fully conversant with the foreign language may be accepted. Such a person is generally one who holds or has held a post in the diplomatic or consular service, and by reason of such service can be deemed to have a thorough knowledge of the foreign and English languages. The direction of the registrar should first be obtained and it may be necessary for the person making the translation to make an affidavit setting out his qualifications and verifying the translation. A notarial translation which contains, not a copy of an original English will, but a re-translation of it, should be accompanied by a photographic copy or other duly verified copy of the original.

A will or codicil in the Welsh language will normally be translated by an official of the probate registry without charge, and the document should be given to the registrar of the registry from which it is intended that probate shall issue, who will arrange for the translation to be made. A notarial or other verified translation will be accepted if more convenient to avoid delay or for some other reason, in which case the applicant will be reimbursed out of the account of the issuing probate registry for notarial charges not exceeding 70p per folio of 72 words. The probate copy inserted in the grant will consist of a copy (photographic, typed or fiat as the case may be) of the original document together with a copy of the translation into English.

15.2 Entitlement to an English grant (Probate Rule 29)

(a) Probate

Where a will, written in the English or Welsh language, can be shown to be formally valid in accordance with any law to which reference may be made (see p 13 et seq), probate thereof will issue to any executor named therein. He will be regarded as having full rights of executorship and no inquiry as to the extent or duration of his powers will be made save in so far as they are limited by the terms of the will.

Where it is required to obtain a grant of representation in England and Wales in respect of the estate of a person who has died domiciled in Scotland or Northern Ireland instead of, or before, obtaining a grant in the country of domicile, the oath or supporting affidavit by the executor must additionally show (*a*) that no confirmation, or grant, has been issued in the country of domicile and (*b*) the reason why it is desired to obtain a grant in England and Wales instead of, or before, obtaining representation in the country of domicile (see p 220). The grant is limited to estate in England and Wales and further limited until representation be granted in Scotland, or Northern Ireland, unless the registrar has specifically directed otherwise.

If the will describes the duties of a named person in such terms as to constitute him the executor according to the tenor, probate will also issue to that person, whether the will is in the English or Welsh language or in some other language. However, an appointment purporting to be that of an executor in a foreign language will not of itself entitle the person so appointed to a grant of probate.

Application for a grant of letters of administration with will annexed may be made by the attorney of the executor in the usual way (see head 10.1). This applies also to a foreign corporation which, if an individual, would be entitled to a grant of probate (see p 202). It is immaterial whether or not the will has already been proved in the place of domicile unless a grant has already been made in this country to the person entrusted.

The renunciation by an executor of his right to probate of the will in the country of domicile does not operate to prevent him from applying for and obtaining probate of the will in England and Wales; on an application by other executors named in the will, power will be reserved to the renouncing executor in such circumstances.

(b) Administration

Where the deceased died on or after 1 January 1926 domiciled in a country other than England and Wales and intestate, or leaving no person entitled or willing to take a grant of probate, the ordinary rules for determining the entitlement to a grant of administration do not apply, subject to one exception. Instead, a grant will issue by order of the court. This is so even if the applicant would have been the person entitled to the grant under the rules applicable if the deceased had died domiciled in England and Wales (*In the Goods of Kaufman* [1952] P 325). However, where the whole of the estate in England and Wales consists of immovable property, a grant limited to such property may issue to the persons entitled under the law which would have been applicable had the deceased died domiciled in England and Wales.

It may not always be necessary to obtain a separate English grant to administer the estate in England and Wales (*a*) if in the circumstances application can be made for a grant of representation obtained in some other country to be re-sealed (see head 17.2) or (*b*) if, in the case of a person who died domiciled in Scotland or in Northern Ireland, a grant has already issued in the country of domicile (see head 17.1).

In considering an application for an order, the court will give preference to the following persons:

(*a*) the 'person entrusted' with the administration of the estate by the court having jurisdiction at the place at which the deceased died domiciled; or

(*b*) the 'person entitled' to administer the estate by the law of the place at which the deceased died domiciled.

The court will not make an order for a grant to issue to a person who is a minor.

(c) *Person entrusted*

A person entrusted must produce documents under the seal, if any, of the foreign court fully establishing that he has been entrusted with the administration of the estate in a manner generally corresponding to the issue of an English grant of representation. Documents in a foreign language must be accompanied by a translation (see head 15.1(*c*)). A person entrusted takes precedence over all others and does not have to clear off executors.

If the powers of the person entrusted are limited as to time under the foreign grant, and it can be shown (*a*) that the grant is required solely for the purpose of collecting English assets, (*b*) that this can be done within the time prescribed, and (*c*) that there are no debts in England, the order and the subsequent grant will contain a similar limitation as to time.

It is to be noted that since and including 1 January 1974 grants of representation in Sri Lanka have been issued by the Public Trustee of that country. A grantee acting under such a grant is not accepted as a 'person entrusted' but will be treated as a 'person entitled', the production of the grant being taken as sufficient proof of his entitlement to administer the estate. Such a grant will, however, be accepted for re-sealing in an appropriate case.

(d) Person entitled

The claim to be a person entitled must be supported by an affidavit of law made by a duly qualified expert (see head 15.1(*b*) and Form 15.1), establishing that the applicant is entitled to administer the deceased's estate according to the law of the latter's place of domicile at the date of his death. The facts upon which the affidavit of law is based must be sworn to by the applicant either in a separate affidavit or in the oath (and see pp 205–207). A person entitled does not have to clear off executors. An applicant who would be entitled to administer the estate by the law of the place of domicile only if he were to obtain a grant of representation in that country or to comply with certain prescribed formalities will not be regarded as a 'person entitled' for the purpose of the application.

Where it is not possible, or it would be unnecessarily expensive having regard to the size of the estate, to provide an affidavit of law, the registrar may be prepared to dispense with this requirement if there is sufficient other evidence as to the applicant's entitlement such as a certificate of inheritance or an act of notariety.

(e) Application under Probate Rule 29 (c)

If there is no person entrusted or entitled, or in special circumstances, the registrar may make an order in favour of some other person or persons. Thus, where the deceased left no estate in the country in which he died domiciled, and there is, therefore, no need to obtain a grant of representation in that country, the person who would be entitled to apply for such a grant may apply for an order under Probate Rule 29 (*c*). An applicant must satisfy the court that the special circumstances of the case justify the making of an order in his favour, eg, in the example quoted, it should be stated why the applicant has not taken the steps necessary to constitute himself the person entrusted and whether he intends ultimately to do so. An affidavit of law is not always necessary and the direction of the registrar should be taken.

In the special case of a person who has died domiciled in Scotland or Northern Ireland, where for some reason it is not desired to extract a grant in the country of domicile, for instance because the deceased left no estate there, or where it is required to obtain a grant of representation in England and Wales before taking a confirmation or grant in the country of domicile, application should be made under Probate Rule 29 (*c*), except (i) where the application is to be made by the executor or by an attorney of the executor (see p 210 under Probate), or (ii) where the whole of the estate in England and Wales consists of immovable property (see p 211 under Administration). The usual practice is applicable and additionally it must be shown in the oath or supporting affidavit (*a*) that no confirmation, or grant, has been issued in the country of domicile and (*b*) the reason why it is desired to obtain a grant in England and Wales instead of, or before, obtaining a grant of representation in the country of domicile. The grant is limited to the estate in England and Wales and further limited until representation be granted in Scotland, or Northern Ireland, unless the registrar has specifically directed otherwise. If a confirmation or grant, containing a statement as to the domicile of the applicant, has already issued in the country of domicile, there is no need to apply for a further grant in England and Wales (see head 17.1).

(f) Application under Probate Rule 29 (d)

Where it is required that the grant should be made to at least two individuals, application may be made for an order for the grant to issue to such person as the registrar may direct jointly with the person entrusted or entitled or with any other person.

(g) Procedure

The application for an order of the court may be made ex parte to a registrar of the Principal Registry (through the Probate Department), or to a district probate registrar when application for the grant is to be made at a district probate registry, by lodging the affidavits in support, together with the will (if any), or an official copy thereof, the foreign grant of representation (if any) and any other necessary documents. The registrar has power to make orders irrespective of the amount of the estate but in any particular case he may require the application to be brought before a registrar of the Principal Registry or a judge by summons or before the court on motion. The order will direct that a grant issue to the 'person entrusted' or 'person entitled' or to the applicant or applicants by name.

Alternatively, when application is being made by the person entrusted or entitled, it is permissible to lodge the documents in support of the application with the papers to lead the subsequent grant at either the Principal Registry or a district probate registry. The contents of the applicant's affidavit may then be included in the oath. The oath is in the usual form (see Forms 4.4 and 5.4) subject to the modifications indicated in the notes thereto. If the registrar makes the order, and the papers to lead the grant are without defect, the grant will issue without further application having to be made. It may sometimes be convenient to adopt this procedure when application is to be made under Probate Rule 29 (*c*) (or 29 (*d*)), but the oath must be so worded as to give a sufficient title and must not be inconsistent with the order made; otherwise it will have to be amended to recite the making of the order and re-executed (see the note to para 8 of Form 4.4, at p 103). The facts leading to the order should be set out in a separate affidavit.

If there is no person in existence who will succeed to estate in England and Wales passing under a total or partial intestacy by the law of the deceased's domicile, the estate may become bona vacantia (*Re Barnett's Trusts* [1902] 1 Ch 847; but see also *In the Estate of Maldonado, decd* [1954] P 223, and *Re Mitchell* [1954] Ch 525). The applicant must, therefore, either show that there are kin or other persons who are entitled to share in the estate under the foreign law or lodge the Treasury Solicitor's consent to the issue of a grant.

(h) Grant to attorney

A grant will be made by order to the attorney of a person entrusted or entitled until further representation be granted. Should the donor of the power later apply for a direct grant to himself, he must obtain a further order of the court and he will be required to lodge an affidavit showing either that he is still the person entrusted or that he is still entitled to administer the deceased's estate according to the law of the place of domicile.

(i) Minority and life interests

The existence of a minority or life interest is determined according to the law applicable to the circumstances of the particular case. If there is such an interest, the grant will usually have to be made to at least two individuals or a trust corporation (see head 6.2), notwithstanding that the law to which reference has to be made would allow a grant to be made to one individual. Usually it will be sufficient to state in the oath that minority or life interests do or do not exist. However, if it is alleged that there is no minority or life interest, but it would appear from the will or otherwise that there might be such an interest, the position should be clarified by an affidavit of law (see head 15.1(*b*)).

Chapter 16

Amendment and Revocation of Grants

On good cause being shown, a grant of representation will be amended or revoked by order of a registrar of the Principal Registry. If the grant issued from a district probate registry, the application may also be made to any district probate registrar (s 105 of the Supreme Court Act 1981; Probate Rules 42 and 2 (2)). Except in special circumstances, for instance where the grantee cannot be found, the order will not be made save on the application, or with the consent, of the person to whom the grant was made.

When an error is discovered in a grant, it depends on the nature of the error whether the registrar will allow the grant to be amended or require it to be revoked. Unimportant errors in the names of the deceased or the grantee, or in addresses or dates, may be put right by amendment but if, for instance, the true surname of the deceased is quite different from that appearing in the grant, revocation is necessary. In cases of doubt the direction of the registrar should first be obtained.

16.1 Amendment

Application for the amendment of a grant is made by lodging in the registry (with the Record Keeper if application is made in the Principal Registry) the original grant, together with an affidavit by the grantee setting out the nature of the error, the reason for it and the amendment required. No fee is payable. An application by a solicitor may be sent through the post; no correspondence fee is payable. If the error is in the name of the deceased or in the date of death or is otherwise of substance, a fresh guarantee may have to be given or the original guarantee altered and re-executed by the sureties. If satisfied, the registrar makes an order and the grant is amended in the registry. An application for amendment of the probate copy of the will is made in a similar manner.

If the grant is found to be inaccurate or deficient by reason of an official error and it is returned (with any official copies which may have issued) to the registry within fourteen days of the date thereof, it will be re-written provided that it has not been registered. Otherwise, it must be amended by order but no affidavit will usually be required.

(a) Amendment as to value of estate

When it is required that an alteration in the amount of the estate be noted on the grant, application should be made to the Capital Taxes Office, by forwarding a corrective account (CAP Form D-3; see p 231) and the original grant. Where a grant of administration has issued before 1 January 1972 the Inland Revenue authorities may need to be satisfied that sufficient security to cover the increased estate has been given; for the procedure, see p 175.

(b) Notation of appointment of additional personal representative

See head 6.3.

(c) Notation of order of the court

Where an order has been made under the Inheritance (Provision for Family and Dependants) Act 1975 (except under s 15(1)) the grant is sent by the court to the Principal Registry, together with an office copy of the order, for a memorandum of the order to be prepared. The memorandum is filed with the original will and a photographic copy thereof is attached to the original grant, which is then noted to that effect. No fee is payable. The memorandum is prepared in all cases where a final order is made, including an order embodying terms of compromise.

Similarly, where an order has been made under s 20(1) of the Administration of Justice Act 1982 for rectification of a will after the grant has issued, a copy of the order is sent to the Principal Registry for filing and a memorandum of the order is thereupon endorsed on, or permanently attached to, the original grant (RSC, Ord 76, r 16(2)).

(d) Notation as to redemption of life interest

The surviving spouse of an intestate dying on or after 1 January 1953 may, under s 47A of the Administration of Estates Act 1925, as amended, require the deceased's personal representatives to redeem his or her life interest. Where the surviving spouse is the sole personal representative and elects to have the life interest redeemed, he or she must give written notice of election, usually within twelve months of the date of the grant, by filing the prescribed notice (Form 7 of Sched 1 to the Non-Contentious Probate Rules 1954) with the Record Keeper of the Principal Registry or in the district registry from which the grant issued (Probate Rule 56). The notice should be in duplicate if filed in a district registry. The original grant should be lodged at the same time and a notation is made thereon. No fee is payable for filing the notice.

16.2 Revocation

In addition to the instance already mentioned where the nature of an error on the face of the grant is too serious to allow of amendment, a grant will be revoked if some or all of the facts upon which its issue was based were false. Thus, revocation will be ordered where the grantee was not in fact a person entitled to the grant, where a will has been found after the issue of a grant based on an intestacy, where a will admitted to proof is subsequently found not to have been properly executed, or where the 'deceased' is found to be alive. (For the position when an executor or administrator becomes incapable owing to mental illness, see head 9.2(*d*).)

Application for revocation of a grant may be made by the grantee or, with the consent of the grantee, by a person having a right to a new grant. If on an application by someone other than the grantee, the latter's consent cannot be obtained, the order will not be made save in special circumstances, for instance where the grantee's whereabouts are unknown. Otherwise it may be necessary to apply to the Chancery Division by writ for revocation of the grant, or in an appropriate case for the appointment of a judicial trustee (see head 13.3). In the normal case the grant, an affidavit of facts and such further evidence in support as may be required should be lodged in the registry (with the Record Keeper if application is made in the Principal Registry). No fee is payable. The application may be sent through the post if made by a solicitor; there is no correspondence fee. If satisfied, the registrar makes an order and the grant is cancelled and retained in the registry. In the special case where a grant of probate is to be revoked because of the death of one of several executors before the grant was sealed and a new grant is to be issued to the surviving executor or executors (see p 7), the affidavit to lead the order for revocation may also serve as the oath to lead the new grant. The will may be referred to as that which has already been proved and it need not be marked, nor need a copy be annexed. It is not necessary to lodge a fresh Inland Revenue account in such circumstances and the values of the estate to be quoted in the affidavit should be those appearing in the original grant. This procedure is not applied where the original grant is one of administration, with or without will annexed, but in suitable cases, for instance where the applicants are the surviving grantees, the registrar may dispense with the swearing of a further oath provided the applicants lodge a consent to the issue of the new grant, endorsed with a cross-reference to the oath filed to lead to the original grant.

If the person having possession of the original grant refuses to hand it over or to lodge it in the registry, he should be served with a citation to bring in the grant, issued out of the Principal Registry. Failure to obey the citation is punishable by committal for contempt. Where the grant cannot be produced because it has been lost or is held in some other country, it may still be revoked but the applicant may be required to bring it into the registry when found or available.

The court has power of its own motion to call in a grant of representation where it appears that the grant ought not to have been made, or that it contains an error, and, if satisfied that the grant would be revoked at the instance of a party interested, the court will revoke it (even if it cannot be called in) (s 121 (1) and (2) of the Supreme Court Act 1981).

Section 27 of the Administration of Estates Act 1925 provides that where a grant of representation is revoked, payments made and acts done in good faith in the course of administration of the estate are to be treated as valid.

(For the cancellation of a re-sealing see head 17.2(*e*).)

Chapter 17

Recognition of Grants: Re-sealing

When a person has died leaving estate not only in England and Wales but also in certain Commonwealth countries, British possessions or trust territories, it may be found more convenient, instead of taking out a separate grant in each country in which property is situated, to apply for a grant of representation obtained in one of these countries to be re-sealed in each of the other countries. The re-sealing of a grant enables the grantees to administer the estate of the deceased in the country in which re-sealing has been effected. Before 1 January 1972 it was possible to apply for Scottish confirmations and Northern Irish grants to be re-sealed in England and Wales and for English grants to be re-sealed in Scotland and Northern Ireland. This practice was abolished by the Administration of Estates Act 1971 under which a grant of representation issued in any one of those three countries in respect of the estate of a person who has died domiciled in the country of issue will be recognised in both the other two countries, provided that the grant contains a statement of the deceased's domicile (ss 1, 2 and 3 of the Act of 1971).

17.1 Recognition of grants under the Administration of Estates Act 1971

In the case of a person who has died domiciled in Scotland, a confirmation granted whether before or after 1 January 1972 in respect of all or part of the deceased's estate and containing a statement as to his Scottish domicile will be treated in England and Wales, without being re-sealed, as if it were an English grant issued to the executors named in the confirmation in respect of the property of the deceased set out in the inventory attached to the confirmation (s 1 of the Act). The inventory may include real estate situated in England and Wales or in Northern Ireland. 'Confirmation' includes an additional confirmation, and a certificate of confirmation relating to one or more specified items of the deceased's estate will similarly be accepted as the equivalent of an English grant in respect of those items provided that it is noted with the deceased's Scottish domicile. A confirmation or certificate of confirmation which satisfies the conditions will be treated as a grant of probate where the executors are executors nominate, and in all other cases as a grant of letters of administration. However, a chain of representation will not arise in respect of executors nominate (see head 3.1). Where a confirmation or additional confirmation contains or has appended thereto a note or a statement of property in England and Wales held by the deceased in trust, the executors will be as competent to deal with such property as they are in respect of other property specified in the confirmation.

Similarly where a person has died domiciled in Northern Ireland, a grant of probate of his will or of letters of administration in respect of all or part of his estate, whether issued before or after 1 January 1972 will be treated in England and Wales, without being re-sealed, as if it had been issued by the court in England and Wales provided that it contains a statement of the deceased's Northern Irish domicile. In this case, however, a chain of representation may arise in respect of a Northern Irish grant of probate (see head 3.1).

It follows that where a person died domiciled in Scotland or Northern Ireland and leaving estate in England and Wales the usual procedure will be for representation to be obtained in the country of domicile, in which case the confirmation or grant will be recognised in England and Wales without the necessity of obtaining a further grant. However, if it is not necessary to obtain representation in the country of domicile or if it is desired to deal with the English estate before obtaining representation in the country of domicile, application must be made for a grant in the usual manner and the grant will be limited unless otherwise directed to the estate in England and Wales and until representation is granted in the country of domicile (see p 210).

It is also provided by the Act that where a person has died domiciled in England and Wales, an English grant of probate or letters of administration, which contains a note of the deceased's domicile, will have the same effect in respect of the deceased's estate in Scotland as if it were a Scottish confirmation issued to the executor or administrator named in the grant and will be treated in respect of the deceased's estate in Northern Ireland as if it had originally been issued by the court in Northern Ireland (ss 3 and 2 of the Act). This applies to grants issued before as well as after 1 January 1972. A grant issuing after that date will always contain a note of the deceased's domicile but where the grant has issued prior to 1 January 1972 and omits the statement of domicile it will be necessary to apply for a notation of domicile to be placed on the grant. The application is made to the registry from which the grant issued (the Record Keeper in the case of the Principal Registry). It must be supported by an affidavit setting out that the deceased died domiciled in England and Wales, that he left assets in Scotland or Northern Ireland as the case may be (or giving such other reason requiring the notation of domicile to be made), that a grant has issued in England and Wales, and that a notation of domicile is required thereon. No fee is payable, nor is there a correspondence fee if the application is made by post. The registrar will then order the notation to be made on the grant.

A document purporting to be a confirmation or grant of representation issued under the seal of the appropriate court is to be taken to be such a confirmation or grant without further proof, and a duplicate of a confirmation or a copy of a grant issued under the seal of the appropriate court is to be received in evidence in the same manner as the confirmation or grant of which it purports to be a duplicate or copy (s 4 of the Act).

17.2 Re-sealing under the Colonial Probates Acts 1892 and 1927

By virtue of the Colonial Probates Act 1892, as modified by the Colonial Probates (Protected States and Mandated Territories) Act 1927, grants issued out of certain Commonwealth countries, British possessions or trust territories may be re-sealed in England, whereupon they have the same effect throughout the United Kingdom as if they had originally been obtained in England. Re-sealing is within the discretion of the court and will be carried out only in respect of grants issued in territories to which the Act has been applied by Order in Council. The various Orders in Council have been consolidated in the Colonial Probates Act Application Order 1965, Sched 1 to which contains the list of countries to which the Act of 1892 has been applied. These countries together with any other countries subsequently added to the list, are as follows:

Alberta
Anguilla
Antigua and Barbuda
Australian Capital Territory
Bahamas
Barbados
Belize (formerly British Honduras)
Bermuda
Botswana (formerly Bechuanaland)
British Antarctic Territory
British Columbia
British Sovereign Base Areas in Cyprus
Brunei
Cayman Islands
Christmas Island (Australian)
Cocos (Keeling) Islands
Cyprus (Republic)
Dominica
Falkland Islands and Dependencies
Fiji
Gambia
Ghana
Gibraltar
Grenada
Guyana (formerly British Guiana)
Hong Kong
Jamaica
Kenya
Kiribati (formerly Gilbert Islands)
Lesotho (formerly Basutoland)
Malawi
Malaysia
Manitoba
Montserrat
New Brunswick
New Guinea Territory
New South Wales
New Zealand
Newfoundland
Nigeria
Norfolk Island
North West Territories of Canada
Northern Territory of Australia
Nova Scotia
Ontario
Papua

Prince Edward Island
Queensland
St Christopher-Nevis
St Helena
St Lucia
St Vincent
Saskatchewan
Seychelles (Republic)
Sierra Leone
Singapore
Solomon Islands
South Australia
Sri Lanka (formerly Ceylon)
Swaziland
Tanzania
Tasmania
Tortola (formerly Virgin Islands)
Trinidad and Tobago
Turks and Caicos Islands
Tuvalu (formerly Ellice Islands)
Uganda
Victoria
Western Australia
Zambia
Zimbabwe (formerly Rhodesia)

It is to be noted that the Act of 1892 still applies to the Republic of South Africa, by virtue of s 2 (1) of, and para 1 of Sched 2 to the South Africa Act 1962.

Once an Order in Council has applied the Act to a particular territory, grants issued in that territory may be re-sealed irrespective of the date of their issue.

(a) Who may apply

The application should be made by the person or persons to whom the grant was made, or by any person authorised in writing to apply on his or their behalf (Probate Rule 41). All the grantees should join in the application or authorisation, but, if this is not possible, the consents of those who have not done so should be lodged; otherwise a sufficient reason may have to be given by affidavit, eg, that such grantees have died.

The authorisation of a person who is applying on behalf of the grantee need not be in the form of a power of attorney, so long as it is in writing (for powers of attorney, see Chapter 10 and Form 10.4). There is no prescribed form of wording but it must be clear that the authority conferred thereby extends to an application to re-seal the colonial grant for the purpose of administering the deceased's estate in England and Wales.

Where the colonial grant has been made to the attorney of the person entitled, it is not necessary to lodge the original or a certified copy of the power of attorney for inspection in the probate registry. If the power is limited to the deceased's property out of England and Wales, the grant will not be re-sealed.

(b) Title of grantee

A grant will be accepted for re-sealing if it has been made in circumstances similar to those in which a grant would have been made in England and Wales, that is to say:

(*a*) where it was made by the court having jurisdiction at the place where the deceased died domiciled; or (*b*) where it was made by a court other than the court of the deceased's domicile, provided that it was given (i) to the person entrusted with the administration of the estate by the court of the deceased's domicile, or (ii) to the person entitled to administer the estate by the law of the deceased's domicile (in which case an affidavit of law may be required), or (iii) in respect of a will admissible to proof (see p 13 et seq), to the executor named in that will in the English or Welsh language or, whatever the language used in the will, to the person given such duties in that will as to constitute him executor according to the tenor.

If a grant has been made in circumstances other than those just described, it will not be re-sealed except by leave of a registrar of the Principal Registry. In such a case the circumstances in which the grant issued may have to be recited in an affidavit in support of the application.

In New Zealand a trustee company is permitted in certain circumstances to file an election to administer as an alternative to obtaining a grant of representation, whereupon it is deemed to be the personal representative of the deceased. Such an election may be re-sealed in England and Wales on a certificate being lodged that the election is still in force, together with an undertaking not to proceed with the administration of the estate in England and Wales if the circumstances change so as to make the election invalid. Elections or similar documents having the same effect as a grant, obtained in other countries to which the Colonial Probates Acts apply, may also be re-sealed on production of a copy of the local ordinance which validates this procedure.

The leave of a registrar of the Principal Registry must also be obtained for the re-sealing of a limited or temporary grant. This requirement does not apply to a grant expressed to relate to personal estate only. A grant expressly limited to estate within the jurisdiction of the issuing court will not be re-sealed. A grant issued by the court of domicile may be re-sealed although made to a corporation which is not a trust corporation and which has its principal place of business out of England and Wales (*Re McLaughlin* [1922] P 235).

(c) Procedure

Notice of the application for re-sealing does not have to be advertised unless, on consideration of the application, the registrar gives directions for such advertisement to be made.

The papers in support of the application should be lodged at the Principal Registry, either by the grantees or their duly authorised agent in person or by their solicitor with the Receiver of Papers. Alternatively, the papers may be sent through the post to the Receiver of Papers (see p 5) or application may be made through the Personal Application Department (see p 10). Any court fees required to be paid (see Appendix 1) including any departmental fees should be paid at the same time by enclosing with the papers a crossed cheque made payable to 'HM Paymaster General'. The papers required are as follows:

(i) The original grant; a duplicate or a certified copy will be accepted, also an exemplification if containing all the essential parts of the grant.
(ii) If the original grant does not include a copy of the will to which the grant relates, a copy of the will certified as correct by or under the authority of the court which issued the grant.
(iii) A plain copy of the grant and of the will, if any; alternatively, a photographic copy will be prepared in the registry at a charge of 25p per sheet.
(iv) Where it is sought to re-seal a grant of administration, and if required by the registrar, a guarantee by sureties (see below).
(v) An Inland Revenue account, accounting for the tax, if any, payable in respect of the deceased's property in the United Kingdom. This must have been controlled by the Capital Taxes Office and any tax paid (see head 18.3). The account is usually made by the person making the application, but this may be done by the grantee although someone else is applying on his behalf.
(vi) An authorisation in writing, if appropriate.

The registrar may require the application to be supported by an oath made by the person making the application. The statement as to the domicile of the deceased contained in the Inland Revenue account is usually accepted as sufficient. A statement is necessary to show that there is a good and sufficient reason for re-sealing the grant when there is no estate in England and Wales.

(d) Guarantee

The duties laid upon a personal representative (by s 25 of the Administration of Estates Act 1925, as amended by s 9 of the Administration of Estates Act 1971, and see head 1.5) are similarly placed upon a person to whom letters of administration have been granted in a country to which the Colonial Probates Act 1892 applies as soon as such a grant is re-sealed (s 11 (2) of the Administration of Estates Act 1971). To ensure the proper performance of those duties the court may require as a condition of re-sealing letters of administration issued in any such country that one or more sureties should guarantee that they will make good, within prescribed limits, any loss which any person interested in the administration of the deceased's estate in England and Wales may suffer in consequence of a breach by the administrator of his duties in administering it there (s 11 (3) of the Administration of Estates Act 1971). A guarantee will be required when the grant has been made to a person or for a purpose such that a guarantee would have been required had application for a grant of administration been made in England and Wales (Probate Rule 41 (2A)—see head 11.1). It is to be noted that whether or not a guarantee is required may depend on the status of the grantee, not on that of the duly authorised agent; in this respect a guarantee will be required in many cases because the grantee resides out of the United Kingdom. However it is possible that in the exercise of his discretion to dispense with a guarantee in special circumstances the registrar may be prepared so to dispense when the application for re-sealing is made by one of the persons listed in Probate Rule 38 (2) (see head 11.2). In a case where a guarantee would normally, or is likely to, be required, the registrar may be prepared to dispense with such a requirement on production of a certificate by the appropriate officer of the court from which the grant issued to the effect that security has been given in a sum sufficient to cover the property which will be covered by the re-sealing.

The guarantee must be in the prescribed form (Form 2 in the Schedule to the Non-Contentious Probate Rules—see below).

Form 17.2 Surety's guarantee under Colonial Probates Acts 1892 and 1927
(*For heading and title, see Form* 2.11)

1 Whereas , of died on the day of , 19 , and
2 letters of administration of his estate were on the day of , 19 , granted by the to and and are about to be sealed in England and Wales under the Colonial Probates Acts 1892 and 1927. Now therefore:
3 1 I/We of and of hereby [jointly and severally] guarantee that I/we will, when lawfully required to do so, make good any loss which any person interested in the administration of the estate of the deceased in England and Wales may suffer in consequence of the breach by the administrator(s) of his/her/their duty—

(*a*) to collect and get in the estate of the deceased which is situated in England and Wales and administer it according to law;

(*b*) when required to do so by the court, to exhibit on oath in the court a full inventory of the estate which is situated in England and Wales and, when so required, to render an account of that estate.

2 The giving of time to the administrator(s) or any other forbearance or indulgence shall not in any way affect my/our liability under this guarantee.
4 3 The liability under this guarantee shall be continuing and shall be for the whole amount of the loss mentioned in paragraph 1 above, but (my) (our aggregate) total liability shall not in any event exceed the sum of £
5 Dated this day of , 19 .
Signed, sealed and delivered by the above-named
in the presence of

LS

A Commissioner for Oaths (or Solicitor).

1 The name and address of the deceased and the date of death are inserted here.

2 The full names, addresses and descriptions of the administrators must be inserted here together with the description of the court by which the grant was issued.

3, **4** and **5** See the notes to para **3**, **4** and **5** of Form 11.3.1, at p 172 et seq.

(e) Cancellation of re-sealing

Where a grant which has been re-sealed is subsequently found to have been issued incorrectly, it is the practice of the court to cancel the re-sealing on application being made by a person interested. The procedure for making the application is similar to that for revoking a grant (see head 16.2). Since 1 January 1982 the court has had power of its own motion to call in a grant or other document which has been re-sealed where it appears that the document ought not to have been re-sealed, and if satisfied that the re-sealing would be cancelled on the application of a person interested, to cancel the re-sealing accordingly (s 121 (3) of the Supreme Court Act 1981). If the document cannot be called in, the court may cancel the re-sealing notwithstanding (s 121 (4) of the Supreme Court Act 1981).

Chapter 18

Inland Revenue Accounts

[NOTE—Liability for capital transfer tax is a subject in itself and has been dealt with fully elsewhere, eg, *Dymond's Death Duties*. However, inasmuch as an Inland Revenue account may have to be lodged with the papers to lead a grant of representation, a short account of the various forms and of the procedure for filing them is given below.]

18.1 Capital transfer tax

Capital transfer tax is a tax in respect of the estates of persons dying on or after 13 March 1975 (s 49 (1) of the Finance Act 1975). It is a tax levied on the value transferred by a chargeable transfer (s 19 (1)). A transfer of value is defined (s 20 (2)) as any disposition made by a person as a result of which the value of his estate immediately after the disposition is less than it would be but for the disposition, and the amount by which it is less is the value transferred by the transfer. Unlike estate duty, which it replaced, the tax applies not only to transfers on death (on or after 13 March 1975), the deceased being deemed immediately before his death to have made a transfer of the value of his estate, but also to gifts and other gratuitous transfers made in the lifetime (after 26 March 1974) and to transfers relating to settled property. There are a number of exemptions specified in the statute, and certain types of property are excluded in special circumstances. Generally, where the deceased died domiciled in the United Kingdom, all his property wherever situated is liable to the tax, but if he died domiciled elsewhere, only property situated in the United Kingdom is subject to tax.

Where capital transfer tax becomes chargeable on the death of a person, it is levied on the value of his estate; 'estate' for this purpose being the aggregate of all property to which the deceased was beneficially entitled, less property specifically excluded (s 23). It includes property over which the deceased had a general power of disposition. The value of an asset is taken to be what it would fetch if sold in the open market at the relevant time (s 38).

The general rule is that no grant of representation may issue, and no grant issued outside the United Kingdom may be re-sealed, until the applicant has prepared and lodged an account containing full details of all the property in respect of which he is liable for the payment of capital transfer tax and of its value, and has either paid such tax or shown that no such tax is payable (s 109 (1) of the Supreme Court Act 1981). The account has to be delivered within twelve months from the end of the month in which the death occurred or, if later, within three months beginning with the date on which the applicant commenced to act as personal representative. If any errors are discovered therein at a later date, these must be corrected within six months of discovery. The deceased's personal representatives are in general liable for the payment of tax chargeable on the estate by reason of the death of the deceased, including property which though comprised in a settlement has devolved on, or vested in, the personal representatives (s 25 (5)). When the deceased has died on or after 15 March 1983 there is an option to pay the tax by ten equal annual instalments commencing six months after the end of the month in which the death occurred. In respect of deaths before 15 March 1983 there are options to pay the tax by eight yearly or sixteen half-yearly instalments. The option is exercisable only in respect of land of any description and buildings wherever situated, and certain other types of property, namely the net value of a business or an interest in a business, including a profession or vocation, if carried on for gain, timber and various kinds of shares or securities in a company (para 13 of Sched 4). On sale of the property the tax becomes payable in full. In determining the rate of tax payable, it is necessary to take into account all transfers of value including lifetime gifts made after 26 March 1974, unless they are exempt from tax; this may result in a higher rate of tax being chargeable than if only the value of the estate passing on death had to be considered. Subject to the instalment option, the personal representatives must pay all the tax for which they are liable on delivery of the account and they may at the same time pay any tax chargeable on the death for which they are not liable, if requested to do so by the persons liable for such tax. Where the applicant does not know the amount or value of any property passing on the death of the deceased, he must disclose the existence of such property and, so far as he is able, give an estimate of its value. He may be required to undertake to bring in an account as soon as the amount or value is ascertained and to pay any tax thereon (see also p 78).

However, in respect of persons dying on or after 1 April 1981, it is no longer necessary to deliver an Inland Revenue account in order to apply for a grant of representation where the estate is an excepted estate, unless the Capital Taxes Office so requires by a notice in writing issued to the applicant within the prescribed period (Capital Transfer Tax (Delivery of Accounts) Regulations 1981, as amended by the Capital Transfer Tax (Delivery of Accounts) (No 3) Regulations 1983). An 'excepted estate' is defined as meaning the estate of a person immediately before his death where—

(*a*) the value of the estate is attributable wholly to property passing under that person's will or intestacy or under a nomination of an asset taking effect on death or by survivorship in beneficial joint tenancy;
(*b*) the total gross value of that property did not exceed £40,000 (or £25,000 in the case of a death before 1 April 1983);
(*c*) of that property not more than 10 per cent of the total gross value or £2,000 (or £1,000 in the case of a death before 1 April 1983) whichever figure is the higher, represented value attributable to property then situated outside the United Kingdom;
(*d*) that person died on or after 1 April 1981, domiciled in the United Kingdom and without having made any chargeable transfer during his lifetime.

The 'prescribed period' in relation to any person is the period beginning with that person's death and ending thirty-five days after the making of the first grant of representation in respect of that person in England and Wales (not being a grant limited in duration, in respect of property or to any special purpose). Transfers which do not have to be reported are those gifts which amount individually to over £250 and which in any one financial year when added together do not exceed £3,000 (or £2,000 before 5 April 1981). Where an estate includes joint property, the total gross value of that property must be taken into account to determine whether or not the value exceeds £40,000 (or £25,000 in the case of a death before 1 April 1983). If it is discovered at a later date that an estate claimed to be an 'excepted' estate is not so, an Inland Revenue account should be delivered to the Capital Taxes Office within six months of discovering that fact.

If there is any doubt as to whether an estate qualifies as an excepted estate and therefore an Inland Revenue account will not be needed, a preliminary inquiry may be made at the Capital Taxes Office. The view taken by the Capital Taxes Office is that where a first grant of representation would give the executors or administrators full powers to deal with the whole of the estate, that is a case where the estate may be treated as an excepted estate provided all the other conditions are satisfied. A grant to an attorney or for the use and benefit of minors will be regarded as coming within this category. On the other hand, on an application for a grant pending suit, or for an ad colligenda grant, or for a grant in respect of settled land or limited to other property, an Inland Revenue account will be required. Again, whenever application is being made for a second grant in the same estate the Capital Taxes Office will expect an Inland Revenue account to be lodged. This applies to grants de bonis non, grants of double probate, grants following a cessate grant, grants following a pending suit grant, or an ad colligenda grant, or a settled land grant, and grants made after the revocation of a first full grant.

18.2 The forms of account

The applicant for a grant of representation in respect of the estate of a person dying on or after 13 March 1975 is not required to swear to, or to affirm, the truth of any account of the deceased's estate which he has to render to the Capital Taxes Office. However the account, which is referred to as the Inland Revenue account, must be signed.

When application is to be made for a first grant of representation, the following forms are to be used in appropriate cases:

(*a*) CAP Form 200, where the deceased died on or after 13 March 1975 domiciled in England and Wales, Scotland or Northern Ireland. The new print of this form is for use where the deceased died on or after 27 March 1981.

(*b*) CAP Form 201, where the deceased died on or after 13 March 1975 domiciled otherwise than in the United Kingdom; in this case a full statement of all the facts in support of the claim to a foreign domicile should be annexed to the account. In the case of a death between 13 March 1975 and 14 March 1983 a person who was not domiciled in the United Kingdom at the relevant time may be treated for the purposes of capital transfer tax as if he had been domiciled there if (i) he was domiciled in the United Kingdom on or after 10 December 1974 and within three years immediately preceding the relevant time; or (ii) he was resident in the United Kingdom on or after 10 December 1974 and in not less than seventeen of the twenty years of assessment ending with the year of assessment in which the relevant time falls; or (iii) since 10 December 1974 he became and remained domiciled in the Isle of Man or the Channel Islands, having immediately before been domiciled in the United Kingdom. Sub-paragraphs (i) and (ii) still apply in the case of a death on or after 15 March 1983, but sub-paragraph (iii) has been deleted. The new print of this form is for use where the deceased died on or after 27 March 1981.

(*c*) CAP Form 202, a single-sheet form of account for use where the deceased died on or after 13 March 1975 domiciled in England and Wales, Scotland or Northern Ireland and the gross estate in the United Kingdom, including nominated property and the entirety of jointly held property passing by survivorship, does not exceed £12,000 when the deceased died before 27 October 1977, or £20,000 when the deceased died between 27 October 1977 and 25 March 1980, or £40,000 when the deceased died on or after 26 March 1980, or when the deceased died on or after 27 March 1981 (the current form) where the total net value of the estate after deducting any exemptions and reliefs claimed does not exceed the threshold above which capital transfer tax is payable at the date of death (subject to the provisions in respect of excepted estates).

Form 213 which accompanies CAP Forms 200 and 201 contains a comprehensive set of notes and instructions for their completion. Instructions for the completion of CAP Form 202 are contained in the form itself.

Form 22 (CTT) is for use where no grant of representation is required in respect of a small estate but a certificate of exemption from tax is required (see p 1).

If further estate is discovered, or an error is found in the details disclosed in the original form, a corrective account, CAP Form D-3, may have to be submitted. Application may be made to the Capital Taxes Office to dispense with a corrective account in an appropriate case.

The form to be used on an application for a second or subsequent grant of representation depends on the nature of the grant sought:

(*a*) When the application is for a grant of double probate, or a cessate grant, or a grant de bonis non, CAP Form A-5C is at present appropriate (for an exception, see p 163). If further estate has been disclosed, details of this must be given in a corrective account, and tax paid thereon if necessary.

(*b*) In other cases, eg, on an application for a full grant following a grant of administration pending suit or ad colligenda bona, or for a new grant following the revocation of the previous grant or for a general grant following a grant limited to settled land, CAP Form 200 or 201, as appropriate, should be used (not CAP Form A-5C). Where application is made following the revocation of the previous grant, capital transfer tax, if payable, may be paid again, leaving it to the previous grantee to claim a refund; alternatively, application may be made to the Capital Taxes Office by letter for the transfer of the receipt and tax stamp to the new account. If the latter course is followed, and the applicant for the new grant did not pay the tax originally, the letter should show that the tax was paid out of the deceased's estate or the consent of the former grantee should be obtained.

The Capital Taxes Office does not require the value of assets and liabilities brought into the body of an account, whether as an individual item or as a total carried from a separate schedule, to include any odd pence. Items in a separate schedule, eg, a list of stocks and shares, should include pence but the odd pence in the total figure may be omitted. Pence will be retained however in the calculation of capital transfer tax, and any interest thereon.

18.3 Procedure

All the current forms of Inland Revenue account and instructions may be obtained from the Controller, Capital Taxes Office, Inland Revenue, Minford House, Rockley Road, London W14 0DF, by personal or postal application. CAP Forms 200 and 202, and CAP Form 213, may also be obtained by personal application to the London Chief Post Office, King Edward Street, London EC1 1AA, to certain branch post offices in the Metropolitan Postal District and to head post offices outside that district, and to the Stamps Office, Room 2, South-West Wing, Bush House Strand, London WC2B 4QN.

With certain exceptions, it is not necessary for the Inland Revenue account to be submitted to the Capital Taxes Office for examination and assessment of tax prior to the issue of a grant; the present practice is to require the solicitor to assess the tax himself. This procedure does not apply where:

(i) it is claimed that the deceased died on or after 13 March 1975 domiciled outside the United Kingdom;

(ii) exemption from tax is claimed in respect of articles considered to be of national, scientific, historic or artistic interest, or land or buildings of outstanding interest;

(iii) tax is to be paid out of deposits in the National Savings Bank, or out of the proceeds of national savings certificates or premium savings bonds to be encashed before the grant;

(iv) the grant is required only in respect of settled land or is one for which CAP Form 200 or Form 202 is inappropriate;

(v) it is desired to pay the tax by instalments on unquoted shares or securities (see p 228).

In these cases the Inland Revenue account and any other appropriate forms, whether or not capital transfer tax is payable, should be sent or taken to the Controller, Capital Taxes Office, Lynwood Road, Thames Ditton, Surrey KT7 0EB, for examination and assessment if necessary. Where tax is payable, in order to save time the tax and interest may be estimated and a remittance for that amount sent with the account; if in order the remittance will then be transmitted to the Central Accounting Office.

In all other cases, where tax is payable the solicitor should assess the tax and interest payable on delivery of the account by completing the pages headed 'Assessment of Tax' and 'Probate Summary' at the end of CAP Form 200. When the application for a grant is to be made at the Principal Registry the completed account, together with the warrant and a remittance for the tax and interest, must be sent by post to the Central Accounting Office (Cashier), Inland Revenue (4), Barrington Road, Worthing, West Sussex BN12 4XH. After stamping and return, the account should be delivered to the Principal Registry with the papers to lead the grant. If the application is being made in a district probate registry, the Inland Revenue account, together with the warrant and remittance, may be sent to the Central Accounting Office at the Worthing, Sussex address, or alternatively directly to the registry with the papers to lead the grant, and the registrar will arrange for the tax to be paid. If CAP Form 202 is used, it should be lodged at the registry with the papers to lead the grant. If it is difficult to assess the tax and interest without prior reference to the Capital Taxes Office, the signed account should be sent to that department with a letter of explanation.

If it is desired to have for retention a copy of the account showing any amendments made by the Capital Taxes Office, a duplicate copy should be lodged with the original, with a letter of request.

Cheques or money orders should be made payable to 'Inland Revenue' and crossed; no special form of crossing is required. In certain circumstances the tax may be paid out of assets belonging to the deceased's estate; inquiry should be made of the Capital Taxes Office in any case where it is desired to do so. A computer print-out receipt will be stapled to the back page of the account.

In the case of deaths on and after 13 March 1975 and up to 31 March 1981, the grant of representation is endorsed with a certificate that an Inland Revenue account has been delivered and showing the gross and net values of the estate. For deaths on and after 1 April 1981 the certificate shows merely the gross and net values of the estate. After the grant has issued the probate registry sends the account to the Capital Taxes Office for retention. If the issue of a grant is a matter of urgency, application may be made in appropriate cases to the Capital Taxes Office to expedite consideration of an Inland Revenue account.

18.4 Estate duty

Where a person has died before 13 March 1975 but on or after 1 August 1894, estate duty was and still is payable on the market value at the date of death of all property, real or personal, settled or not settled, which passes on his death, unless exemption therefrom has been conferred expressly by statute. Duty applies to gifts made during the deceased's lifetime only in limited circumstances. The applicant is required to disclose, so far as lies within his knowledge and belief, the fullest details of all such property, whether or not he is accountable for the duty thereon and whether or not it is under his control. He must swear to, or affirm, the truth of the account of the deceased's estate in the form of an affidavit, known as the Inland Revenue affidavit. A grant of representation will not issue until the applicant has first filed this affidavit as to the total value of the deceased's estate so that duty may be paid thereon. He must pay estate duty, insofar as duty is payable, on all personal property, wherever situated, of which the deceased was competent to dispose at his death, on delivery of the Inland Revenue affidavit (Finance Act 1894, ss 6 (2), 8 (3)); however, where the deceased died on or after 1 April 1971 the applicant has an option to pay the duty by eight yearly or sixteen half-yearly instalments commencing a year after the death in the case of the types of property set out in s 62 of the Finance Act 1971. He may at the same time pay the duty on any other property passing on the death of the deceased, if it is under his control or at the request of the persons accountable for the duty, on delivery of the Inland Revenue affidavit or on a separate C-5 account. He may also pay the duty on any real estate of which the deceased was competent to dispose on delivery of the affidavit but, irrespective of the date of death, he has a similar alternative of paying the duty by eight yearly or sixteen half-yearly instalments commencing a year after the date of death.

The old forms of affidavit may be used whilst they are still available, namely:

(*a*) Form A12, where the deceased died domiciled in England and Wales or Scotland.

(*b*) Form A13, where the deceased died domiciled otherwise than in Great Britain.

If Form A14A, a single-sheet form of affidavit for use where the deceased died on or after 22 March 1972 up to 12 March 1975 domiciled in England and Wales or Scotland and the gross estate does not exceed £12,000 is not available, Form A12 must be used. A comprehensive set of notes and instructions for the completion of Forms A12 and A13 is given in Form 41C. When it is necessary to submit a corrective affidavit (Form D-3) (see p 231), except when a refund of duty is being claimed, the affidavit may be submitted to the Capital Taxes Office signed but unsworn; if the Capital Taxes Office then requires it to be sworn, it will be returned to the solicitor for that purpose. In other respects the practice is very largely the same as that in respect of deaths after 12 March 1975. However, a certificate is endorsed on the grant of representation to the effect that an Inland Revenue affidavit has been delivered and in appropriate cases that estate duty and interest thereon has been paid.

Chapter 19

Dispute over a Will or the Right to a Grant

If contention arises out of the execution, or out of the condition, of a will or codicil, to the extent that the court will be asked to pronounce for or against the validity of the document in solemn form, proceedings have to be taken by issuing a writ in the Chancery Division (s 1 of the Administration of Justice Act 1970). Such proceedings were formerly taken in the Probate Division. Similarly, where a deceased has died intestate, a dispute between two or more claimants over the right to a grant may have to be resolved by commencing an administration action in the Chancery Division. (See also as to rectification of a will, head 2.16.) However, the county court retains contentious jurisdiction in respect of questions as to the grant or revocation of probate of a will, or of letters of administration of the estate, where the value of the deceased's estate is less than £30,000 (s 62 of the County Courts Act 1959, as amended) (see head 19.4).

There are still certain preliminary steps which may be taken in the Family Division, whereby a person may declare a contrary interest, or call upon some other person to take a grant or to produce a will.

19.1 Caveats and warnings

(a) Caveats (Probate Rule 44)

Any person who desires to prevent the sealing of a grant (or the re-sealing of a grant issued in another country) without notice to himself may enter a caveat in any probate registry or sub-registry. (It is to be noted that where a person wishes merely to be notified of the issue of a grant, it is possible to apply for a standing search, see p 257.) A caveat must also be entered as a preliminary to the issue of a non-contentious citation. It is open to a plaintiff to enter a caveat as a preliminary to issuing a writ in the Chancery Division or commencing proceedings in a county court but, unless otherwise directed by registrar's order on summons, the commencement of a probate action, whether or not any caveat has been entered, operates to prevent the sealing of a grant (other than a grant of administration pending suit) just like a caveat. The effect of entering a caveat is to place a notice on the records of the court that nothing is to be done in the estate of the deceased without reference to the caveator and no grant will be sealed if the registrar has knowledge of an effective caveat; however a caveat will not be effective to prevent the sealing of a grant on the day on which the caveat is entered. The entry of a caveat does not prevent the issue of a grant to the caveator himself.

A caveat may be entered by any person having an interest in the estate, or by his solicitor, by attending, and completing the form in the caveat book, at the Probate Department in the Principal Registry (see p 5) or at a district probate registry. Alternatively a notice in the proper form (see below) may be sent through the post to any registry (including the Principal Registry). A fee of £4 is payable; a cheque or postal order should be made payable to 'HM Paymaster General'. Entry by post is made at the risk of the caveator and must be on the form prescribed by the rules (Form 4 of Sched 1 to the Non-Contentious Probate Rules 1954). An address for service within England and Wales must be given and, if the caveat is entered by a solicitor, the name of the caveator must be disclosed on the form. Two or more persons wishing to prevent the sealing of a grant must enter separate caveats. Notice of the entry of a caveat in a district probate registry is immediately given to the Principal Registry, where an index of all current caveats is kept. Search for entry of a caveat in the Principal Registry may be made by personal attendance, when the applicant will be allowed to inspect and make a copy of an effective caveat (inspection fee, 25p), or by post, when the applicant will be supplied with a typed copy on request (copy, 25p).

Form 19.1 Caveat

(*For heading and title, see Form* 2.11)

1 Let no grant be sealed in the estate of
late of
deceased, who died on the day of , 19 , at
2 without notice to
Dated this day of , 19
3 Signed
whose address for service is:—
Solicitor for the said

1 Give the full names and last address of the deceased, including any alias names.

2 Insert the name of the person by whom or on whose behalf the caveat is being entered.

3 The caveat is signed by the caveator's solicitor or by the caveator in person. The address for service must be within England and Wales. If the caveator is in person, substitute 'in person' for the last line.

A caveat ceases to be operative at the end of six months from the date of entry, except that, unless otherwise directed by order of a registrar of the Principal Registry made on summons, (*a*) a caveat in force at the commencement of proceedings by way of citation or motion remains in force until the person shown to be entitled by the decision of the court in such proceedings applies for a grant, provided that the person who entered the caveat had notice of the proceedings (but if no appearance to warning has been entered it may be withdrawn), (*b*) where appearance to a warning has been entered, the caveat remains in force up to the commencement of an action, unless removed by order of a registrar made on summons. An action no longer keeps a caveat alive. When the writ issues, a copy thereof is sent to the Principal Registry by the Chancery Master and notice of the action is then given by the registry to any person who has entered a caveat in the estate. Similar notice is given to any person entering a caveat thereafter, until the action is finished, and notice of the entry of the caveat is also sent to the Chancery Master. A similar procedure is followed whenever the Principal Registry is notified by letter from the Chancery Master of the production to him of a probate counterclaim in a non-probate action. On application for a grant, in pursuance of the court's decision in the action, any effective caveat entered by a person who has had notice of the action expires. A caveat may be extended for a further period of six months beginning from the date of expiry by lodging at the registry in which it was entered a written application for the extension; there is no prescribed form. The application may be made personally by attending at the registry and signing a form of endorsement on the caveat. Alternatively a written application may be sent by post quoting the caveat number. A fee of £4 is payable for the renewal of the caveat in this way; a cheque or postal order should be made payable to 'HM Paymaster General'. Such application may be made only in the sixth month following the date of entry or the date of the last renewal. Notice of a successful application for the extension of a caveat in a district probate registry is sent immediately to the Principal Registry. A successful application for extension made, or received in the registry, on the date upon which the caveat is due to expire operates to prevent the sealing of a grant. Apart from the procedure for extending a caveat just described, no further caveat may be entered during the lifetime of a caveat save by leave of a registrar of the Principal Registry. However, another caveat may be entered by the caveator at any time after the previous caveat has expired except that where a caveat has ceased to be effective by reason of the failure of the caveator to take any further step after service of a warning upon him (see p 239), or by reason of the application for a grant by the person shown by order or decree of the court to be entitled thereto (see p 239), no further caveat may be entered by the caveator except by leave of a registrar of the Principal Registry. The further caveat remains operative for six months from the date of its entry.

The issue of a grant of representation to the caveator does not render his caveat inoperative; it is marked to the effect that a grant has issued and may then expire with the passage of time.

(b) *Warnings (Probate Rule 44)*

Any person who finds his application for a grant blocked by a caveat may choose either to warn the caveator or immediately to issue a writ in the Chancery Division making the caveator a defendant. The latter course may be preferable if the caveator's interest is known and it is clear that no agreement can be reached between the parties.

A caveat may be warned only from the Principal Registry. The warning in the prescribed form (Form 5 of Sched 1 to the Non-Contentious Probate Rules 1954) must state the interest of the person at whose instance it is to issue and, if he claims under a will, the date of the will; it must give an address for service in England and Wales. It calls upon the caveator within eight days of service upon him to enter an appearance and to set forth his interest in the estate contrary to that of the person issuing the warning, or, if he has no contrary interest, to issue and serve a summons for directions returnable before a registrar.

The form of warning is completed in the Probate Department and the signature of the registrar added. There is no fee. It must be served on the caveator by leaving the original or a true copy thereof at the address given in the caveat as an address for service, or by sending it to the caveator at that address by prepaid registered post.

(c) Appearance to warning (Probate Rule 44)

If, after service of the warning upon him, the caveator still wishes to oppose the issue of a grant, he may enter an appearance to the warning, in the form prescribed (Form 6 of Sched 1 to the Non-Contentious Probate Rules 1954), in the Probate Department of the Principal Registry, either in person or through his solicitor and within eight days of service of the warning upon him or at any time thereafter provided a step in default has not been taken by the other party. The form of appearance is obtainable at the registry. An appearance will not be accepted unless the caveator can show a good cause of action, viz, an interest contrary to that of the person warning the caveat. The appearance must give an address for service within England and Wales and a copy bearing the registry seal must be delivered or sent by the caveator to the person warning at the latter's address for service. No fee is payable for entering an appearance.

If the caveator cannot show a contrary interest but nevertheless still wishes to oppose the sealing of a grant, he must, within eight days of service of the warning upon him or at any time thereafter, provided no step in default has been taken by the other party, issue and serve a summons for directions returnable before a registrar (see head 20.2).

(d) Subsequent procedure (Probate Rule 44)

If the contention persists after an appearance to the warning, the next step is the issue by one or other of the parties of a writ to commence an action in the Chancery Division (or in a county court: see head 19.4).

If the caveator wishes to remove the caveat because the parties have come to an agreement or for some other reason, he may withdraw it. There is no fee for withdrawal. A caveat cannot be withdrawn, however, where the caveator has entered an appearance to a warning. If the caveat has been warned, but no appearance has been entered, notice of the withdrawal must be given by the caveator to the person warning. Withdrawal may only be carried out at the registry in which the caveat was entered, and the receipt given at the time of entry must be surrendered. Where a caveat entered at the Principal Registry is preventing the issue of a grant in a district registry and the caveat is withdrawn, notice thereof will be sent to the district registry. The applicant for the grant will be asked whether he wishes to proceed with his application.

If the period of eight days allowed after service of the warning has expired, and no appearance has been entered and no summons for directions has been taken out, the caveat can be removed at the instance of the person warning by filing in the Probate Department of the Principal Registry an affidavit as to service of the warning and showing that no summons has been served on him (there is no filing fee). The search for appearance and the check that the time has expired will be carried out in the registry immediately the affidavit is lodged. It is advisable to wait whilst this is being done, as the caveat is not cleared off until the official search has been made. If the caveat was entered in a district registry, notice of the removal of the caveat will be sent to the district registry.

After an appearance has been entered to the warning, the caveat remains in force until the commencement of an action, except that it may be removed by order of a registrar of the Principal Registry made on summons (see head 20.2). If, therefore, the parties have come to an agreement after an appearance has been entered to the warning, application may be made to the registrar in this way for an order for discontinuance of the proceedings, for a grant of representation to issue to a named person if entitled thereto and that on application for such a grant by that person the caveat do cease to have effect. Where proceedings by way of citation or motion have been taken, a caveat in force at the commencement of such proceedings remains effective until the person shown to be entitled by order of the court made in such proceedings applies for a grant (but a caveator who has not entered an appearance to a warning may always apply to withdraw his caveat) Thereupon, all caveats entered by parties who had notice of the proceedings cease to be effective. If the caveat is not referred to by number in the order, the solicitor should lodge with the papers a certificate that the caveators had notice of the proceedings. The commencement of a probate action operates to prevent the sealing of a grant (except for a grant of administration pending suit), irrespective of whether a caveat has been entered, until application for a grant is made by the person shown to be entitled thereto by the decision of the court in the action; thereupon any caveat entered by a person who had notice of the action (see p 237) ceases to be effective. There is no jurisdiction in the Family Division to make an order for the discontinuance of proceedings on a probate action. An order by the Chancery Division disposing of a probate action by agreement without a formal pronouncement in respect of a will may be for discontinuance or may stay all proceedings save for the purpose of carrying out the agreed terms, and is regarded as authorising the issue of a grant notwithstanding the existence of the probate action.

If two claimants, having an equal right to a grant of letters of administration, cannot agree as to which of them is to take the grant, the dispute must be brought by summons before a registrar of the Principal Registry, the parties attending before him either in person or by their solicitors or counsel. Where such a summons has been issued, a grant in respect of the deceased's estate will not be allowed to issue until the summons has been finally disposed of.

19.2 Citations (Probate Rules 45 to 47)

An application for a grant may have to be preceded by the issue of a citation. This necessity will arise if (i) there are persons who, having a right to a grant in respect of the deceased's estate, delay or decline to apply for a grant and refuse to renounce their right; or (ii) an applicant for a grant has knowledge of the existence of a purported testamentary document but wishes to proceed in reliance on an earlier will or an intestacy.

(a) Citation to accept or refuse a grant

A person beneficially interested or a creditor must cite (but see p 193) all persons having a prior right to take a grant if those persons are unwilling to renounce their right in his favour (see Form 19.2, below) (for the order of priority, see pp 87 and 114). A person who would have a beneficial interest in the estate only if the persons having a prior right to a grant were dead or renounced their interest will not be allowed to cite. If such a person wishes to obtain a grant, he must apply to the court for an order for a discretionary grant to be made to him under s 116 of the Supreme Court Act 1981 (see head 13.6). If a creditor cannot swear that there are no kin he must cite the kin in general (see Form 19.2, below) and notice of his application must be given to the Treasury Solicitor, or as the case may be.

Any will referred to in a citation should be lodged in the Probate Department of the Principal Registry before the citation issues, unless the registrar is satisfied that it is impracticable to require it to be lodged. He may require a subpoena to bring in will to be served on the person who has possession of the will (see head 19.3).

Where power to make a grant to an executor has been reserved, he may be called upon to accept or refuse a grant by citation issued at the instance of the executors who have already proved the will or of the executors of the last survivor of deceased executors who have proved.

Form 19.2 Citation to accept or refuse a grant

IN THE HIGH COURT OF JUSTICE,
Family Division

Elizabeth the Second, by the grace of God, of the United Kingdom of Great Britain and Northern Ireland and of Our Other Realms and Territories Queen, Head of the Commonwealth, Defender of the Faith:

1 To of in the county of
.
2 Whereas it appears by the affidavit of sworn the day of ,
19 , that of died on the day of , 19 ,
3 having made and duly executed his last will and testament dated the day of , 19 (now remaining in the Principal Registry of the Family Division), and thereof appointed you the said the sole executor
4 and therein named the said a residuary legatee and devisee
5 Now this is to command you the said that within 8 days after service hereof upon you, inclusive of the day of such service, you do cause an appearance to be entered for you in the Principal Registry of the Family Division of our High Court of Justice at Somerset House, Strand, London WC2, and accept or refuse probate of the said will, or show cause why letters of administration with the said will annexed of all the estate which by law devolves to and vests in the personal representative of the said deceased should not be granted to the said
6 And take notice that in default of your so appearing and accepting and extracting probate of the said will as aforesaid our said Court will proceed to grant letters of administration, with the said will annexed, of the said estate to the said , your absence notwithstanding.

Dated at London this day of , 19 , and in the year of our reign.

(Signed)

Registrar.

Extracted by
of , Solicitor.

1 Insert the full name and address of each person who is being cited. If a creditor is required by reason of an intestacy to cite the deceased's kin in general because he cannot swear that there are no kin the citation is addressed to 'the kin (if any) who are entitled to share and all other persons having or claiming any interest in the estate of deceased'.

2 Insert the name of the deponent to the affidavit in support, followed by the name of the deceased, his last address and the date of his death.

3 Set out in this paragraph the title of the citee to a grant in respect of the deceased's estate, clearing off any person who has a prior right. For instance, if the deceased left a will and the citee is not an executor, substitute after the reference to the deceased's will 'whereof he did not appoint an executor (*or*, whereof he appointed , sole executor who died in his lifetime, *or as the case may be*) and therein named you the said the sole residuary legatee and devisee for life (*or as the case may be*)'.

If the deceased died intestate, substitute for the whole of this paragraph 'intestate leaving you the said his lawful widow and relict and one of the persons entitled to share in his estate'. If it is necessary to clear kin who have a prior right to the citor, insert after 'intestate' the words 'without issue (or parent) or any other person entitled in priority to share in his estate by virtue of any enactment'. Where a creditor is citing the kin in general, the paragraph should read 'intestate, a widower (*or as the case may be*) without known issue, parent, brother or sister of the whole or half-blood or their issue, grandparent, uncle or aunt of the whole or half-blood or their issue, or any other person entitled in priority to share in his estate by virtue of any enactment.'

4 Alter this paragraph as appropriate to give the title of the citor (see p 87 and p 114); for instance on an intestacy, substitute 'and the said his lawful son (*or as the case may be*) and the only other person (*or* one other of the persons) entitled to share in the said estate'. In the case of a creditor, substitute 'and that the said is a creditor of the said deceased'.

5 Eight days is the time allowed for appearance if personal service of the citation is effected in England and Wales, one month if service is to be effected therein by advertisement. A citee who is not an executor is required to accept or refuse 'letters of administration (with the said will annexed) of all the estate which by law devolves to and vests in the personal representative of the said deceased' or to show cause why 'the same' should not be granted to the citor, and this paragraph should be altered accordingly, the words in brackets being omitted in the case of an intestacy.

6 Similarly 'letters of administration (with will annexed)' should be substituted for 'probate of the said will' if the citee is not an executor; the words 'with will annexed' should be left out of this paragraph if the deceased died intestate.

(b) Citation to take a grant

Where an executor has intermeddled in the deceased's estate without proving the will, he may be cited to show cause why he should not be ordered to take a grant of probate at the instance of any person interested in the estate and at any time after six months have elapsed from the date of death of the deceased, provided that proceedings as to the validity of the will are not pending.

(c) Citation to propound

If an applicant for a grant knows of the existence of a document purported to have been executed by the deceased as a testamentary document, he must cite the executors, if any are appointed in the document, and all persons beneficially interested thereunder to propound it. Before the citation will issue, the document must be lodged in the Principal Registry. If the person in whose custody it is refuses to give it up or to bring it into the registry a subpoena to bring in will must be served on him, calling upon him to lodge the document in the Principal Registry or in a named district probate registry (see head 19.3). The registrar may dispense with the requirement if satisfied that it is impracticable to require the document to be lodged.

If the executor appointed in the will has knowledge of a purported codicil thereto but doubts its validity, his proper course is, not to cite those interested under the codicil to propound it, but himself to issue a writ in the Chancery Division to prove the will in solemn form, and either to ask that court to pronounce against the codicil or to leave it to those interested under the codicil to persuade the court to pronounce for its validity (*In the Estate of Muirhead* [1971] P 263).

(d) Issuing a citation

Citations may issue only from the Principal Registry. The draft citation, a draft affidavit in support, to be made by the applicant, or one of the applicants, and setting out all the circumstances which call for the issue of the citation, and any other necessary documents, may be lodged in the Probate Department of the Principal Registry for the form of citation to be settled. At the same time a caveat must be entered in the deceased's estate (see head 19.1). After the draft has been settled, the affidavit, which must verify every fact set out in the citation, should be sworn by the applicant, and a fair copy of the citation, the settled draft and affidavit in support are then lodged in the registry. In special circumstances, the registrar may accept an affidavit in support sworn by the applicant's solicitor. The only fee now payable, namely £5 for settling the citation, must be paid at this time. The citation is then signed by the registrar, sealed and sent to the citor's solicitor by post. Additional sealed copies may be obtained on request.

Alternatively an application for the issue of a non-contentious citation may be made through the post. The draft citation and affidavit should be sent to the Receiver of Papers at the Principal Registry, for the citation to be settled, together with a photographic copy of any relevant will or codicil, or the originals of such documents. Original testamentary documents should be sent by registered post and will be retained by the registry unless their return is requested, for instance in order to exhibit them to the supporting affidavit. The settled drafts are returned by the registry to the solicitor, who must then enter a caveat if he has not already done so (see head 19.1). He should arrange for the affidavit to be sworn and then return to the registry the sworn affidavit, a fair copy of the citation, the settled draft citation, any relevant original wills or codicils in his possession and the receipt for entry of the caveat, together with a cheque, payable to 'HM Paymaster General' for the fee (see above). The sealed citation is sent to the solicitor in due course, with the receipt for caveat.

(e) Miscellaneous requirements

The affidavit in support of a citation by a creditor to accept or refuse must set out the value of the estate, the amount and nature of the debt, and whether any, and if so what, security is held for the debt.

If a minority or life interest arises in the deceased's estate, the affidavit in support should usually show that at least two persons are applying for a grant (see head 6.2) or should set out the name of a proposed co-grantee and that he has a good title to the grant. In default of this, the citation will contain a limitation to the effect that in default of appearance a grant will be made to the citor and to his co-grantee 'if entitled thereto'.

The affidavit in support of a citation to take probate directed against an executor who has intermeddled must show that the deceased died more than six months previously and how the citee has intermeddled.

Where a citor is a person under disability, the procedure prescribed by RSC, Ord 80, is to be followed (except that the term 'next friend' is not used). Since the citation may result in the issue of a grant of representation to the citor, it is appropriate that the person who it is proposed should act as guardian should be the person entitled to apply for a grant on behalf of the citor (see heads 9.1 and 9.2), provided that such a person has no contrary interest. Under the provisions of RSC, Ord 80, r 3, an order appointing a guardian is usually not required but the following should accompany the documents to lead to the issue of the citation:

(i) a written consent by the proposed guardian to act as such (this may be incorporated in the supporting affidavit);
(ii) where the proposed guardian is the person authorised by the Court of Protection, an office copy under seal of the authorisation;
(iii) in the case of a minor a certificate by the solicitor that he knows or believes the citor to be a minor and that the proposed guardian has no contrary interest;
(iv) in the case of a patient, unless there is a person authorised by the Court of Protection, a certificate by the solicitor that he knows or believes the citor to be a patient, giving the grounds of his knowledge or belief, that there is no person authorised by the Court of Protection and that the proposed guardian has no contrary interest.

A similar procedure should be followed where an appearance to a citation is to be entered on behalf of a person under disability.

The guardian of a person under disability must be represented by a solicitor.

(f) Service

Citations must as a rule be personally served by leaving a copy of the citation with the party cited, producing the original to him if so requested. A certificate of service must be endorsed on the citation after service. Service on a minor who is not also a patient is effected by serving the father or guardian of the minor, or if he has no father or guardian, the person with whom the minor resides or in whose care he is at the time. Service on a patient is effected by serving the person authorised, failing whom the person with whom the citee resides or in whose care he is.

Where personal service is difficult or impossible, application may be made to a registrar, supported by an affidavit as to the facts, for his directions as to some other mode of service or as to the giving of notice by advertisement. The latter course is usual if the whereabouts of the citee are not known.

Application for the advertisement to be drafted is made by lodging the original sealed citation in the Probate Department of the Principal Registry and paying the fee of £5. A draft abstract of the citation to be advertised should also be lodged for settling, unless the citation is to accept or refuse a grant, when the advertisement will be drafted in the registry. The attempts which have been made to trace the citee must also be recited in an affidavit in support, but if it is known at the time application is made for the citation to issue that substituted service will be necessary, these facts may be included in the affidavit in support of the citation. The registrar will give directions as to the newspapers in which insertion is to be made, the number of insertions and the time which is to be allowed for appearance to the citation.

(g) Appearance to citation

A citation to accept or refuse a grant or to take a grant or to propound a will calls upon the citee to enter an appearance at the Principal Registry within a specified number of days (if service is to be effected in England and Wales eight days, or one month in the case of substituted service by advertisement) and to take the appropriate action. An address for service in England and Wales must be given on the prescribed form of appearance (Form 6 of Sched 1 to the Non-Contentious Probate Rules 1954), which must be filed in the Probate Department of the Principal Registry by personal attendance within the eight days (or as the case may be), or at any time thereafter if no step in default has been taken. The person appearing must send or deliver a sealed copy of the form to the citor or his solicitors. Forms of appearance are obtainable in the registry.

(h) Subsequent procedure

The procedure subsequent to the issue and service of a citation depends on the action, if any, taken by the party cited, for instance:

(1) If no appearance has been entered to a citation to accept or refuse a grant by the party or any of the parties cited, the citor may apply to a registrar of the Principal Registry ex parte for an order for a grant to himself, except where the citation was directed to an executor to whom power had been reserved. In that case, the registrar should be asked for an order that a note be made on the grant that the citee has been duly cited and has not appeared and that all his rights in respect of the executorship have wholly ceased. The application should be supported by an affidavit or affidavits showing that the citation was duly served, the original citation being exhibited thereto, and that search has been made in the appearance book (in the Probate Department) and no appearance has been entered. It must show how the person served was identified by the server and must be supported by any further affidavit necessary to complete the identification,

eg, an affidavit as to handwriting in respect of an acknowledgment of service. When notice of the citation has been advertised the copies of the newspapers containing the insertion should be lodged, together with the settled abstract, the original citation and an affidavit as to non-appearance. There is no fee payable. The application is made by lodging all the documents at the Probate Department of the Principal Registry. If, after service of the citation upon him, the citee signs a renunciation, the citor may apply for a grant without first obtaining the registrar's order. If the citor is a person under disability, it may be necessary for application to be made also for an order assigning guardians to take a grant on his behalf (see pp 160 and 162).

(2) If a party cited to accept or refuse a grant enters an appearance but then fails to take further steps within a reasonable time, the citor may apply to a registrar of the Principal Registry on summons for an order for a grant to himself or, in the case of a citee to whom power has been reserved, for an order striking out the appearance and for the endorsement on the grant of the appropriate note (see (1), above). The summons must be served on the party cited (see head 20.2).

(3) If no appearance has been entered to a citation to take probate directed to an executor who has intermeddled or if appearance has been entered but no further steps have been taken within a reasonable time thereafter, the citor may apply to a registrar of the Principal Registry on summons for an order requiring the citee to take a grant within a specified time or for a grant to himself or to some other person specified in the summons. An affidavit of service and non-appearance (see (1), above) will be required, if appropriate. The summons must be served on the party cited, as must also the resulting order. Disobedience to an order requiring him to take a grant will render the party cited liable to committal. In special circumstances the court has been prepared to pass over an executor who has intermeddled and to allow a person with an inferior right to take the grant (*In the Estate of Biggs* [1966] 1 All ER 358).

(4) If no appearance has been entered to a citation to propound a will, the citor may apply to a registrar of the Principal Registry ex parte for an order for a grant to himself, or to such other person as is entitled thereto, on the footing that the will is invalid (*In the Goods of Morton, Morton* v *Thorpe* (1863) 3 Sw & Tr 179). If appearance has been entered but no further steps have been taken to propound the will within a reasonable time thereafter, the citor may apply to the registrar by summons, served on those parties cited who have entered an appearance, for a similar order. An affidavit of service and non-appearance (see (1), above) will be required if appropriate.

(5) If a party cited has entered an appearance and wishes to take a grant, he must first obtain an order of a registrar of the Principal Registry giving him leave. The application is made ex parte by lodging with the Probate Department an affidavit setting out that the applicant has been cited, has appeared and is willing to take a grant and that he has not been served by the citor with notice of any application for a grant to himself. An

appearance to a citation to propound may, however, lead to the issue of a writ to commence an action.

If no appearance is entered on behalf of a citee who is a person under disability, application supported by affidavit should be made to a registrar of the Principal Registry for directions as to whether a guardian should be assigned to represent the citee (see RSC, Ord 80, r 6 and p 244).

19.3 Examination of person; subpoena to bring in will

When a person is known or reasonably believed to have knowledge of the whereabouts of a will or other testamentary document, or to have such a document in his possession or under his control, but he refuses to divulge such information, or to deliver up the document, there are two courses open to a person interested in the document. In the first place application may be made to the High Court, whether or not any legal proceedings are pending, for an order that such person should be required to attend to be examined in open court as to his purported knowledge. Unless the application is made in the course of a probate action, it may be made to a registrar on summons (see head 20.2). On the attendance of that person in open court he may be required to answer questions as to his knowledge of the document in question and, if appropriate, to bring in the document as directed by the court (s 122 of the Supreme Court Act 1981, replacing s 26 of the Court of Probate Act 1857). Failure to attend for examination or to answer any question or to bring in any document makes the person guilty of contempt and therefore liable to committal.

Alternatively a person known or reasonably believed to have a testamentary document in his possession, custody, or power may be required to bring in the document by the issue and service upon him of a subpoena (s 123 of the Supreme Court Act 1981, replacing s 23 of the Court of Probate Act 1858). Application for leave to issue a subpoena to bring in the will where there is no probate action pending is made by lodging in the Probate Department of the Principal Registry an affidavit of facts together with two forms of the subpoena duly completed. An order of the registrar is no longer drawn up, nor is any fee now taken. The subpoena duly sealed may be collected some two to three days later. It should be stated at the time of the application whether the person named in the subpoena is to bring the will to the Record Keeper at the Principal Registry or to a convenient district probate registry or elsewhere as the court thinks fit. The subpoena must be served personally and should be endorsed with the penal notice (see RSC, Ord 45, r 7 (4)). If the will is not in the possession or under the control of the person served with the subpoena, he should file an affidavit to that effect in the registry. Disobedience to the subpoena makes that person guilty of contempt of court and liable to committal, or the court may order such person to attend before it for examination.

19.4 Application for trial in a county court

When it has become necessary to take proceedings in order to resolve a matter in dispute in connection with an application for the grant or revocation of probate or letters of administration, those proceedings may in the appropriate circumstances be taken in the county court for the district in which the deceased had a fixed place of abode at the time of his death (s 62 of the County Courts Act 1959). Before such proceedings can be commenced, application must first be made to a registrar of the Principal Registry for his minute to found the jurisdiction of the county court. The application is made ex parte supported by an affidavit (see head 20.1). The registrar has to be satisfied that the value of the deceased's estate was at the time of his death less than £30,000, exclusive of what he was possessed of or entitled to as a trustee and not beneficially, but after making allowances for funeral expenses and for debts and incumbrances, and that the deceased was resident within the jurisdiction of a particular county court.

The fact that the registrar has signed his minute does not of itself prevent the issue of a grant, nor does it extend the life of a caveat in the same way as the commencement of contentious proceedings. The solicitor should therefore inform the Probate Department of the Principal Registry so soon as he has commenced proceedings in the named county court.

(As to the procedure after the county court has made an order, see p 80.)

Chapter 20

Applications to the Court

Applications for an order of the court are usually made as follows:

(*a*) ex parte to a registrar of the Principal Registry or to a district probate registrar; or

(*b*) on summons to a registrar of the Principal Registry or to a judge; or

(*c*) on motion to the court.

20.1 Ex parte applications

An ex parte application to a registrar of the Principal Registry is made by lodging the affidavits and other supporting documents in the Probate Department or by sending them by post to the Department. No fee is payable in respect of the application. The registrar's order will be ready for collection at the Probate Department in about a week's time, except that an order for leave to swear the presumed death of a person will not be handed out to the applicants. In the case of an application lodged by post, the order will be sent by post to the solicitor. At the time of making the order the registrar will indicate whether or not he requires a guarantee by sureties (see head 11.1). If the registrar is not satisfied, a note of the points raised on the application will be found at the Probate Department or will be sent to the solicitor in the case of a postal application. The order and affidavits in support of the application must be filed with the papers to lead the grant. Most ex parte applications may be made in the alternative to the registrar of a district probate registry when application for a grant has been, or is proposed to be, made in a district probate registry. A similar procedure is followed, the relevant papers being lodged at the registry and the order being obtained from that registry.

In a foreign domicile case, an alternative procedure is available, under which the documents in support of the application may be left at the registry with the papers to lead the grant (see p 213). In such a case, a separate attendance to collect the order is not necessary.

It is required that the affidavit in support of an application for an ex parte order, or one of the affidavits if there are several, should be made by the proposed grantee, or by one at least of the proposed grantees. The order will name the proposed grantee or grantees. If thereafter application for a grant is to be made by someone other than the person or persons named in the order, it will be necessary to apply to the registrar for an amendment of his order, or for its rescission and the issue of a fresh order.

An ex parte application for a registrar's order may be made irrespective of the amount of the estate:

(i) for an order for a discretionary grant under s 116 of the Supreme Court Act 1981 (see head 13.6);
(ii) for leave to swear the presumed death of a missing person (see p 142);
(iii) for an order for a grant limited to part of the estate (see head 13.7);
(iv) for an order for a grant ad colligenda bona (see head 13.4);
(v) for an order for a grant to the applicant in a foreign domicile case (see p 213);
(vi) for the assignment of a guardian to a minor (see p 160);
(vii) for an order for a grant for the use and benefit of a person entitled who is mentally or physically incapable (see pp 162, 164);
(viii) for an order giving leave to omit offensive or libellous words from probate (see head 2.15);
(ix) for an order for rectification of a will, if unopposed (see head 2.16);
(x) for an order admitting to proof a copy, completed draft, reconstruction or declaration of the contents of a lost will (see head 2.22);
(xi) for an order (by a registrar of the Principal Registry) in favour of the citor, no appearance having been entered to a citation to accept or refuse a grant (see p 245) or to a citation to propound a will (see p 246);
(xii) for an order (by a registrar of the Principal Registry) in favour of a citee who has appeared and wishes to take a grant (see p 246);
(xiii) to add an additional personal representative under s 114 (4) of the Supreme Court Act 1981 (see head 6.3);
(xiv) to join with a person entitled to a grant a person entitled in a lower degree or with no right at all (see head 6.1).

The registrar may direct, for instance when other persons ought to be given notice of the application so that they may have the opportunity of being heard to contest it, that the application should be made by summons to a registrar (in which case it will be heard by a registrar of the Principal Registry) or to a judge, or that it should be brought before the court on motion (Probate Rule 60).

When no other procedure is prescribed, any non-contentious probate matter may be referred to a registrar of the Principal Registry for his decision. Application should be made to the Probate Department, where a note will be prepared for submission by the solicitor to the registrar. Such a matter may also be referred to a district registrar, who in any case of doubt or difficulty will refer it to a registrar of the Principal Registry for directions.

20.2 Summonses

(a) Registrar's summons

An application to a registrar on summons is made to a registrar of the Principal Registry and in the following instances:

(*a*) Where there is a dispute between persons entitled to a grant in the same degree (see p 240).

(*b*) For directions at the instance of a caveator who has no interest contrary to the person warning but who wishes to oppose the issue of a grant to that person (see p 238).

(*c*) For the removal of a caveat (see pp 236, 239).

(*d*) For an order in favour of the citor where the person cited to accept or refuse or to take a grant has entered an appearance but failed to take any further step (see p 246).

(*e*) For an order in favour of the citor where the person cited to propound a will has entered an appearance and thereafter has failed to take any further step within a reasonable time (see p 246).

(*f*) For leave to sue on a guarantee by sureties (see p 175).

(*g*) For an order directing a person to attend to be examined in open court (see p 247).

(*h*) For an order directing an administrator to exhibit an inventory of the estate and to account for his administration (see head 1.5).

A registrar of the Principal Registry or a district registrar may require any other application which is made to him to be brought before a registrar of the Principal Registry by summons (Probate Rule 60)

The summons is drawn in duplicate and should set out the nature of the application and be endorsed with the name and address of the issuing solicitor (see Form 20.2). Both forms are taken to the Probate Department of the Principal Registry where the original is sealed; except in the case of a consent summons (see below) the solicitor will then be asked to take both forms to the clerk to the Registrar for the Day who will insert the day and time when returnable and return the sealed copy summons to the solicitor. There is no fee for the summons nor for filing any affidavit lodged in support of the application.

A copy of the summons, together with a copy of each supporting affidavit, must be served on the party to whom it is addressed at least two clear days before the day on which the summons is to be heard by leaving it at, or by sending it by prepaid registered post or by recorded delivery to, that party's address for service, or if there is no address for service that party's last known address (Probate Rules 63 and 64). Saturdays, as well as Sundays, bank holidays, Christmas Day and Good Friday, are excluded in reckoning the period of two clear days. Service may be effected between 12 noon on a Saturday and midnight on the following day or after 4 pm on any other weekday, but will then count as service on the next following weekday. A registrar may at or before the hearing dispense with service of the summons on any party on such conditions as he considers necessary; or he may direct, where no other provision is made by the Probate Rules, that the summons is to be served on such person or persons as he may direct.

Summonses are now specially fixed for hearing before a registrar at the Principal Registry. If it is intended that counsel should appear at the hearing of the summons, the copy lodged in the registry should be marked to that effect; all other parties should be notified that counsel will be appearing. Similarly, any party served with a non-counsel summons who wishes to appear by counsel should notify the party taking out the summons.

At the time and on the day named the solicitor for the party issuing the summons should attend on the registrar with the original summons. If the party summoned does not appear within fifteen minutes after the time appointed, the registrar may proceed to hear the application but will require to be satisfied by an affidavit of service or an acknowledgment of receipt of the copy summons that it has been duly served. If the party issuing the summons does not attend at the time appointed, the registrar may be asked to mark the summons as to the attendance of any party summoned, together with his costs.

If the hearing of the summons is adjourned by the registrar, it must be restored to his list for hearing by obtaining a restoration slip from the Probate Department, completing it and submitting it to the clerk to the registrar for a further hearing date to be given; notice of the date and time of the hearing must be given to the other party.

Counsel appearing for a party on a summons should ask at the end of the hearing for a certificate for counsel; otherwise his costs may not be allowed on taxation. Whenever it is intended to ask for an order for the costs of the application, a specific application for such costs should be included in the form of summons.

In the special case where the opposite party or parties to the summons consent to an order in the terms sought, it is unnecesssary for any of the parties to attend the hearing of the summons. The summons in duplicate, endorsed with, or accompanied by, the written consent, should be lodged in the Probate Department of the Principal Registry, together with any other relevant documents. The signature of any party in person should if possible be verified by the affidavit of a person acquainted with his handwriting. No return date is fixed but the documents are passed to a registrar for consideration. If there are minor matters which require attention before the order can issue, these will be noted on the summons which will be returned to the solicitor for him to put them right. If the registrar requires the parties to attend before him, a hearing date will be inserted in the original summons which will be returned to the solicitor. He should give notice of the appointment to all other parties. The subsequent procedure is then as for an ordinary summons.

In all cases an addressed envelope should be left with the summons in the registry, and the order will be sent to the solicitor by post.

(b) Judge's summons

An appeal against any decision or requirement of a registrar of the Principal Registry or of a district registrar lies to a judge by summons (Probate Rule 62). If any other party was represented before the registrar, the summons must be issued within seven days of the decision complained of and made returnable on the first available day. A copy must be served on such other party not less than two clear days before the return day (Probate Rule 63).

An application to a judge on summons may also be made at the direction of a registrar of the Principal Registry or a district registrar (see above). The summons is issued out of the Principal Registry for hearing before a judge in London.

The procedure for the issue of a summons returnable before a judge is similar to that in respect of a registrar's summons (see subhead (*a*), above and Form 20.2, below). Both forms should be taken to the Probate Department of the Principal Registry where the original is sealed; the Probate Department will then obtain a day and time for hearing from the Clerk of the Rules at the Royal Courts of Justice, insert these particulars and return the sealed copy summons to the solicitor. The hearing takes place in the judge's chambers at the Royal Courts of Justice. During the Long Vacation, a registrar of the Principal Registry may exercise the powers exercisable by a judge in chambers (Probate Rule 61). Leave must be obtained from a registrar before a summons can be put in the Vacation Judge's list. These are usually taken once a week on a day notified in the Vacation Notice.

Form 20.2 Registrar's or judge's summons
(*For heading and title, see Form* 2.11)

1 Let all parties concerned attend before one of the Registrars in chambers at the Principal Registry of the Family Division, Somerset House, Strand, London,
2 on day the day of , 19 , at o'clock in the noon on the hearing of an application on the part of
3 that
4 and for an order as to the costs of this application.
5 Dated the day of , 19 .

To	This summons was taken out by
	of
Solicitor or Agent for	Agent for
	of
	Solicitor for

1 A summons for hearing before a judge should read '... attend before one of the Judges of this Division in chambers at the Royal Courts of Justice, Strand, London'.

2 The day and time are inserted by the registry (see subhead (*a*), above).

3 The nature of the application should be stated in this paragraph.

20.3 Motions

It is sometimes necessary to apply to the court on motion for an order, for instance, for committal for disobedience to a court order (see RSC, Ord 52), or when a registrar has so directed (see p 250). Where an application is likely to be strenuously contested with a large number of affidavits being filed and the possibility that all the deponents will be cross-examined, consideration should be given to the application being made on motion in the first place; there can then be a preliminary hearing before a registrar with a view to directions being given for the filing of pleadings to define the issues and to some restriction being placed on the number of affidavits to be filed (*Van Hoorn* v *Van Hoorn* (1979) 123 SJ 65).

The application is commenced by filing a case on motion, a notice of motion (if necessary), supporting affidavits and any other relevant documents in the Probate Department of the Principal Registry not later than seven clear days before the day on which the motion is to be heard. There is no fee payable on the motion or for filing any documents.

The case on motion (and other documents) should be headed 'In the Estate of   deceased' and it should set out the names, addresses and nature of the interest of the applicants and of the persons to be served with notice of the motion, the nature of any proceedings which have already been taken by such persons and the circumstances which require an order of the court. The case should conclude with a prayer setting out the nature of the order desired.

The notice of motion should set out the date, place and time of the hearing, the nature of the order desired and briefly the grounds on which the application is based.

Copies of the notice and of the supporting affidavits should be served on all persons having an interest likely to be affected by the making of the order by leaving them at, or by sending them by prepaid registered post or by recorded delivery to, the address for service or, if there is no address for service, the last known address of the persons concerned. If the application is for committal the documents should be served personally on the person who is to be committed.

Service must be effected at least five clear days (ie, excluding the day of service, Saturdays and Sundays) before the day named in the notice for the hearing (Probate Rule 63). A day and time for hearing the motion will be fixed by the Clerk of the Rules. If the registrar considers that any of the documents lodged are defective, he may strike the motion out of the list unless the defect can be remedied in time.

At the hearing, the parties must appear by counsel unless they are acting in person. Copies of the order drawn up by the registrar may be ordered from the registry two days after the hearing.

To restore an adjourned motion to the list for hearing, it is necessary to file a notice of adjourned motion together with any additional affidavits in the Probate Department and to serve notice on all interested parties. The subsequent procedure is as for an original motion.

An appeal from an order on motion must be made within four weeks from the date on which the order was signed, entered or otherwise perfected, to the Court of Appeal, unless leave is obtained from the judge or the Court of Appeal to extend the time (see RSC, Ord 59, for the general procedure). The notice of appeal must be served within the prescribed time on all interested parties. The appellant must then apply within seven days after service of the notice to set the appeal down and must give notice of having done so within two days thereafter.

Chapter 21

Engrossments, Searches and Copies

21.1 Engrossments

The copy of the will annexed to the grant is usually a photographic copy of the original prepared in the registry. However, it may be necessary to supply an engrossment (Probate Rule 9) if the registrar considers that the original will is not suitable for photographic reproduction, or if the will contains alterations which are not admissible to proof (see p 23) or includes irrelevant matter or if the court has made an order for rectification of the will under s 20 (1) of the Administration of Justice Act 1982 (see head 2.16). The engrossment must be supplied by the applicant's solicitor. Foreign wills are often accompanied by superfluous matter and it is advisable to refer such wills in advance to the Probate Department of the Principal Registry or to the district registry to ascertain whether an engrossment will be required. Where some out of a number of testamentary documents are suitable for photography but not the others, the registrar should be asked whether or not he requires an engrossment of all the documents to be prepared. Similarly, when it is necessary to obtain a fiat copy of one of several testamentary documents, the registrar may be prepared to direct that it is unnecessary to prepare fiat copies of the other documents.

In preparing an engrossment the following should be noted:

- (i) A fiat copy (see p 23) in particular should be made bookwise on durable paper following continuously from page to page on both sides of the paper (Probate Rule 9 (3)). Like all documents for use in the High Court the paper used should be size A4 ISO.
- (ii) The writing, typing or printing must be clear and distinct, containing no alterations, interlineations or erasures. An erasure is fatal to the acceptance of an engrossment.
- (iii) The spelling, abbreviations in the will and dates and numbers must be copied as written.
- (iv) Whilst a strict facsimile is not necessary, the punctuation, spacing and division into paragraphs of the original must be reproduced.
- (v) The initials of the testator and witnesses in the margin of the will authenticating alterations are not copied.
- (vi) Incorporated documents are engrossed immediately after the document in which reference to them is made.

(vii) A notation on the will that it has been pronounced for in an action must be reproduced.

(viii) When there has been an order for rectification the form in which the will is to be proved must be strictly followed.

As an alternative to a typewritten engrossment, the registrar has a discretion to allow a facsimile copy produced by photography in the following circumstances:

(*a*) where a complete page is, or complete pages are, to be excluded;

(*b*) where, by masking them out, it is possible to exclude words on the same page below the testator's signature;

(*c*) where the original has been altered but neither re-executed nor re-published and there is in existence a photocopy of the original executed document.

If part or the whole of a will has been written in pencil, a copy of the will or of the pages or sheets containing the pencil writing, in which the words which appear in pencil in the original are underlined in red ink, must be lodged with the will (Probate Rule 9 (4)). The copy may be a photographic copy.

21.2 Searches and copies

Short details of every grant of representation issued in England and Wales are contained in the calendars which are open to inspection in the Principal Registry and various district probate registries (s 111 of the Supreme Court Act 1981). Calendars held in the district probate registries which relate to grants issued before 1 January 1929 may have been transferred to the appropriate local record office. A weekly list of grants is now produced by computer and is available for inspection, usually on the Friday following the week to which the list relates. The search is made in person; no fee is payable for the search but there is an inspection fee of 25p for each document (Fee 7). On a postal application in the Principal Registry for a copy of a grant there is a handling fee of £1 in respect of each estate (Fee 9).

There is an additional facility whereby on application for a standing search the applicant will be sent, without the need for further application, an office copy of any grant of representation in respect of an estate which tallies with the description given, and which grant either issued not more than twelve months before the receipt of the application for the search or issues within a period of six months after that date. The application must be made to the Principal Registry by lodging with, or sending by post to, the Record Keeper a request in the prescribed form (see Form 21.2 below) together with the fee of £2 (Fee 5). The form should include all alternative names for the deceased; there is no additional fee. The application may be renewed at the expiration of the period of six months on payment of a further fee of £2; the form of receipt given by the Record Keeper includes provision for the extension of the period of search. An application by post should be sent to 'The Record Keeper, Principal Registry of the Family Division, Somerset House, Strand, London WC2 1LP'. Payment of the fee is by crossed cheque or postal order made out to 'HM Paymaster General'. Advantage may be taken of this service where a person has no wish to prevent the issue of a grant of representation but wants to know when such a grant issues so that, for instance, he may commence proceedings against the deceased's legal personal representatives. Up to 1 October 1975 when the standing search was introduced, the only course open to such a person was to enter a caveat, the subsequent removal of which sometimes led to trouble and delay.

Form 21.2 Application for a standing search
(*For heading and title, see Form* 2.11)

I (*or* We) apply for the entry of a standing search so that there shall be sent to me (*or* us) an office copy of every grant of representation in England and Wales in the estate of:
Full name of deceased:
Alternative or alias name:
Full address:
Exact date of death:
which either has issued not more than 12 months before the entry of this application or issues within six months thereafter.

Signed:
Full address:
Reference No (if any):

Original wills and other documents filed on an application for a grant (other than the Inland Revenue account) are also open to inspection subject to the control of the High Court (s 124 of the Supreme Court Act 1981). There is a fee of 25p for inspecting an original will or any other document, including a copy will (Fee 7); there is no fee payable for the search. When it is desired to carry out searches for research or similar purposes, a permit may be obtained from the President of the Family Division which will allow the holder to search records which are over 100 years old without payment of the prescribed inspection fees. There are also facilities for the production of a proved original will in another court or for inspection and examination by the police or at the request of a solicitor or researcher. Enquiry should be made at the registry where the will is kept.

An office copy, or a sealed and certified copy, of any will or part of a will which is open to inspection, or of any grant of representation, may be obtained on payment of the prescribed fees (see below) (i) from the registry in which the will is kept or from which the grant issued, or (ii) when the will or other document is kept in some place other than a registry, from the Principal Registry, or (iii) with the approval of the Senior Registrar, from the Principal Registry when the will was proved in, or the grant issued from, a district probate registry (s 125 of the Supreme Court Act 1981). In addition to the fee for the copy, there is an additional fee of £1, in respect of each estate, for handling a postal application in the Principal Registry for a copy of a will or grant (Fee 9). Copies of other documents filed on an application for a grant (except the Inland Revenue account) may also be obtained. Copies of the record of the grant may be ordered and paid for at the time of the application for the grant.

The records of Exeter and the former registries at Taunton and Wells were destroyed by enemy action in 1942. Applications for copies of these records should be made to the Record Keeper of the Principal Registry.

Copies of the will or of the record of a grant or of the record of re-sealing will usually be photographic copies (Fee 8 (*a*)), bearing the seal of the registry, and, unless required to be sealed and certified, will be issued as office copies. When such office copies are available for issue, it is not possible to obtain copies (whether photographic or typed) certified under the hand of a registrar to be true copies, unless it is desired that the copies should also bear the seal of the court (Fee 8 (*b*)). A sealed and certified copy of the testamentary dispositions of the deceased will include all the documents admitted to probate, whether they were proved together or separately. When photographic office copies are not available, typed copies certified to be true copies (Fee 8 (*a*)) may be obtained, as well as unofficial or 'plain' copies (Fee 8 (*a*)) and sealed (and certified) copies (Fee 8 (*b*)). Other types of copies obtainable are an exemplification and a copy signed by a registrar and countersigned by the President of the Family Division (Fee 8 (*c*)). Photographic, office or sealed and certified copies of documents in a foreign language which are retained in the registry may be obtained without an English translation, if so required. Plain copies of an unproved will which has been retained in the registry, eg, a will marked 'Probate refused', or of a will containing alterations which have not been admitted to probate, or which has been rectified by order of the court, or of a memorandum which has been filed but not incorporated with the will, may be obtained on request; the copy will be marked to show that the original document was not admitted to probate at all or in that form. A duplicate grant (Fee 3) will issue only on the written request of the grantee or the extracting solicitor, who must state the reason why it is required; the application may be made through the post. If two or more duplicates are required, the reason for this should be given because the request will be referred to a registrar for his approval. The fees quoted are those set out in the Non-Contentious Probate Fees Order 1981, as amended by the Non-Contentious Probate Fees (Amendment) Order of 1981 and the Non-Contentious Probate Fees (Amendment) Order 1983 (see Appendix 1).

When copies of the record of a grant are ordered from the registry of issue they will usually be sealed with the seal of the registry. Such copies must be accepted by limited companies for the purpose of the registration of stocks and shares and will be accepted in evidence in any part of the United Kingdom without proof, as will copies of confirmations given under the seal of office of any commissariat in Scotland and copies of grants issued under the seal of the High Court in Northern Ireland (s 4 of the Administration of Estates Act 1971, and see p 221).

Unless special leave is granted, no copies of any documents may issue if an action for the revocation of the grant is pending in the Chancery Division. Where a grant has been revoked only plain copies of the grant may issue.

Chapter 22

Deposit of Wills of Living Persons

On 16 May 1972 the Convention on the Establishment of a Scheme of Registration of Wills (Registration Convention) was concluded at Basle, Switzerland. Sections 23 to 25 of the Administration of Justice Act 1982 are based on the terms of the Registration Convention being applied to England and Wales, Scotland and Northern Ireland but have still to be brought into effect. The Principal Registry is to be a registering authority with the duty of providing and maintaining depositories for the custody of the wills of living persons, and it will also be the national body under the Convention for the purpose of arranging for the registration of wills in other contracting states and of receiving and answering requests for information from the national bodies of those other states. Wills already deposited under s 172 of the Supreme Court of Judicature (Consolidation) Act 1925, or s 126 of the Supreme Court Act 1981 (see below), will be treated as if deposited under s 23 of the Administration of Justice Act 1982.

Meanwhile the circumstances under which a testator during his lifetime may at present deposit his will for safe keeping in the Principal Registry are governed by the Wills (Deposit for Safe Custody) Regulations 1978 made under the authority of s 172 of the Supreme Court of Judicature (Consolidation) Act 1925, now replaced by s 126 of the Supreme Court Act 1981. The regulations came into effect on 1 February 1979 but apply also to wills lodged in the registry before that date under the previous regulations.

The will and any codicils, or a codicil on its own, may be deposited on the personal attendance of the testator, or of an agent specifically authorised in writing by the testator for such a purpose, at any probate registry or sub-registry (in the Principal Registry with the Record Keeper). If the will is deposited in a district probate registry it is then sent to the Principal Registry for safe keeping. Alternatively the will may be sent by registered post by the testator, or by his duly authorised agent, but in this case it must be sent directly to the Record Keeper at the Principal Registry. A will brought into a probate registry, or sent by post to the Principal Registry, must be enclosed in a sealed envelope bearing an endorsement in the prescribed form (see Form 22.1, below). There is a fee of £1 payable on deposit (Fee 6); if payment is made by crossed cheque or postal order it should be made out to 'HM Paymaster General'. A certificate of deposit in the form prescribed by the regulations is given or sent to the testator and where the will is deposited by an agent to that agent also; a copy of the certificate is filed with the envelope containing the will. As a precaution the testator ought to keep a copy of his will in his possession.

Form 22.1 Endorsement of envelope containing will

1 This sealed packet contains the last Will and Testament bearing date the day of 19
2 of me of
in which of
and of
are appointed Executors, which I hereby lodge for deposit in the Principal Registry of the Family Division for safe custody.
I undertake to notify the above named Executors of their appointment and of the deposit of the will.
I certify that the date of my birth was the day of 19
3 Dated this day of 19
(signed) Testator.
Signed in the presence of

1 If appropriate insert after 'Testament' the words 'and first codicil thereto (*or as the case may be*)' and give the dates of all the testamentary documents which are to be deposited in the registry. If a codicil alone is being lodged the wording should be amended accordingly, for example 'First Codicil to the last Will and Testament'.

2 Insert the full name of the testator and his address followed by the full names and addresses of the executor or executors. Amend or substitute the reference to 'will' according to the nature of the documents deposited (see **1** above). It is most important that the testator should carry out his undertaking by telling his executors that he has appointed them executors of his will which has been deposited in the Principal Registry.

3 If the testator intends to bring the will into the registry personally he has to sign the endorsement in the presence of an officer of the registry who will then sign as the witness. In all other cases the testator must arrange before the will is brought into or sent to the registry to sign the endorsement in the presence of a witness who must give his address.

The testator may at any time ask for the return of his will. The request must be made in writing and the certificate of deposit must be produced at the same time. A printed form of application can be obtained from the Principal Registry on request (see Form 22.2, below). Provided the registrar is satisfied as to the identity of the testator and that it is proper for the will to be returned, it will be given out in return for a signed form of receipt. The testator is required in the form of receipt to give an undertaking to notify his executor that he has withdrawn the will from deposit in the registry. No fee is payable on withdrawal in this way. Otherwise the will is retained in the Principal Registry until the death of the testator.

Form 22.2 Application for withdrawal of will from deposit (during lifetime of testator)

(*For heading and title, see Form* 2.11)

1 WHEREAS on the day of 19 a sealed envelope containing the Will bearing date
2 of me of
was deposited for safe custody in the Principal Registry of the Family Division pursuant to Section 126 of the Supreme Court Act 1981 I produce herewith the official Certificate of Deposit issued by the Registry
3 Now I the testator hereby request that I be permitted to withdraw my said Will from deposit in the Registry for the following reason namely:
Dated the day of 19
(signed) Testator.

1 Insert, if appropriate, after the word 'Will' the words 'and first codicil thereto (*or as the case may be*)' and give the dates of all the testamentary documents which have been deposited in the registry.

2 Insert the name and present address of the testator. If he has changed his address since depositing the will insert after his present address the words 'formerly of' and state his address at the time of deposit. If the will was deposited before 1 January 1982, substitute 'Section 172 of the Supreme Court of Judicature (Consolidation) Act 1925'.

3 Insert the name of the testator and after the word 'Will' any necessary reference to codicils. The usual reason for withdrawal will be that the testator intends to make a new will.

A record is kept of all wills deposited in the Principal Registry and a search is always made therein before a grant issues in respect of a deceased person's estate. After the death of the testator, application may be made to the Record Keeper at the Principal Registry for the sealed envelope containing the deposited will to be opened by a registrar and for the will and any other testamentary document contained therein to be handed out to the applicant. A printed form of application is available from the Principal Registry (see Form 22.3, below). Before giving out the will the registrar will require to see a copy of the death certificate in respect of the testator, or such other evidence as is available, and, unless he directs otherwise, the original certificate of deposit of the will. He must also be satisfied that the applicant is either the executor or any other person who intends to prove the will or, where the will has been effectively revoked or a grant of representation in the testator's estate is not required, a person who is entitled to possession of the will. The registrar may require the person intending to prove the will to attend at a registry for that purpose. Before a deposited will is handed out, a copy is made and retained in the Principal Registry. The applicant is required to sign a receipt for the will and in appropriate cases he has to give a written undertaking to lodge the will on any application for a grant of representation to the testator's estate. No fee is payable on a deposited will being released in this way.

Form 22.3 Application for withdrawal of will from deposit (after death of testator)

(*For heading and title, see Form* 2.11)

1 WHEREAS on the day of 19 a sealed envelope containing the Will bearing date
2 of of
was deposited for safe custody in the Principal Registry of the Family Division pursuant to Section 126 of the Supreme Court Act 1981
3 I produce herewith (i) the official Certificate of Deposit issued by the Registry (ii) the official Certificate of the Death of the testator
4 Now I the
hereby request that I be permitted to withdraw the said Will from deposit in the Registry for the following reason namely:
5 [I undertake to prove the said Will]
Dated the day of 19
(Signed)

1 See the note to para 1 of Form 22.2, above.

2 Insert the name and last address of the testator. If he had changed his address since depositing the will insert after his last address the words 'formerly of' followed by his address at the time of the deposit. If the will was deposited before 1 January 1982, substitute 'Section 172 of the Supreme Court of Judicature (Consolidation) Act 1925'.

3 If the original certificate of deposit is not available give the reason why it cannot be produced. Where it is not possible to attach an official death certificate, other evidence of death must be produced (see head 7.1).

4 Give the name of the applicant, followed by the qualification which entitles him to ask for the will to be released and the reason for making the request. Usually he will be an executor who wishes to prove the will. Insert after the word 'Will' any appropriate reference to codicils.

5 The form of undertaking should be deleted or modified to suit the particular circumstances (see p 263).

Appendix 1

Fees

(Extracted from the Non-Contentious Probate Fees Order 1981, as amended (see p 259).)

2—(1) In this Order, unless the context otherwise requires—
"assessed value" means the value of the net real and personal estate (excluding settled land if any) passing under the grant as shown—
- (i) in the Inland Revenue affidavit (for a death occurring before 13 March 1975), or
- (ii) in the Inland Revenue account (for a death occurring on or after 13 March 1975), or
- (iii) in a case in which, in accordance with arrangements made between the President of the Family Division and the Commissioners of Inland Revenue or regulations made under section 94 (1) (*a*) of the Finance Act 1980 and from time to time in force, no such affidavit or account is required to be delivered, in the oath which is sworn to lead to the grant;

and in the case of an application to re-seal a grant means the said value, as so shown, passing under the grant upon its being re-sealed;

5—(1) Where it appears to the Lord Chancellor that the payment of any fee specified in the Schedule would, owing to the exceptional circumstances of the particular case, involve undue hardship, the Lord Chancellor may reduce or remit the fee in that case.

(*Note: Responsibility for dealing with such applications has been delegated to a registrar of the Principal Registry in relation to a matter proceeding, or to be commenced, in the Principal Registry, or to the registrar of the district probate registry in which the matter is proceeding or to be commenced. The application should be made before the fee is paid.*)

(3) Where any application for a grant is withdrawn before the issue of the grant, a registrar may reduce or remit a fee.

(4) Where, on application for a grant by a personal applicant, the papers leading to the grant are prepared by the applicant himself, a registrar may remit up to one-half of the fee prescribed by Fee No 2.

(5) Fee No 7 shall not be taken where a search is made for research or similar purposes by permission of the President of the Family Division for a document over 100 years old filed in the principal registry or a district registry or another authorised place of deposit.

APPENDIX 1

SCHEDULE

	Item	Fee
	Application for grant: general	£
1	On an application for a grant (or for re-sealing a grant) other than an application to which fee No 3 applies:	
	(*a*) if the assessed value does not exceed £10,000	No fee
	exceeds £10,000 but does not exceed £25,000	40·00
	exceeds £25,000 but does not exceed £40,000	80·00
	exceeds £40,000 but does not exceed £100,000	2·50 per £1,000 or part thereof
	(*b*) if the assessed value exceeds £100,000	250·00
	and, for every additional £100,000 or part thereof a further fee of	50·00
	Personal application fee	
2	On application for a grant by a personal applicant (or for re-sealing such a grant if the application is prepared in the registry) save where Fee No 3 (*a*) is payable, in addition to any other fee:	
	(*a*) if the assessed value does not exceed £500	1·00
	exceeds £500 but does not exceed £1,000	2·00
	exceeds £1,000 but does not exceed £5,000	5·00
	(*b*) if the assessed value exceeds £5,000, for each £1,000 or part thereof	1·00
	Special applications	
3	On an application for:	
	(*a*) a grant in respect of an estate exempt from estate duty by virtue of section 71 of the Finance Act 1952 or from capital transfer tax by virtue of paragraph 1 of Schedule 7 to the Finance Act 1975 (exemption for members of the armed forces, etc);	
	(*b*) a grant limited to settled land;	
	(*c*) a grant limited to trust property;	
	(*d*) a duplicate grant;	
	(*e*) any second or subsequent grant (including one following a revoked grant) in respect of the same deceased person, other than a grant preceded only by a grant limited to settled land, to trust property or to a part of the estate	2·00
	Caveats	
4	For the entry of a caveat or the extension of a caveat	4·00
	Search	
5	On an application for a standing search to be carried out in an estate, for each search period of six months	2·00
	Deposit of wills	
6	On depositing a will for safe custody in the principal registry or a district registry	1·00
	Inspection	
7	On inspection of an original will or any other document, including a copy of a will	0·25

	Copies of documents	
8	(*a*) For a copy of all or part of any document, whether or not issued as an office copy, for each page	0·25
	(*b*) For a sealed and certified copy of any document	1·00
	And for each page after the first, a further fee of	0·25
	(*c*) For an exemplification of a copy signed by a registrar and countersigned by the President of the Family Division, including the fees for preparing the necessary documents	5·00
	Postal application	
9	For handling a postal application in the principal registry for a copy of a will or grant, in respect of each estate	1·00
	Oaths and guarantees	
10	Save on a personal application for a grant:	
	(*a*) for administering an oath, for each deponent to each affidavit	2·00
	(*b*) for marking each exhibit	0·50
	(*c*) for superintending and attesting execution of a guarantee, for each surety	1·00
	Taxation of costs	
11	For taxing a bill of costs in the principal registry, inclusive of the registrar's certificate	The same fees as are payable in an action
	Settling documents	
12	For perusing and settling citations, advertisements, oaths, affidavits or other documents, for each document settled	5·00

Appendix 2

Probate Registries of the Family Division of the High Court of Justice

Principal Registry
Somerset House, Strand, London WC2 1LP
Personal Application Department: 5th Floor, Golden Cross House, Duncannon Street, London WC2N 4JF
(01) 214 3015 and 3116
Probate Department: Principal Registry, Somerset House, Strand, London WC2 1LP
(01) 405–7641 Ext 3659

District Probate Registries

Registries	*Sub-registries*	*Registrar*
Birmingham Cavendish House, Waterloo Street, Birmingham B2 5PS 021–236–6263 and 4560	*Stoke on Trent* 3rd Floor, Norwich Union House, Trinity Street, Hanley, Stoke on Trent ST1 5PZ 0782–23736	A N Teasdale
Brighton 28 Richmond Place, Brighton BN2 2NA 0273–684071	*Maidstone* 3rd Floor, 5–11 London Road, Maidstone, Kent ME16 8HP 0622–51737	G R Garrett
Bristol The Crescent Centre, Temple Back, Bristol BS1 6EP 0272–23915 and 24619	*Bodmin* Market Street, Bodmin, Cornwall PL31 2JW 0208–2279	P L Speyer
	Exeter 94 Fore Street, Exeter, Devon EX4 3HZ 0392–74515	

Ipswich
17/19 Cornhill,
Ipswich, Suffolk IP1 1DF
0473–53724

Norwich
65 Cathedral Close,
Norwich, Norfolk
NR1 4DN
0603–26648 and 23839

Peterborough
Clifton House,
Broadway,
Peterborough PE1 1SL
0733–62802

E R Alexander

Leeds
Devereux House,
East Parade,
Leeds LS1 2BA
0532–431505

Lincoln
Mill House,
Brayford Side North,
Lincoln LN1 1YW
0522–23648

Sheffield
4th Floor,
Belgrave House,
Bank Street, Sheffield
S1 1QN
0742–29920 and 78317

C S Fisher

Liverpool
3rd Floor,
India Buildings,
Water Street,
Liverpool L2 0QR
051–236–8264

Chester
5th Floor,
Hamilton House,
Hamilton Place,
Chester CH1 2DA
0244–24636

Lancaster
Mitre House,
Church Street,
Lancaster LA1 1HE
0524–65911

J D Hemingway

Llandaff
Probate Registry
of Wales,
49 Cardiff Road,
Llandaff, Cardiff
CF5 2YW
0222–562422

Bangor
Garth Road,
Bangor, Gwynedd
LL57 1EA
0248–362410

Carmarthen
14 King Street,
Carmarthen, Dyfed
SA31 1BL
0267–236238

Gloucester
3 Pitt Street,
Gloucester GL1 2BJ
0452–22585

D W Jones

Manchester
9th Floor, Astley House,
23 Quay Street,
Manchester M3 4AT
061–834–4319

Nottingham
Castle Gate House,
Castle Gate,
Nottingham NG1 7BU
0602–501337

M A Moran

Newcastle upon Tyne 2nd Floor, Plummer House, Croft Street, Newcastle upon Tyne NE1 6ND 0632–618383	*Carlisle* 2 Victoria Place, Carlisle CA1 1ER 0228–21751 *Middlesbrough* 12–16 Woodlands Road, Middlesbrough, TS1 3BE 0642–244770 *York* Duncombe Place, York YO1 2EA 0904–24210	A Bertram
Oxford 10a New Road, Oxford OX1 1LY 0865–241163	*Leicester* Government Buildings, Newarke Street, Leicester LE1 5SE 0533–546117	Miss M L Farmborough, LL B
Winchester 4th Floor, Cromwell House, Andover Road, Winchester, Hants SO23 7EW 0962–53046 and 63771		A K Biggs

Appendix 3

Questionnaire

The following series of questions is designed for use as a handy and speedy means of selecting the various points which must be dealt with whenever instructions to apply for a grant of representation are first taken by the practitioner. Then, during the preparation of the papers to lead the grant and immediately before they are lodged in the probate registry, the questionnaire may be used to check their accuracy and to ensure that everything which should have been done has been done. Generally, the questions have been so framed that, if the answer is 'yes', action is necessary to deal with the point or to correct an error, and if necessary reference may be made to the text at the page indicated; however, it has not always been possible to adhere to this rule. To avoid having to refer to questions which are clearly not applicable in the particular circumstances, the questionnaire has been divided into sections under the headings which appear below.

	Questions
Wills	
Death before 1 January 1964	1–2
Death on or after 1 January 1964	3–9
General	10–44
Entitlement to a grant	
General	45
Probate	46–54
Administration—general	55–63
with will annexed	64–73
intestacy	74–77
The oath	
Generally	78–105
Where a will is being proved	106–118
Where there is an intestacy	119–124
Guarantee by sureties	125–134
Colonial re-sealing	135–145
Miscellaneous	
Generally	146
Renunciations	147–151
Powers of attorney	152–157
Inland Revenue accounts	158–161
Documents to be lodged at the registry	162–171

APPENDIX 3

Wills

	Death before 1 January 1964	*Page*
1	Where the deceased died domiciled in England and Wales:	
	(*a*) has the will been executed in accordance with the Wills Act 1837?	12, 16
	(*b*) if not, can it be admitted to proof as a privileged will?	48
	(*c*) or if not, and the deceased was a British subject, can it be admitted to proof under s 1 or 2 of Lord Kingsdown's Act?	12
	(*d*) or if not, is the will valid according to the law of the deceased's domicile at the date of execution?	13
2	Where the deceased died domiciled out of England and Wales:	
	(*a*) is the will valid according to the law of the deceased's domicile at the date of death?	12
	(*b*) or if not, and the deceased was a British subject, can it be admitted to proof under s 1 or 2 of Lord Kingsdown's Act?	12
	(*c*) or if not, is the will valid according to the law of the deceased's domicile at the date of execution?	13
	(*d*) is the will valid to pass immovable property in England?	12
	Death on or after 1 January 1964	
3	By what law is the formal validity of the will to be established?	13
4	If the will is to be tested by English law:	
	(*a*) has the will been executed in accordance with the Wills Act 1837?	16
	(*b*) if not, can it be admitted to proof as a privileged will?	48
	(*c*) or if not, and the deceased was a British subject, can it be admitted to proof under s 1 of Lord Kingsdown's Act?	15
	(*d*) is the will that of a mentally disordered person?	53
5	If the will is to be tested by foreign law:	
	(*a*) has it already been proved in a foreign court?	206
	(*b*) has it been lodged with a foreign notary?	206
	(*c*) is an affidavit of law necessary?	207
6	Is part only of the will valid?	23, 56
7	Does the country to the law of which reference is to be made possess two or more distinct law systems?	14
8	Have all the means by which the testator has expressed his testamentary intentions, whether in writing, orally, or otherwise, been taken into account?	16
9	Is the will an 'international will'?	59
	General	
10	Does the will neither deal with real or personal property in England and Wales nor appoint an executor?	16
11	Was the testator under the age of eighteen years when he made the will?	16
12	Did the testator marry after making the will?	54
13	Is there no attestation clause, or are there blank spaces therein?	17
14	Has the attestation clause been so completed that it does not show clearly:	
	(*a*) who signed the will?	17
	(*b*) that it was signed, or the signature acknowledged, in the presence of at least two witnesses?	17

		Page
105	On an application by a trust corporation:	
	(*a*) is it stated that the corporation is a trust corporation?	200
	(*b*) is it stated that the corporation has power to take a grant?	200
	(*c*) is it stated that the nominee is empowered to execute papers on behalf of the corporation?	200

Where a will is being proved

(*Note*—See also Nos 119 to 124 below, if there is an intestacy as to part of the estate)

106	Are the applicants named in the oath in an order other than that in which they appear in the will?	67, 99
107	Is there any doubt as to the identity of an applicant because of:	
	(*a*) a difference between his true name and the name by which he is described in the will?	68
	(*b*) an insufficient description in the will, eg, 'my wife', 'Capt Smith', etc?	69
	(*c*) a misrecital in the will of his relationship to the deceased?	68
108	Has there been a failure to mark the will?	70
109	Is a copy of the will being proved?	71
110	Are several paper-writings being proved?	71
111	Does the true name of the deceased differ from the name appearing in the will?	72
112	Does the deceased's signature on the will differ markedly from his true name?	72
113	Is the address of the deceased different from the address in the latest testamentary writing?	72
114	Is there any limitation on the power of the applicant to act as executor or administrator?	75
115	Has there been an order of the court relating to the will?	80
116	Should the relationship of the applicant to the deceased be stated?	74, 101
117	Where the will is claimed to be privileged:	
	(*a*) have the facts justifying the claim been stated?	43, 51, 80
	(*b*) has the domicile of the deceased at the date of execution been stated?	73
118	Are the facts determining the choice of the law by which the validity of the will is to be established sufficiently set out (in the oath or a separate affidavit)?	205

Where there is an intestacy

119	Has the word 'lawful' been omitted from the recital of the relationship of the applicant to the deceased?	133
120	Where appropriate is it stated that the applicant is related by the whole or half-blood?	133
121	If the applicant is taking per stirpes, has his parent been cleared off?	133
122	Where the marriage of the deceased had been dissolved or annulled:	
	(*a*) are the details stated?	117, 130
	(*b*) is it stated that the deceased did not thereafter remarry?	130
123	Where there was a legal separation between the deceased and his spouse, has any necessary limitation been recited?	119, 131
124	Is it claimed that there is no life interest after the permitted deductions have been made?	134, 138

Page

Guarantee by sureties

125 Are the circumstances such that a guarantee may be required? 170
126 Are the names, addresses and descriptions of the applicants and sureties recited in full and correctly (see Nos 80 to 82)? 172
127 Is any surety resident outside the United Kingdom? 172
128 Has there been any substitution of sureties in the guarantee? 173
129 Has the limit of liability been altered? 174
130 Have the full name, address and date of death of the deceased been recited? 172
131 Are there any alterations which have not been initialled by the commissioner or solicitor? 174
132 Have any necessary limitations been omitted? 173
133 Has the date of the guarantee been omitted? 172
134 Does the signature of either surety disclose an additional forename not recited previously? 172

Colonial re-sealing

135 If the application is not made by or on behalf of all the grantees, have the others been accounted for? 222
136 If the application is made on behalf of the grantee, is there a sufficient authority by him in writing? 222
(See also *Powers of attorney*, Nos 152 to 157.)
137 If the grant was made to an attorney is the power limited to property out of England? 222
138 Is the grant a limited or temporary grant? 223
139 Was the grant made by a court other than that of the deceased's domicile? 223
140 Is there no estate in England? 224
141 Does the document to be re-sealed contain a copy of the will, if any? 224
142 If appropriate, has security been given in the country from which the grant issued sufficient to cover the English estate? 225
143 Are the circumstances such that a guarantee by sureties may be required? 224
(See also *Guarantees*, Nos 125 to 134.)
144 Has the Inland Revenue account been submitted to the Capital Taxes Office? 224
145 Is a plain copy of the grant available or to be ordered? 224

Miscellaneous

Generally

146 Is there any unexplained discrepancy in the rendering of the name of a person or of an address which appears more than once in the same document or in more than one document?

Renunciations

147 Is it necessary for an executor who is renouncing to renounce his right to a grant in another capacity? 146
148 Has the renunciation been witnessed? 148
149 Has the renunciation been dated? 148

Index

References to forms are italicised.